A RAPID READING BOOK for
FRESH
ELECTRICAL
ENGINEERING
GRADUATES

A RAPID READING BOOK for
FRESH ELECTRICAL ENGINEERING GRADUATES

For JOB ASPIRANTS

CHANDRA

PARTRIDGE
A Penguin Random House Company

To order additional copies of this book, contact
Partridge India
000 800 10062 62
www.partridgepublishing.com/india
orders.india@partridgepublishing.com

Foreword

This book is intended for GRADUATE ENGINEERS fresh out of colleges—particularly from the not so well known engineering colleges across the world in developing and under developed countries—on the look-out for jobs. It is important for them to cross the first hurdle, viz, go through the selection process.

Interviewers usually are experienced professionals and have very little time to gauge the "quality" or "technical competence" of the candidate during the interview process. Either they tend to ask 'abstract' questions that the student might not have had opportunities to explore or very basic questions that the student may not have assimilated. Also the 'width' of the knowledge apart from the 'depth' is often assessed since a combination of the two is what is relevant in real life.

This book is not targeted for those who intend to migrate to "non-core" areas such as software development etc. This is essentially for those who LOVE ELECTRICAL ENGINEERING and would try and stick to that profession.

This is NOT intended to be a text book. The written presentation is original, but the technical contents and diagrams are certainly not—and cannot be so in a book of this nature. They are inspired by the learnings the author was privileged to have in the course of his work life. It is meant for relaxed and easy reading. It merely 'skims' the top to lead you into the depth. This has been deliberately so designed to be reasonably simple & brief so as not to overwhelm you with "yet another book"; but at the same time be comprehensive enough to cover the vast field in which you are likely to work for the next forty years.

So here you go, ENJOY reading this and do not stop after you finished reading. EXPLORE further. Unlike this book, please be aware that there are hundreds of quality text books available that will help you to further probe in areas that excite you.

Your feed back will be invaluable in improving this book and will be most welcome.

BEST OF LUCK DURING YOUR NEXT INTERVIEW.

Warm Regards
N.V.Chandrasekharan
Chennai, India

About the Author

N.V.Chandrasekharan graduated in Electrical Engineering from The University of Calcutta, India, in the year 1971 in the top rank, winning the Calcutta University Gold Medal.

Later while pursuing a career in a Consulting Engineering Company in their New Delhi branch in India he acquired an MBA degree from the Faculty of Management Studies of the University of Delhi in 1987.

Spanning a career span of over four decades, the author, prior to his retirement from active service in 2012 had opportunities to pursue Engineering in India & abroad in various roles in large Companies including a few MNCs in the Power, Oil & Gas and a few other sectors.

- ❑ Consulting Engineering Companies—Development Consultants, India, The Kuljian Corporation, Philadelphia, USA and Parsons, Oman
- ❑ Owner organization as Owner's Engineer—Petroleum Development, Oman
- ❑ Engineering division of large International Contracting Companies—Petrofac and Foster Wheeler

The author's experience has been in

- ❑ Setting-up, growing and developing the functioning of Engineering Disciplines, in particular the Electrical Department.
- ❑ Overviewing FEED (Front End Engineering Design) and Detail Electrical Engineering effort by a large team of Engineers & Designers in a multi discipline environment for Large projects in

the Oil & Gas and Power Sectors to ensure delivery to Quality, Budget and Schedule with value addition in the technical areas

❑ Conducting training programmes on various APPLICATION ENGINEERING ASPECTS

The author—in the context of engineering organisations—can claim to be reasonably

❑ Well versed in managing a large multidisciplinary team (had opportunity upto 1000 nos) typical in the Engineering offices that provide support to overseas offices.

❑ Leading, developing and enhancing the capability of an Engineering organisation to deliver

❑ Developing Vision statements, conducting workshops, setting-up Mission goals, tracking action plans and helping achieve them by setting up KPIs etc. typically required by an Engineering Organisation for sustaining long term growth.

The author is currently a Senior Member of IEEE, an organisation where he has been a member since 1981.

The author's passion, arising out of his experience in assessing students fresh out of campus, is to help 'ordinary' fresh engineering graduates who are otherwise keen, to be "battle ready" to perform well in the selection process of various engineering organizations and improve their chances of bagging a job at the entry level in the 'core' engineering sector in ELECTRICAL ENGINEERING.

The author resides with his wife Lata in Chennai, while his elder son lives with his wife and two children in Sydney, Australia, the younger son resides with his wife at Chennai.

CONTENTS

1

Load List & Maximum Demand

As an Application Engineer for Electricals in a Project your first task will be to seek and find out what are the connected LOADS are going to be and have a clear understanding of each of the load to be able to assess the total demand so that ALL the associated electricals are adequately selected to ensure a properly engineered system.

To achieve the above you need to understand different types of loads:

Continuous loads are all loads that may be continuously required for normal operation of the plant.

Intermittent loads are loads that may be required to operate only intermittently such as filling pumps, valves etc

Stand-by loads are loads that are brought on line during normal power outages—say under emergency conditions.

Types of loads

You may have a Motor, a Heater, a "group" load that is not so much defined when you begin your assessment, Lighting load, Small power load (Power sockets) etc. The rated power needs of each—estimated or as per vendor name plate details—will have to be provided by the other concerned discipline in the project team viz., Process & Mechanical disciplines in a well co-ordinated way.

Here you need to be aware that the 'estimated' load provided by them for a pump or compressor will usually be the "absorbed normal" load which will be based on mechanical design calculations for the power absorbed by the load and therefore might have a design margin typical in such assessments.

The name plate rating of the electrical drive motors are determined to be higher than the above needs by 10 to 15% depending on the confidence level on the calculated absorbed power. Usually 15% is added, but a cautious approach for larger ratings is important in order not to inflate the needs that may prove to be expensive. The rating for the motor chosen will be next available "standard" rating and this in turn will further provide some more margin.

Now you need to factor-in the "efficiency" of the particular load to work out what will be the input power needs. Motors have efficiencies of 0.8 to 0.9 depending on their ratings and the operating points of the load. Manufacturer's typical data on this are usually available. Note that an oversized motor will have poorer efficiencies since it will have to operate at lesser than its name plate rating (at say 75% load) than if it were sized accurately. Hence computation of "input power" is usually done as per the absorbed power with efficiency values of the nearest motor rating.

Power Factor of the load will determine the quantum of KVA and kW needs. As you all know a resistive load such as a heater will have pf of 1 while motors have pf values of 0.75 to 0.9 depending on the rating. Higher the rating better is the pf. Manufacturer's catalogues will provide a go-by.

Thus input power needs for the electrical load

= {Absorbed normal kW/η} where η is the efficiency.

The KVAr needs for each loads are determined by their pf values.

You can now add up all the kW and KVAr needs for ALL the loads using a spread sheet.

TOTAL kVA demand = $\{(\text{Total input kW})^2 + (\text{Total input kVA}_r)^2\}^{0.5}$

The GRAND TOTAL kVA demand for the project can then be worked out by applying the Diversity factor for the continuous or intermittent or stand by as discussed earlier. The values chosen varies from project to project. Typically those are:

100% for continuous loads
30% for intermittent loads
10% for stand by loads

GRAND TOTAL kVA demand =

100% of TOTAL kVA demand for CONTINUOUS LOADS +
30% of TOTAL kVA demand for INTERMITTENT LOADS

PEAK TOTAL kVA demand =

100% of TOTAL kVA demand for CONTINUOUS LOADS +
30% of TOTAL kVA demand for INTERMITTENT LOADS +
10% of TOTAL kVA demand for STAND BY LOADS

A further factor is added sometimes to allow for "growth" in the load as the design progresses. This is as high as 25% in the "Front End Engineering Design" (FEED) stage of a project and can be brought down to just 10% towards the Detailed Engineering stage when most of the individual needs of various plants & systems are clearly known or even ordered.

A well constructed spread sheet can define all the computations and values tweaked to suit a particular case.

Demand computation can be made for each load centre/each switch board and total values added up for the entire project.

The importance of assessing the Maximum demand should be appreciated in the context of finalising ordering of main transformers, in-plant power generation equipment, applying to utilities for power requirements, tie-in needs for overhead lines etc. or simply working out preliminary cost estimates for the project electricals.

Foot Note:

Compilation/Review of Load list has generally been my first task for any project in any organization where I had anything to do with detailed engineering. However note that each organization had a unique way of looking at it—and rightly so. Every organization use their own home-grown spread sheets finely evolved over the years to address their needs in a systematic and error free manner.

Stepping back from the din it might appear to me that

Consultants probably estimate the loads rather pessimistically, always 'guesstimatng' them to be on the safer side. This can ofcourse be justified that they usually come early in the project when the needs of the project are yet to be firmed up in concrete terms. Better practices adopted by some firms call for review & recasting this even much later in the project.

EPC Contractors, with responsibility of achieving tidy bottom lines, tend to estimate loads to the bone to keep the capacities and cost low and 'just meet' the Owner specified needs.

PMC firms usually play the role of ensuring that the EPC contractor's estimates meet the minimum needs.

2

Single Line Diagrams (SLDs)

Single Line Diagram (SLD) is the language of Electrical Engineers. If you are playing any role in any project make sure you have a reasonable understanding of the SLD of the project.

For any switchgear, at any voltage, as a MINIMUM, the SLD should represent the power distribution.

Also pay attention to the 'Symbology' that we shall discuss separately.

For a clear understanding it is recommended that, **this chapter should be revisited by the reader** on completion of reading the book.

Typically **Minimum** information to be shown in any SLD is indicated below:

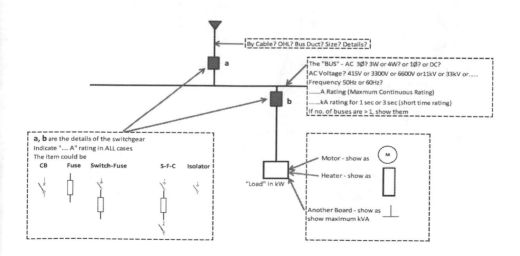

We shall now briefly discuss various SLDs commonly used in the Industry:

Key SLD
EHV Switchyard SLD or Main Receiving Station (MRS) SLD
HV switchgear SLDs
MV switchgear SLDs
LV switchgear SLDs
LV MCC SLDs
LV DB SLDs
UPS DB SLDs
Lighting & Small power SLDs
Trace Heating SLDs
Etc.,

Each will have its own nuances, but basic ingredients that need to be shown are similar.

Key SLD

Show ALL buses and connections.

Briefly mention the 'location' of the board, 'tag no.' of the board.

Show Bus couplers, if any for each of the board and indicate whether they are kept OPEN or CLOSED (NO or NC) during normal operation.

Show all Generators & Transformers with kVA & voltage ratings.

Do NOT show cable sizes, CTs, VTs, Protection & Metering to avoid clutter.

Showing Ampere ratings of feeders is optional.

Arrange bus depiction using different thicknesses/colour—highest for largest voltage and all similar voltage rates bus to be arranged in one row with the highest voltage rated bus appearing in the top most row.

Similarly rated transformers should appear on one row as far as possible.

Remember, a neat depiction of the key SLD will convey clarity of thought on the entire power distribution.

EHV switchyard SLD

Decide on the breaker and the bus configuration and depict them appropriately.

Arrangement shown shall also be physically same as in the switchyard. This is an important requirement of some clients from safety point of view.

Typically show the following:

Rating of ALL devices shown in the SLD shall be indicated.

For Bus bars the short time current rating (in kA) and its duration (1 sec or 3 sec) shall be shown

Incomers	Bus bar	Bus Section	Outgoings
Lightning Arresters			
Isolators		Isolators	Isolators
Circuit Breakers		Circuit Breakers	Circuit Breakers
CTs		CTs	CTs
VTs		VTs	VTs
			Transformers

Show Protections

Metering
Synchronisation
Interfacing with SCADA etc.

HV SLDs/MV SLDs

Rating of ALL devices shown in the SLD shall be indicated.

For Bus bars the short time current rating (in kA) and its duration (1 sec or 3 sec) shall be shown.

Incomers	Bus bar	Bus Section	Outgoings
Source details			
Transformer details			
Bus Duct/cable details			
Isolators			Isolators
Circuit Breakers (D/O)		Circuit Breakers (D/O)	Circuit Breakers (D/O)
CTs		CTs	Earth switches
VTs		VTs—D.O or Fixed	kW or kVA details
D/O or Fixed Earth Switches			CTs or CBCTs
			VTs
			Name of Destination board or Load
			Cable details

Some transformer feeders might have latched-in HV contactors backed up by HV fuses.

Some outgoing motor feeders might use contactors backed up by Fuses.

Show equipped spares and vacant spares in the ends of the bus.

Show the feeder arrangements symmetrically as far as possible.

LV Switchgear

Rating of ALL devices shown in the SLD shall be indicated.

For Bus bars the short time current rating (in kA) and its duration (1 sec or 3 sec) shall be shown.

Incomers	Bus bar	Bus Section	Outgoings
Source details			
Transformer details			Switch
Bus Duct/cable details			Fuse or Fuse-switch
Isolators			Isolators
Circuit Breakers		Circuit Breakers—D/O or Fixed	Air Circuit Breakers—D/O or Fixed or MCCBs
CTs		CTs	CTs
VTs		VTs—D.O or Fixed	kW or kVA details
D/O or Fixed			CTs
Protection			Name of Destination board or Load
Metering (Local & Remote)			Cable details
			Protection
			Metering (Local & Remote)

LV Motor Control Centres (MCCs)

Rating of ALL devices shown in the SLD shall be indicated.

For Bus bars the short time current rating (in kA) and its duration (1 sec) shall be shown.

Forward/Reverse loads shall show two sets of contactors

Contactor ratings for Capacitors, Heaters, inchng loads, lighting loads shall be assessed correctly and notings indicated accordingly

Incomers	Bus bar	Bus Section	Outgoings
Source details			
			Switch
Bus Duct/cable details			Fuse or Fuse-switch
Isolators			Contactors (identify duty in a note)
ACB/MCCB		ACB/MCCB	TOL relay range
CTs			
VTs			
D/O or Fixed		D/O or Fixed	D/O details
Protection			Name of Destination board or Load
			Load "nomenclature"
Metering (Local & Remote)			Cable details
Ammeters with MDIs, selector switches			Protection
			Metering (Local & Remote)

LV Distribution Boards (ACDBs)

Rating of ALL devices shown in the SLD shall be indicated.

For Bus bars the short time current rating (in kA) and its duration (1 sec) shall be shown.

Incomers	Bus bar	Bus Section	Outgoings
Source details		Switch	Switch
cable details			Fuse or Fuse-switch
Isolators			MCBs
Metering—3 Ammeters with selector switch? With MDIs?			MCCBs
			Load description
			Cable details

UPS DBs

The depiction shall be similar to ACDBs.

Show battery sources with AHr ratings, autonomy time and connecting cable sizes (always 1c cables).

Lighting & Small Power DBs

Show lighting transformers (if used) on the Incomer side with rating, voltage ratio and taps.

Show clearly the buses that are controlled by photo electric cells and show the contactor used with ratings checked for correct application.

Show unswitched bus for fixtures fed from it that has a built-in battery back-up.

Show voltmeters and Ammeters with MDI for ammeters as relevant.

Show destination lighting fixture groups with appropriate distances and cable sizes. Such information will ensure correctness of application.

Circuits having MCBs with residual current operated devices (for E/F protection) shall be thoroughly checked for Earth Loop impedance to ensure that the MCBs will trip for E/F at the remotest part of the circuit.

Modern Control System interface

We shall discuss these yet again later.

As we shall see separately, it is very common to have ALL the utilisation circuits and most of the ELECTRICAL distribution paraphernalia to be also (sometimes solely) controlled from computer screens, remotely located in control rooms.

Motor drives/Heaters etc.—from Process Control Room.
The screens might have the P&ID displayed where the pumps/ valves etc. are displayed adjacent to which there will be ON-OFF controls and TRIP indications.

Incomers/Bus couplers—shall be displayed on screen with relevant SLDs, with controls, Indication and other metering & protection information shown.

All the above only means that the interface needs shall need to be shown appropriately in the SLDs.

Typically all LV MCCs shall have one set of ON & OFF signals going out and ON & OFF command signals coming in from an INTERFACE BOX/PANEL usually located adjacent to the MCC room—called Control Equipment Room. The reason is to minimise the cabling distance which if it exceeds will, due to capacitance effect cause mal operation of the switchgear devices.

The interface panels have galvanically isolated solid state relays where interlocks taking into account operational needs are wired up. Quite often the interface panels have dedicated "system" cables wired up to the Digital Communication System (DCS) logic panels where the operational logic needs and Alarm needs are built up within. These shall include among other needs—Hi level/Lo level trips, interlock between drives, Hi/Lo temp trips etc.

In Electrical parlance most of the time the MCCs are therefore termed as "dumb panels" from where the drives can seldom be switched ON unless the particular module is under "testing".

Extend the same to understand how an Intelligent Electrical Control System (ECS) can facilitate switching operations for the board to ensure reliable & optimal plant operation, managing "starting' of large motors within the contracted MVA demand etc.

Foot Note:

My own experience emboldens me to pass a rather sweeping statement. Firms—be it consultants or contractors or owners—whoever can ensure that their engineers as a matter of routine can prepare an SLD with good quality, integrity & completeness have definitely an edge over others. No loose ends are thus left and all issues are successfully addressed by them without any post construction surprises.

If you have learnt how to prepare a good SLD and how to review one thoroughly—you have done it!

3

Transformers

Two independent coils linked by a common magnetic core (field) causes mutual induction and hence, if the number of turns are different it causes voltage transformation since the voltage induced-per-turn has to be the same.

In industrial parlance we have slightly different nomenclatures:

Power transformers	-	If they are "large" with ratings above 10 ~ 15 MVA sizes
Distribution transformers	-	for sizes > or = 500 kVA
Other purpose	-	Converter/rectifier transformers
$E_1 I_1$	=	$E_2 I_2$, neglecting losses that are insignificant
E_1	=	$4.44 f N_1 \varnothing$
E_2	=	$4.44 f N_2 \varnothing$
		Where E_1 & E_2 are the voltages induced, f is the system frequency
		$\varnothing$ is the induced flux in the common core
		N_1 & N_2 are the no. of turns in the windings
$\therefore E_1/E_2$	=	N_1/N_2

Losses and Efficiency

In a transformers we have

    Iron loss or core loss
    Copper loss or winding loss
    Stray losses or dielectric losses

Iron loss is due to the eddy current losses in the core caused by the alternating magnetic flux. This is directly proportional to the square of the lamination thicknesses of the core. That is why thinner the core lesser is the iron loss.

Copper loss is the I^2R loss in the windings and therefore varies directly as the square of the current, i.e., varies with the load.

"No Load Loss" is thus more due to the Iron loss and since the load is nil, there wouldn't be any copper loss other than a small amount of no load current.

Typically in a transformer $I_{n.l}$ is $1/20^{th}$ of $I_{f.l}$.
∴ no load Cu loss is $1/400^{th}$ of that due to Full load current and is neglected for practical considerations.

$$\therefore \text{ Total loss} = P_{\text{iron loss}} + x^2 P_{\text{Cu loss}}$$

Where x is the loading factor and its value is unity at full load.

Also the losses varies as per the power factor of the load since the I^2R losses hinges heavily on the p.f.

Transformers being static equipment are highly efficient close to 98% at 0.8 pf.

In general terms

Efficiency $\eta = 1 - [(\text{Total per unit loss})/(\text{Output p.u} + \text{Total pu. Loss})]$

Regulation

Given by the % term $\{(V_{n.l}-V_{f.l})/V_{f.l}\}* 100$

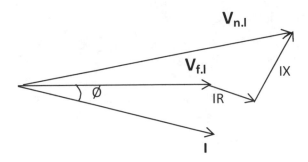

Construction

Core type transformers are more common and shell type transformers that are less common. The former has winding outside a core.

The dielectric medium is usually oil, but can be SF_6 or solid epoxy depending on applications.

The winding is usually a preformed construction, of copper. However Aluminum windings are also prevalent and for lower ratings Al foil wound transformers are offered in the market for certain commercial advantages.

The wound core is immersed in full in a tank filled with oil. The tank is designed to withstand full vacuum to take care of sudden leak of oil.

The insulation of the winding depends on the Voltage rating and usually impregnated paper with epoxy bonding is used to avoid voids in the wrapping since otherwise there may be corona induced at high voltages.

The terminals are "taken out" through oil filled bushings.

Conservator

Conservator is a separate "tank" connected above to the main tank that allows for expansion/contraction of oil such that the main tank is always full of oil well on top of the windings inside it. Seeing oil level in the conservator gives the operating staff an idea of the status of "heating" of the transformer caused by its load.

In hermetically sealed transformers there is therefore no conservator provided.

Cable boxes in transformers

Instead of bushings at the tank top, cable boxes are often provided, depending on specific needs. In many cases the tank assembly is designed in such a way that the transformer assembly can be removed without disconnecting the cabling to facilitate quicker maintenance.

Winding connections or Vector Group

The connections can be Yy, Dy, Yd, yY and so on. The capital letter signifies the HV side and the smaller letter the LV side of the transformer.

The above notations are incomplete since we need to add the relative phasor positions as well as the information on whether the neutral is brought out for further connection. Note that the neutral is usually brought out to satisfy system grounding needs about which we shall discuss separately in another chapter.

In such notations the smaller hour hand signifies the LV side while the larger minute hand signifies the HV side and unlike in the clock the phasors rotate anti clockwise as per convention.

Thus if we have Dyn11 it means the Phase connection is in 11 O'clock signifying

LV side leads HV side by 30^0 and its neutral is available for connection

If we have a YNyn0 connection it means a 12 O'clock connection signifying

Both HV & LV side are in phase and neutrals on both sides are available for connection.

You try figuring out for other commonly used phasor connections as follows:

Dyn1, ynD11, YNyn6 and so on

As an exercise to understand, you should also work out from basics as to how the HV & LV windings are actually connected.

Radiators

Radiators are needed to cool the oil just like as we have in cars. Some of the common modes are AN ON, AF ON, AF OF where N means "natural" and F means "Forced". Thus AN means 'air natural', i.e, no assisted air cooing by fans; ON means oil cooling by natural convection within the tank with no external pumps used for oil circulation that will then be identified as OF.

Momentary/short time overloading of transformers

You can now appreciate that the loading of a transformer rated xx MVA (ONAN) can be increased significantly later by installing external fans/pumps to give YY (OFAF) ratings. This will avoid replacement of transformer saving huge capital expenditure, though as you can appreciate there will be additional losses due to the power consumed by the devices plus make the equipment somewhat less reliable. For very large transformers such as Generator step-up transformers

AFON designs are common with a number of radiator cooling fans automatically switched on depending on the loading as well as ambient temperature that manifests ultimately as "oil temperature".

Large sized system stand-by loads that very rarely come into picture can be started during their testing by permitting the transformers to get over loaded for a short while by just switching on the cooling fans rather than investing in a large sized transformer with a large ONAN rating to account for the stand by loads. In any case all transformers have an inherent short time overload capability even without recourse to above in view of the large thermal capacity inherent in their design.

Tap Changers

Usually the HV side of the windings come with "taps" that permit alteration of the turn ratios to have a different voltage in the LV side to meet the system needs. By automating this operation—taking signals from the LV side voltage—we can ensure a steady voltage on the distribution side.

Such operation is called auto on-load tap changing (OLTC).

Naturally operation of tap changers causes contact wear and sparking that needs to be contained within the oil tank. To minimise current ratings the taps are therefore on the HV side. The tap changes its position without interrupting the supply voltage on the "flag cycle" principle.

Note how the resistor elements in the two outer arms of the sliding switch, bridges the two tap positions as the tap changer progresses from position 1 to 2 in a seamless manner.

Cheaper option is an off-circuit tap changing (OCTC) that allows operation of the taps only under no load. OCTC is often provide to contend with starting of large motors where prior to starting we need to ensure that the motor side voltage is at the desired minimum value.

Non automated OLTCs on a Generator transformer help manually adjust—with the generators running—the system voltage to desired value around which the AVRs of the generators will operate without reaching their capability limits.

Large Generator Transformers

Transformer sizes are limited by the transportation and handling limitations. Often these are the heaviest electrical equipment at site. So for Generator transformers above the 500 MVA range it is sometimes common to have three single phase units connected externally. An incidental advantage exploited here is that a 4th unit can be provided as a stand by to readily replace a fauty unit with minimal system outage that is very expensive for large utilities. In fact trends are there to keep the 4th unit in hot stand by connecting it to the overhead lines in the switchyard to keep the oil warm (no load operation).

Parallel operation of Transformers

For two transformers to operate in parallel they must have identical voltages and the phasors on the distribution side to avoid massive circulating currents of large values that might trip the breakers.

Fault levels

The symmetrical three phase short circuit levels on the distribution side of a transformer is dependant on the impedance values of its windings—usually expressed as Z %. Higher Z will result in a lower fault level that is good news for the selection of switchgears but can turn out to be problematic due to high voltage regulation and impose restrictions on the capability to start large motors. Usually values of Z are inherent in the manufacturing process with some variations possible from the "standard" values. Technical specifications by Application Engineers often stipulate a minimum value based on fault level studies and maximum value based on motor starting studies. Usually a $\pm 10\%$ tolerance is allowed by international standards unless explicitly disallowed in the specifications—and that comes with a significant price.

Cost

Transformer offers are usually evaluated based on their Total Life Cycle cost. This takes into account the Net Present Value (NPV) for which we pay for the losses during its entire life cycle of say 40 years. Set norms are prescribed by users for the energy costs, its projected increase rate and the interest rates applicable for the CAPEX. Thus a cheap high copper loss transformer may be acceptable for a rural distribution system since the load varies with time of the day and therefore the copper loss impact will probably be minimal. However the same equipment if used in a process industry that bears a steady load will result in high Life cycle cost to the user. The logic could be the other way for the no-load losses.

Installation of Transformers

Transformers are installed either outdoor or indoor. depending on the practicalities. Indoor transformers needs better cooling arrangements such as provision of exhaust fans and well spaced room size, maintenance access etc.

Dedicated oil pits to hold the occasional oil spillage are dictated by strict safety norms. Since the oil is inflammable the pit is filled with gravel and need regulated disposal so as not to contaminate the environment.

Another aspect is the heavy foundation needed due to the huge weight of the transformer. Compounded with oil pit needs the result is a need to allow a huge volume for holding the oil that makes the foundation typically deep because the area is limited by the external dimensions of the transformer that sits on top of the foundation.

Thus proper designing of transformer foundations in Industrial plants calls for good expertise on the part of the civil engineers who work in close co-ordination with the electrical Application engineer (YOU) to understand the transformer vendor needs.

Foot Note:

My experience teaches me that once you make a decision on the rating and other technical specs of a transformer, it is not reversible later at the late stage of a project. Legacy issues will invariably crop up in a brown field situation, because the transformers might have been selected much before the expansion has been thought through.

In one case while doing a brown field work I had noticed that we were stuck with the vector group being what it was, that prevented parallel operation of two sources much to the lowering of reliability of power supply for the process loads that would mean lost barrels in the event of an outage of even one of the sources.

In another case absence of an on load switching arrangement for the tap changer in a generator transformer meant constraints in operating the generator in parallel with the utility grid and the owner was stuck with the limitation.

4

Generators

In industrial parlance for purpose of these discussions Generators are essentially synchronous machines.

Generators are rated

Either for 'continuous duty' as typically applicable for Utilities or Process industry applications

Or

Rated for 'stand by' operations for a specified duration—as 'Emergency Generators'.

The basic principle is, you have a rotor that has a DC field—either permanent magnet for small machines or and/or a machine with a winding energized by DC called a 'field'. The stator has the 'armature'—a 3 phase winding. On rotation of the rotor—by a prime mover—with its energized field, it cuts through the field and creates an alternating (ac) voltage that is induced in the stator windings. The generator is thus also called an alternator.

The number of 'poles' of the machine are decided by the rotor speed i.e., the speed of the prime mover.

$n_s = 60f/p$ where f is the system frequency (50 or 60 Hz) and p is the no. of pole pairs

Thus the maximum speed of the prime mover at the generator shaft has to be 3000 rpm for a 50 Hz system.

Typically Gas Turbines as prime movers have much higher speeds and therefore need a gear box to drive the alternator. Steam turbine prime movers are designed for lower speeds (1500 rpm) to avoid gear boxes and their inherent cost & maintenance related issues.

Now digressing a bit in our discussions, Hydel units have even lower speeds (300 rpm) and hence require machines wound with large number of poles and so look very large even for small ratings.

For a typical machine output rating P varies as D^2LN

where D is the diameter, L is the length and N is the rpm.

For a given speed and diameter, lower the rating lower is the length.

That is the reason we see in some hydel stations that the alternators are sometimes positioned vertically. However vertical machines are sometimes problematic when it comes to maintenance of the prime mover since the alternator needs to be lifted-off first and this implies a taller power house to accommodate the overhead crane.

Coming back to our typical alternator, suffice to understand that the machine has an armature with 3-phase windings, a field fed from a DC source providing the "excitation power" all mechanically powered from a prime mover.

Two important characteristics of the alternator needs to be understood—The Open Circuit Characteristic and the Short Circuit Characterisitic.

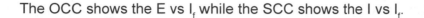

The OCC shows the E vs I_f while the SCC shows the I vs I_f.

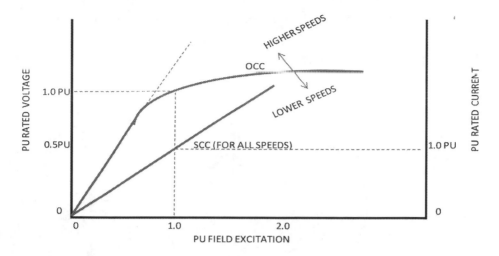

As excitation is increased the open circuit ac voltage at the open circuit terminals keep increasing until a steady state value is reached and any further increase in excitation does not increase the voltage significantly. For the same machine different curves exist for different speeds. The one applicable at rated speed, providing rated open circuit voltage is the rated OCC and the field current I_{fop} read off against this is the rated no load excitation current of the machine.

Similarly as excitation is increased the ac current flowing at the short circuited terminals keep increasing in a linear manner. For the same machine for varying excitation and speed the curve is still the same since the induced voltage in the winding and its leakage reactance are both proportional to speed and hence the value of the current flow caused (given by the ratio) is the same. The value of I_{fsc} read off from the SCC corresponding to rated current gives the full load excitation current of the machine.

The ratio of I_{fsc}/I_{fsc} gves the Short Circuit Ratio of the machine. This parameter is important in studies related to alternator behavior under different system conditions.

Types of Excitation Systems

Two commonly available systems are described below in brief:

Brushless Excitation System

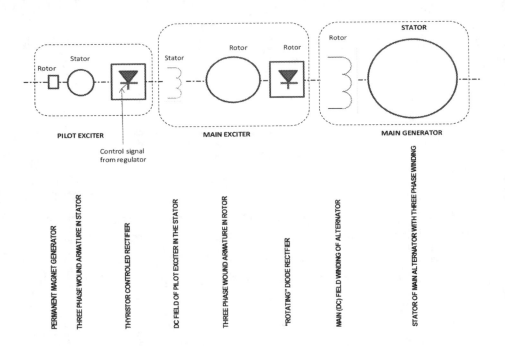

Here a small Permanent magnet Generator mounted on the shaft end induces 3-phase AC voltage that is rectified externally and fed to wound stator. A shaft mounted rotating 3-ph winding in the rotor gets AC voltage induced in it, rectifies them to DC by rectifiers mounted on the rotor itself (rotating rectifiers). This DC feeds the main exciter windings on the rotor and generates the required voltage as described earlier.

We thus have a PMG generator feeding a Pilot exciter that in turn feeds the main exciter—all achieved without using any brush connections. Hence these are known as brushless excitation systems.

Static Excitation system

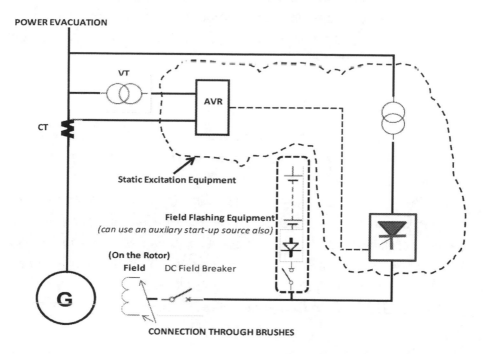

Here a high voltage is drawn from the mains, rectified and fed into the field in the rotor using brushes. Initial excitation is provided from a "field flashing equipment". Once the machine generation approaches rated voltage, the rectifier is fed from a step down transformer drawing power from the machine terminals and compared with the machine voltages to alter the firing angle of the thyristor in the rectifier such that the field current is adjusted accordingly. The advantage of this system is elimination of the need for a pilot exciter but the disadvantage is the use of brushes that present day technologies are however able to cope up with.

Typical alternator output voltages are LV, 3.3kV, 6.6 kV, 11 kV, 13.8 kV and now a days even 33kV for machines used in Ultra MW power stations. Higher values are not practical to build due to limitations in provision of winding insulations in a rotating environment within the machine slots.

Thus the size of the machine is limited by the current carrying capacity of the conductor. Machines with output ratings of 500 or even 800 MVA are common. Sometimes machines are mounted at either end of the shaft of the prime mover, each rated for smaller values off setting the above problem.

Use of Bus Ducts

Large alternator ratings, particularly at lower voltages require large current ratings for connecting cables and thus require a number of cable connections due to limitation in sizes of 1c cables. More the cables, less will be the reliability and also associated difficulties in termination sizes that need to have a large number of cables connected. Using Bus Ducts is a proven alternative. Phase segregated bus ducts are used for smaller machines while phase isolated bus ducts are common for large machines.

We have a separate Chapter on Bus Ducts.

Generator Transformers (GTs)

Usually alternator output is connected to transmission/distribution voltages using Delta/Wye connected transformers—11/33kV, 11/6.6kV, 11/132kV, 11/220kV, 11/400kV etc., as required. Transformer ratings of 250MVA, 500MVA and 1000MVA are common. These are designed for continuous duty, low losses and high performance for obvious advantages.

For large ratings three 1-ph transformers are used to limit individual machine size for ease of transportation and maintenance. One 1-ph unit is often kept as spare to minimise outage time of the large generation plant that can help save huge outage cost by way of loss of tariff.

GTs are usually located adjacent to the Power House from where overhead lines are strung to the switchyard gantry.

It must be noted that there is no need for a GTs for lower rated generators that often 'directly' feed the switchgear by bus ducts or cables via a generator breaker—so long as the Short Circuit rating of the switchgear is not exceeded.

Control of Alternator

Voltage control is achieved by Automatic Voltage Regulators (AVRs). Usually redundant sets are provided for large utilities to ensure that the entire generation is not lost for AVR faults.

Signals to AVR are fed from CTs & VTs from the outgoing generator feeder.

Frequency control is achieved by the governor that regulates fuel supplied to the prime mover that drives the alternator

Parallel operation of generators

Generators providing in-house power generation for plants are often operated in parallel with themselves and with the grid supplied power to ensure reliability of power supply to the plant.

For generators to run in parallel with other units or with the grid it is important that

a) The system frequency is same as the generation frequency
b) The phases are in perfect synchronism
c) The voltages are equal

You must thus be able to visualize a number of machines all feeding a common grid that has a 'maintained' voltage and a 'grid' frequency.

Alternator control under parallel operation

Take the case of one alternator already working in parallel with the 'grid' or 'other machines'.

	Isolated operation	Paralleled operation
Vary I_f	Output Voltage varies	Power Factor of m/c varies since the voltage* is held by the grid
Vary fuel supply (governor)	Frequency varies	Load sharing varies since the frequency* is held by the grid

Note: * If the particular m/c size is much greater compared to the total of all other machines then the Grid voltage and frequency will vary too.

Concept of 'V curves' should be understood in this context.

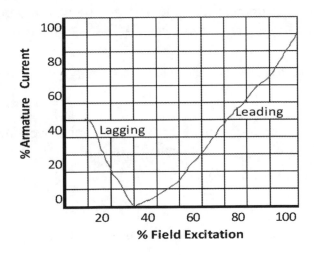

Sudden Load throw off

In a steady state for an interconnected system the generation follows the load automatically.

$$\sum \text{Generated Power} = \sum \text{Operating Loads}$$

Thus if a large load is suddenly thrown OFF, the system might see an over frequency. Similarly if a Large load is suddenly switched ON, the system might see an under frequency

Sudden Tripping of Alternator

If a large m/c trips and its capacity is much greater than other machines feeding the system and if the system load is still there all the other units will see an 'overload' and there is likelihood of a cascade tripping of a the units.

We shall see more on Protection and 'load shedding' schemes for alternators later.

Foot Note:

Choice of generator rating and the machine size option say 2 x 100% or 3 x 50% dictate life cycle operating economics in a process plant. In one project I had experienced a slight increase in the machine size by the vendor at a late stage in the project. That upset the fault level ratings of the MV switchgear that was already finalized. The machines were directly connected to the switchgear—so much so, that a series reactor had to be engineered, procured & installed to 'live with' the switchgear rating.

5

Fault Levels

A good understanding and capability to assess the fault level at any point in an electrical system is very important to ensure that all the related equipment selected adequately meets the Electrical System requirement in a safe manner.

It is strongly recommended that the engineer goes back to the text books to thoroughly understand the topic. A "Rapid Reading" Book such as this can hardly do justice to the topic—other than probably 'de-mystifying' the exercise.

Fault could be due to failure of insulation at any point in the system causing two or more conductors that normally operate at different voltage and phase angle to come in contact, then a 'short circuit' or 'flash' occurs.

Fault can occur for a variety of reasons:

Lighting	Vehicle colliding with OHL support structure
High speed wind	Plane crashing on OHL
Earthquake	Birds causing short circuit
Snow/Frost etc	Sabotage
Insulation contamination	Careless act during maintenance
Insulation breakage	Overloading of cables
Aging	Excess temperature in the vicinity
Falling of a tree	Fire causing insulation damage

Faults can be

3-phase symmetrical short circuit
Un symmetrical short circuit

Why do the AE need to assess the Short Circuit levels?

- For switchgears	:	The fault level needs of the bus bars
- For CBs in switchgears	:	The interrupting duty it has to perform
For isolators/CBs	:	The making duration of a fault
- For cables	:	The SC withstand capability for a specific duration—until the fault is cleared/circuit isolated—without damage to insulation
- For CTs	:	Selection of ALF, Knee point voltage
- For Protection relays	:	To check whether adequate discrimination is there between the upstream & down stream relay so that the right faulty circuit is isolated without outage of the entire system.
- For Reactors	:	To work out ratings of reactors that may be introduced in the system to reduce the SC level

The typical Fault contributors

The sources	:	The Grid The Generators
Rotating equipment (motor loads)	:	Back feeding the fault, acting like a source due to Moment Of Inertia. Larger the motor/larger the no. of motors, more will be its effect in contributing to the fault.
Power Capacitor	:	Can be neglected for practical purposes

Three phase symmetrical faults
  (some basics)

Fault current = System MVA/Impedance (Z)
∴ more the system MVA, more the Fault Level (FL) and
Lesser the system Z, more the FL

We will see some examples as we build up the PU concept.

Take the following cases:

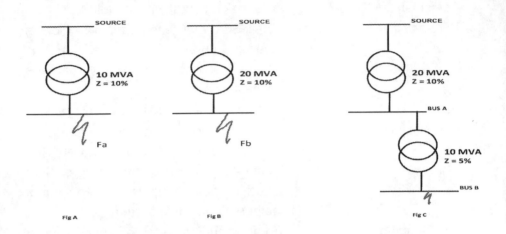

Fig A   Fig B   Fig C

Compare cases in Fig A and Fig B. Assume the source impedance is infinite in both the cases.

$$Fa = \frac{10}{0.10 + 10/\infty} = 100 \text{ MVA, in simple terms} = 10/0.1 \dots \text{(1)}$$

$$Fb = \frac{20}{0.10 + 20/\infty} = 200 \text{ MVA, in simple terms} = 20/0.1$$

$$F_b > F_a \qquad\qquad \text{circa twice.}$$

If system is 1000 MVA,

$$Fa = \frac{10}{0.10 + 10/1000} = \frac{10}{0.10 + 0.010} = \frac{10}{0.110} \dots\dots\dots \text{(2)}$$

If system is 200 MVA,

$$Fa = \frac{10}{0.10 + 10/200} = \frac{10}{0.10 + 0.05} = \frac{10}{0.150} \dots\dots\dots \text{(3)}$$

Note that Fault Levels calculated in (1) > (2) > (3)

34

You can now understand the effect of a "weak" system on fault level values.

PU method

Method—I

$$SC_{BUS-A} \quad = \quad 20/0.10 \qquad\qquad = \quad 200 \text{ MVA}$$

$$
\begin{aligned}
SC_{BUS-B} \quad &= \quad 10/\{0.05 + (10/200)\} \\
&= \quad 10/0.10 \qquad\qquad = \quad 100 \text{ MVA}
\end{aligned}
$$

Method—2

$$
\begin{aligned}
SC_{BUS-B} \quad &= \quad 20/[0.10 + \{0.05*(20/10)\}] \\
&= \quad 20/0.20 \qquad\qquad = \quad 100 \text{ MVA}
\end{aligned}
$$

$$Z_{NEW} \quad = \quad Z_{SELF} \times [\text{Base MVA/Self MVA}]$$

Understand ZBASE

$$Z_{BASE} \quad = \quad (\text{Base kV})^2/\text{Base MVA}$$

∴ if you know Z in actual ohms, you can work out $Z_{PU} = Z$ (in ohms)$/Z_{BASE}$

In PU method fix Base MVA, Base kV then Z_{BASE} is fixed. Rest is Easy. Just remember

$$\text{Fault MVA} \quad = \quad \text{Base MVA}/Z_{EQ}$$

All the above are easily calculated by a system study software, but understanding the basics well will make you a better Application Engineer of the software.

In quick manual calculations we take the liberty of making some simplified assumptions such as

 ➢ Transformer, Generator & Transmission line reactances are >> resistance.
 ➢ Transformer magnetizing elements (shunt) are ignored.
 ➢ All Transformers are considered at 'Normal' tap.
 ➢ For transmission lines, shunt capacitances are neglected.
 ➢ We ignore 'pre-fault' load currents since short circuit amps are >> load currents.

What is the impedance we consider for a Generator in SC calculation?

1) Sub Transient period—lasts for only 2 cycles. The current decays very rapidly during this period. We take 'direct axis sub transient reactance' values.
2) Transient period—for about 30 cycles. Current still decays during this period, but slowly. We take 'direct axis transient reactance' values.
3) Steady state period. Here we take 'steady state reactance'

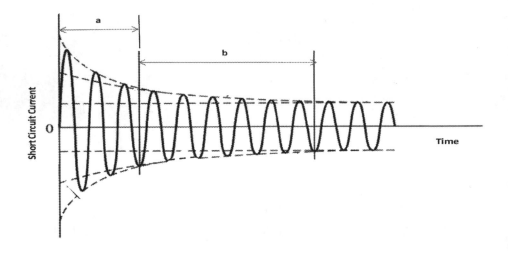

What to do if the SC levels are higher, but the switchgears (with somewhat lower values) are already selected.

Introduce REACTORS!!

Add either series reactors in each feeder feeding the switchgear that has lower ratings or Bus bar reactors as shown below:

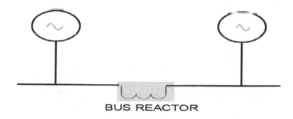

BUS REACTOR

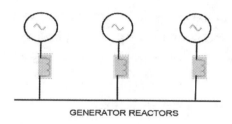

GENERATOR REACTORS

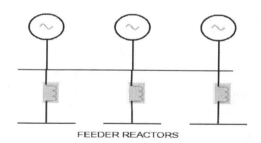

FEEDER REACTORS

Reactors increase the X/R value of the system and can increase the dc component of the Fault current posing limitations on the application of circuit breakers.

Asymmetrical Faults

1) Single line to Ground (SLG) Faults
2) Line to Line Faults (L = Line)
3) LLG Faults

LLL & LLLG faults are symmetrical faults meaning even after the fault, the system stays 'balanced'.

1, 2 & 3 above may occur at

➢ The terminals of the generator or
➢ At any part of the system or
➢ May take place through zero impedance or through an impedance and such impedance can be
➢ Due to arcing (usually negligible in HV system)
➢ Due to Tower Footing Resistance (usually 5 to 20 ohms and are neglected to get conservative results).

Rigorous understanding of unsymmetrical faults need a good study of "symmetrical components" that is briefly described below:

Symmetrical Components (by Fortescue)

Normal symmetrical 3-ph system has

➢ Equal Phasors
➢ Spaced at 120^0
➢ Rotating at system frequency (50Hz) anticlockwise

Any Asymmetrical system will have

➢ A set of +ve sequence phasors like above.
➢ A set of −ve sequence phasors rotating in the opposite direction at twice the frequency.
➢ A set of zero sequence phasors (3 nos.)—all identical.

Thus in a $\triangle$ connected winding if the three phases have equal zero sequence current, nothing can flow in the lines.

For a Y connected winding the current to ground will be three times the zero sequence current if the neutral is grounded. If left ungrounded the zero sequence current will be zero.

The above concepts are important in understanding SLG fault currents in a system having transformer connections with various vector groups.

Fault current computations will involve computation of +ve, −ve & zero sequence impedances (Z_1, Z_2 & Z_0).

For all static equipment $Z_1 = Z_2$
For Rotating equipment Z_1, Z_2 & Z_0 are all different.

This book being of a general nature we will not delve deeper into the computations but advise all Application Engineers to read through in detail from text books.

Foot Note:

I have seen that even many senor engineers in certain roles were unaware of "fault level" issues in quite a few organisations. Suffice to say that if you are not aware of the basics of fault level issues, you are prone to make blunders somewhere sometime.

All organizations are advised to ensure that their engineers have a good understanding of this for SAFETY, if not for anything else.

6

System Grounding

Different countries have adopted different practices in system earthing and have therefore evolved codes that differ.

Selection and design of neutral earthing methods is important and critical since it will affect various other system parameters like

> - E/F withstand capacity requirement
> - Insulation co-ordination needs
> - Surge protection needs
> - Clearance needs
> - Transformer insulation needs (Full? Graded?)
> - Circuit Breaker capability
> - Cable Voltage grade (U_o/U or U/U?)
> - Neutral conductor size in LV system
> - Application of E/F detectors (for high resistance grounded system & unearthed system)
> - Protection relay needs
> - Noise interferences etc.

Unearthed System

Here the neutral point of the system is left unearthed.

However in reality this is a 'capacitive' earthed system due to existence of capacitive coupling with earth—distributed through the entire system. In a balanced normal situation we can see there is no current to earth and the Neutral to Earth voltage is zero. However in a Single Line to Ground (SLG) Fault situation there is no path for the fault current to return to neutral other than through the capacitances mentioned before.

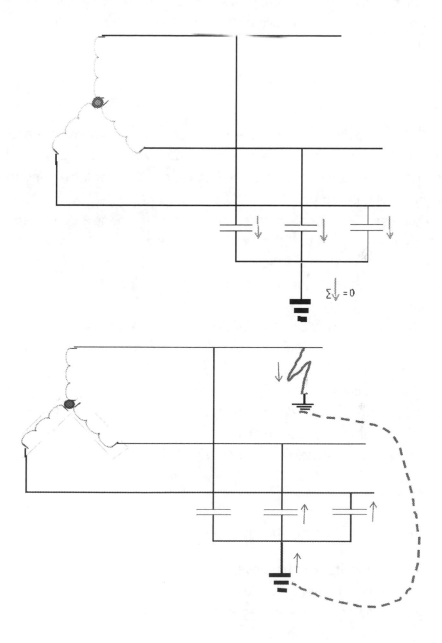

Balanced Normal	On the 1st SLG Fault
There is no current to earth.	The fault current returns via the other two phase capacitances. Hence the Voltage rises.
V_{ph} to N = VLL $/\sqrt{3}$	V_{ph} to N = VLL $/\sqrt{3}$
V_{ph} to E = VLL $/\sqrt{3}$	V_{ph} to E = V_{LL}
N to E = 0	N to E = VLL $/\sqrt{3}$

Per se the first E/F is not a major problem. However if the E/F lingers for a longer time, the healthy phases will be voltage stressed and hence will suffer a second fault causing a LLG fault resulting in a major system outage.

Another likely problem is if the 1st fault happens through some inductance (say a transformer winding) the X & C values may resonate ($X_L = -X_C$) and the neutral to ground potential might reach very high values causing high over voltages across the unfaulted phases.

If the above mentioned 1st fault is of 'intermittent' nature (arcing) it could result in huge transient over voltages (as high as even 700%) and can cause major insulation failures in the system.

Thus sensitive E/F detection devices (to even detect faults as low as 5mA) are recommended for such UE systems. Locating the E/F for a radial system is however tedious.

Therefore UE systems are to be avoided.

Earthed System

Earthed system therefore brings in a lot of advantages.

> Limits voltage in healthy phases within predictable values.
> Allows adequate SLG fault currents that makes detection easy.
> Protecton can be managed with better selectivity.
> Protection can be quicker.

Normally presence of Δ/Y connected transformer in a system isolates the primary & secondary systems and each can be considered as a separate independent system that can adopt its own earthing needs as required.

Types of Earthed System

> - Effectively Earthed system
> - Solidly Earthed system
> - Non effectively Earthed system
>   - Resistance Earthed system
>   - Arc suppression (Peterson coil) Earthed system

Effectively earthed system

Here the system earthing (via low impedance) should ensure that the SLG fault current is $\leq$ 60% of phase current to prevent build up of voltages in the other phases provided for the system the ratio X_0/X_1 is $\leq$ 3 and $R_0 \leq X_1$. This relationship need to exist in all points of the system as defined by zones caused by the isolating transformers.

Solidly Grounded systems

Same as above except that the neutral of the supply system (transformer or Generator) is SOLIDLY grounded without any intervening impedance. The SLG fault amperes are usually very high. However for long OHLs without a return earth wire, the return is via "earth" and increase Z_0 and therefore lowers the magnitude of I_{FAULT}.

Advantages are high & effective ground fault relaying, equipment can have insulation levels of U_0/U thus resulting in lower cost for the cables, transformers etc.

Disadvantages are

> High SLG fault amps that may cause equipment damage and raise safety issues.
> Parallel operation of multiple sources, each having solid ground could cause circulation of 3rd harmonic currents in the equipment. So switching might be necessary so that only one Neutral is earthed.
> High step & touch potential may result due to stray E/F current.
> Flash hazards may result due to imperfect earthing connection

Recommended for ALL

> EHV (>200 kV) Systems
> UHV (>500 kV) Systems
> LV System
> LV EDGs

All MV system Generators may have solid Earthing but will have the above disadvantages too.

Resistance earthed system

Either a simple resistance or through an earthng transformer we can achieve a resistance earthed system.

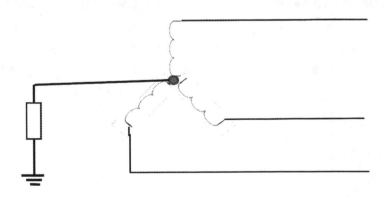

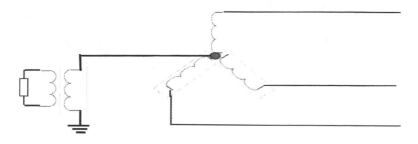

Advantages:

1) Reduce burning effect due to SLG faults. Hence it is easy to repair. This is important for rotating machines in particular.
2) Low fault currents reduces mechanical stresses on the circuit.
3) Reduces stray current induced shock hazard to personnel.
4) Reduce arc/flash hazards.
5) Minimise Transient over voltage.

Two types of resistance earthed systems

- ➢ High resistance earthing
- ➢ Low resistance earthing

In High Resistance earthing the NER is designed to carry not more than 10A. This is usually acceptable for 'alarm only' systems. The current is sufficient to throw up an alarm, but not adequate to cause damage and therefore we can resort to a planned switch off.

Low resistance earthing system help in immediate 'tripping' to prevent equipment insulation damage and its likely escalation into a ph-ph fault.

When resistors are used to earth the system, surge arresters are required for use on unearthed neutral circuits to ensure over voltage protection is there.

Neutral Earthing Resistors (NER)

NERs are commonly used in HV systems. Typically 60 to 300 ohms, depending on system voltage.

$$I_F = [E/\sqrt{3}]/R$$

The fault current values are targeted accordingly. Higher the I_f, lower has to be the R that implies a large cross section of the conductor for the NER. So if a particular value of I_f is targeted as the limiting value, for a given cross section, long lengths might have to be accommodated in the NER. That is why we have physically large sized NER.

If NER values are too high, to limit its physical size a distribution transformer with the secondary housing an 'equivalent value' of resistance as per the turn ratio is a commonly used option.

The current rating of the NER is usually a short time rating equal to the the SLG fault current for 10 seconds even though the protections are expected to come into play much earlier. The continuous current ratings are not of any particular interest and sometimes that itself could be designed for the SLG fault current values.

Use of Peterson coil

Use of Peterson coil is resorted to for transformers feeding long OHLs. This is nothing but a large reactance that nullifies the capacitance caused currents so that the ground fault currents are reasonably small resulting in minimising over voltages and thus preventing insulation failure. The reactance comes with taps to fine tune the X values at site as per actual capacitance of the line measured at site.

Zig-Zag transformers

When the system neutral is not accessible or say it is fed from Delta winding, zig-zag connected transformers are used. Connection details are as follows:

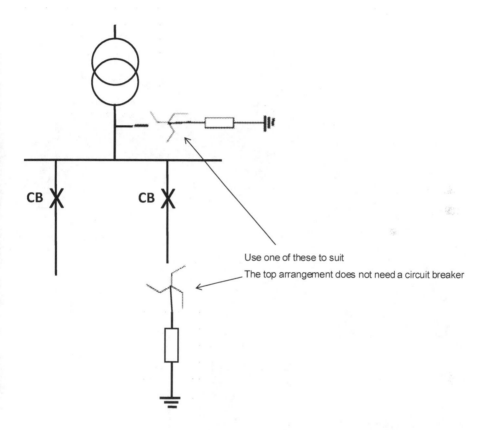

Use one of these to suit
The top arrangement does not need a circuit breaker

Basically zig-zag transformer is like an auto transformer and not a two winding transformer. The windings' construction & connection ensure that the transformer presents a high impedance to the system when there is no fault, allowing only a small magnetising current. However should there be a flow of zero sequence current as in the case of SLG faults it presents a very low impedance causing high E/F currents to flow. Each winding is split into two in the middle and one half is connected in series with that in the next phase.

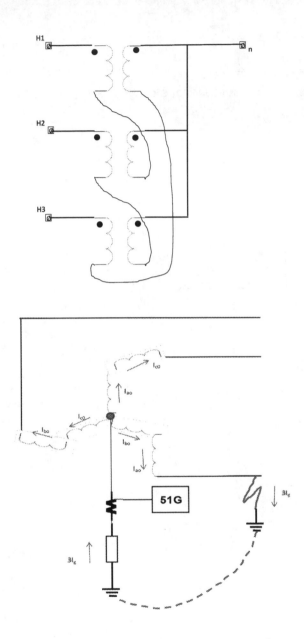

The Resistance connected sometimes provides the desired degree of earthing as discussed earlier.

The transformer rating is for a short time only—for 10 sec or maximum for one minute—since negligible current is carried by it under normal conditions.

Zero sequence diagrams for various commonly used transformer connections are not depicted below. Suffice to summarise that DELTA-STAR wound connection will ensure no fault current will result in the Delta side LINES due to earth faults on the STAR side. However the zero sequence current will circulate in the DELTA winding.

Grounding systems for LV installations

Low voltage systems supplying to consumers are usually solidly grounded. However extending the supply system ground to the consumers are done in different ways.

The categories are defined below using a 3-letter classification (IEC).

Note: 'System' means both the supply & the consumer 'live parts' include neutral conductor also.

First Letter

T　:　The live parts of the system will have one *or more direct connections to ground*.

I　:　The live parts in the system have *no connections to ground or are connected only through a high impedance*

Second Letter

T　:　All *exposed* metal parts/enclosures of electrical equipment are connected to the ground conductor which in turn is connected *to a local ground electrode*

N　:　All *exposed* metal parts/enclosures of electrical equipment are connected to the ground conductor which in turn is connected *to the ground provided by the supply system*

Remaining Letters

C   :   *Combined* Neutral & Protective ground function (*same conductor)*

S   :   *Separate* Neutral & Protective ground function (*separate conductors)*

Common type of systems

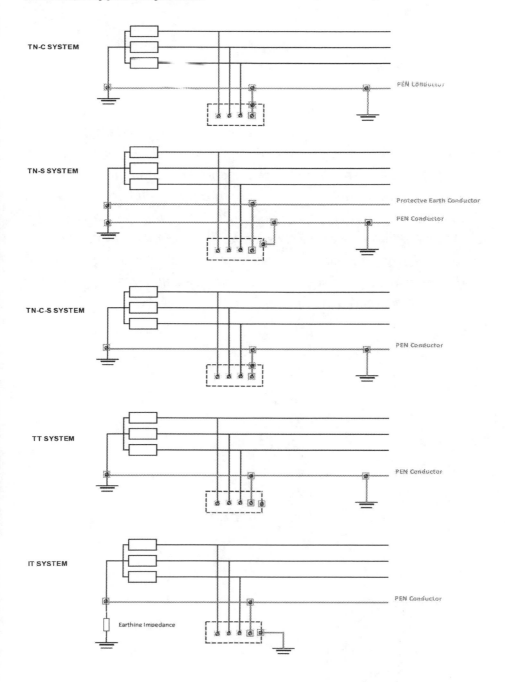

Foot Note:

A good understanding of this chapter makes you be aware of operational/design issues later in your career.

I have experienced in one case where some of the operating engineers in an oil & gas installation were unaware of the consequences of reverse feeding the HV overhead line from the plant (consumer) end from a local generator through a Delta-Star transformer, with the MV star side grounded through a Neutral Earthing Resistor (consumer end). Before going in for a budget constrained de-bottlenecking this issue, I had to spend a considerable amount of time educating the users of the need of going in for the additional simple switching equipment needed and how they need to build it into their operating procedures.

7

Switchgears

Switchgears constitute a very important part of Power Distribution. Hence it is very important for all Electrical Engineers to have a good understanding of the same. We shall therefore devote a considerable length of time in our discussions to have a broad & clear understanding of "Switchgears".

Firstly we shall look at some of the essential devices that constitute a switchgear.

Next we shall look at how the devices are assembled together as a Factory Built Assembly (FBA), that in industry parlance is understood as 'switchgear'.

Later we shall proceed to see the different features of LV switchgear, MV switchgear, HV switchgear and lastly EHV GIS.

Common Devices in Switchgears

Let us have a brief look at the various components that together constitutes an 'assembled switchgear'.

Switch (89)

This is the most fundamental device in making or isolating a circuit from the supply side

Usually switches are not intended for repeated operations and often not even for any operation when the load is connected.

An "off load" switch is thus an 'isolator'—it simply isolates one circuit from the other.

Pre-requisite of a switch is it must **carry** the load current and the short circuit current. Otherwise it should not be used in the circuit.

Can the switch 'interrupt' the fault current? Usually no!!

Can it 'make' on short circuit? In reality this is a requirement for the simple reason that we may have a system short circuit down the line just when we try to 'make' the switch.

Therefore when we specify a switch we need to ask for 'off load isolator' or a 'load break switch' with a full load current rating and with a short circuit making capacity.

Switches also need to have stipulated 'safe' clearances between the source & the load side to ensure that the isolation is 'safe' when it stays open.

Switches mounted on appropriate insulators caters to the various voltage levels encountered in the system.

Switches come with a 'snap action' in making & breaking the circuit to prevent contact erosion.

Switches/or Disconnect switches in out door EHV switchyards are manual and/or motor operated for ease of routine operation. Apart from required electrical clearances, they also need to maintain required 'safety clearances' for maintenance personnel to safely work in the adjacent bays in the switchyard. Obviously these switches need to be of the snap action type while making/breaking to prevent arc induced contact welding.

Contactors (42)

Imagine a switch that has to be repeatedly and remotely operated say for a motor start-stop operation. In a basic sense, this is what a 'contactor' does. It has a solenoid and a power 'contact' as a minimum. On energizing the solenoid, a core is attracted that makes a contact. We thus have a 'compact' switch.

The rated current of a contactor is proportional to the contact area.

Contact material is usually of silver-tungsten alloys. They need have good conducting surface and tough to survive a large number of operations without wear.

Adding an insulated stack of electrically isolated contacts to the main contacts provide the 'auxiliary' contacts. These can be Normally Open (NO) or Normally Closed (NC)—represented by device nos. 42a or 42b.

If the holding power supply is gone, the contacts part and the circuit Is now OPEN.

If you use a 'latching' contactor, you can have it mechanically latched in closed position until another coil is energized to open it.

Contactors are classified in IEC standard for AC1 AC2/AC3/AC4 duties.

AC3 is for 'motor' duty while AC4 is for forward & reverse motor duty that is more onerous than the former.

Obviously more onerous the duty, more expensive it will become. Usually a contactor typically available in the market is so rugged that it can handle 10,000 to 40,000 switching operations.

Lastly—Can contactors interrupt fault currents? Never. It is therefore required to back them up by a fuse or a Miniature Circuit Breaker that can take care of this need.

Crcuit Breakers (52)

As the name implies, these devices can 'interrupt' the load current as well as 'break' the fault current in the system.

Circuit Breakers are however designed for much lesser number of operations compared to contactors—typically 100 ~ 500 times for normal operation and lower in case of fault interruption duties.

Various types based on interrupting medium are as follows:

- ➤ Air Circuit Breakers (ACBs)
- ➤ Oil Circuit Breakers (OCBs)
- ➤ Vacuum Circuit Breakers (VCBs)
- ➤ SF_6 Breakers

Spring charging motor to close/open with great speed are common in the above. However a few with only manual operations are also used depending on the application needs.

All CBs come with 'trip free' mechanism built into the design to ensure that if an operator is holding the closing switch/Push button in the CLOSE position, the trip feature is not defeated.

Also the CB will have 'anti pumping' feature that will not cause CLOSE-TRIP-CLOSE repeatedly when an operator holds the closing switch/Push button for a prolonged duration under fault.

Execution versions can be fixed or Draw out type depending on the application needs.

Typical fault interrupting time is of the order of 40 ~ 50 milli seconds.

CBs used in LV system are usually of the ACB variety. Ratings of LV ACBs are available in the ranges 630A ~ 6000A.

Rated breaking capacities as high as 100kA are available.

Moulded Case Circuit Breakers (MCCBs)

MCCBs are modern compact relatively low amperage devices that perform functions like the above CBs, are more rugged and come with built-in O/C and E/F protections. They are provided with Thermal Overload protection by bi-metallic contacts that separate on flow of current above a setting as also short circuit protection by magnetic tripping action under heavy short circuit currents.

MCCBs also come with 'trip free' mechanism as in the earlier varieties.

MCCBs can also have shunt trip features, Under Voltage release coils, mechanical interlocks, Residual Current Devices (RCDs), Auxiliary switches etc.

Lastly 'current limiting' versions are also available to suit some applications where the breaker interrupts so fast that the prospective fault current is not even reached. Operating time of the order of even 5 msec that the breaker can straightaway replace a fuse.

High Voltage CBs (HV CBs)

Modern HV CBs are usually of the VCB or SF_6 types.

The above indicates the arc interrupting medium.

Earlier Air blast versions and Bulk Oil CBs were common using Air/Oil as the insulating as well as quenching medium and these tended to be very bulky. Minimum Oil CBs (MOCBs) were the next generation breakers that used some oil (about 10% compared to bulk oil types) as the quenching medium, but are now being replaced. These need some maintenance of the contacts, replacement of parts etc that imposes a burden on maintenance and brings down availability.

Sulphur Hexa Fluorde (SF_6) gas is an excellent man made dielectric inert gas. They are colourless, odourless & tasteless in pure state; but if they come in contact with air and being heavier will replace oxygen; so if oxygen levels fall from the usual 29% to less than 13% they can result in suffocation to humans.

Under 2~10 bar pressure they provide a very good quenching medium. SF_6 cooling capability is 1.6 times that of air while its dielectric properties are three times that of air at 1atm. At 3 atm it equals even oil.

It is however important to ensure compete sealing of the assembly since the gas when it comes in contact with moisture loses its dielectric property. The gas is heavy—almost five times denser than air—and so tends to linger at lower levels in vaults, cable trenches etc when they escape out.

Vacuum Circuit Breakers (VCBs)

VCBs now dominate the market in the MV range of switchgears.

It utilises a basic principle that in a vacuum dielectric no electric current can flow. Here the interrupting contacts separate in a vacuum bottle. Due to inherent property of vacuum the contact spacing required is very small—typically 10~20mm. So VCBs are compact.

Since outside pressure is very high vis-à-vis vacuum inside, the contacts remain closed under high pressure resulting in good electrical contact under normal closed conditions.

Modern manufacturing techniques have proven designs that reports very rare vacuum failures.

Modern HV/MV CBs

As we discussed above SF_6 have superior dielectric properties while Vacuum have good interrupting properties. Hence modern CBs have VCBs in an SF_6 insulated enclosures to provide optimal benefits. Such designs are widely used upto 36kV levels.

> VCBs are ideal for large number of operations since there are virtually no arc decomposed products
> VCBs are more compact than any other type of CBs
> Economical
> Easily replaceable
> No maintenance is required

A point that needs to be mentioned is VCBs when breaking large currents too soon may cause voltage spikes in some cases stressing the motor insulation. Using surge suppressers at the motor feeders is a proven remedy.

So as an Application Engineer you need know which type of CB to use and why:

	ACB	OCB	SF_6	VCB
No. of operations	medium	low	medium	High
Medium monitoring needed	N/A	needed	needed	Not possible
Fire risk	none	high	none	None
Health hazard	none	low	low	None

	ACB	OCB	SF$_6$	VCB
Usual for which range of voltage	≤ 1000V	3.3 to 400kV	3.3 to 800kV	3.3 to 36kV

Fuse

Fuses are the basic, most commonly used device in isolating a circuit from fault by burning itself. Modern HRC fuse as against commonly used re-wirable fuse are ceramic cartridges, filled with fine quartz into which precision sized tin alloy is placed. These exhibit consistent fusing characteristics.

On fusing, it along with the filler forms an electrically insulated mass that meets the isolation needs.

Let us briefly go through some we known concepts in a 'fault' situation:

The curve below shows the fault current and operating curves relevant to a fuse.

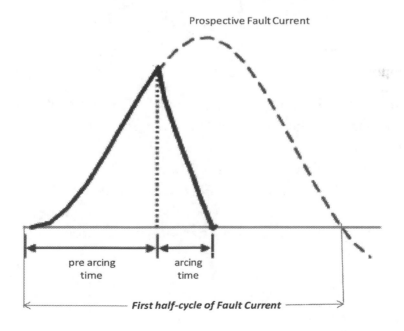

Prospective Fault Current

pre arcing time

arcing time

First half-cycle of Fault Current

Note the Prospective fault current, Pre-arcing time, Arcing time. Discrimination is achieved between two fuses if the pre arcing time of the major fuse is greater than the prearcing + arcing time of the minor fuse.

The I^2t vs time characteristics can be checked to ensure that the I^2t value (i.e., the let through energy) of the major fuse is greater than that of the minor fuse. Also the I^2t capability of the protecting fuse has to be lesser than that of the equipment it is intended to protect.

The cut off characteristics provide the time it takes for a fuse to blow on inception of a particular value of the prospective fault current. Obviously lower the fuse rating, faster will it blow for a particular prospective fault current. An understanding of these will help you to select fuse to suit your application needs.

Compare this with when a CB interrupts a fault and consider its impact on the switchgear design to withstand the Electrodynamic forces.

A fuse can therefore drastically reduce the cost of a switchgear downstream.

Typical operating time is 5 msec and is a function of the fault current and fuse rating.

Earthing Switch (ES)

These are needed for personnel safety. The moment a circuit is de-energised, an Earth switch is 'made' to ground all current carrying parts.

If ES is made switching ON is defeated.

But what if there is a system E/F and the ES is made? Sometimes this becomes a requirement to have in HV/MV switchgears in the sense that the ES need to have a fault *making* capability.

Current Transformers (CTs)

CTs play a very important role in metering & protection and a proper understanding in Application of the right type of CTs becomes necessary

CTs come with bar primary or wound primary. Dual CTs, summation CTs, Torroidal CTs etc. are sometimes used.

CT terminals left open circuited develop a high voltage and it is to be ALWAYS KEPT SHORTED when no devices are connected to it.

CT Primary current

I_{pri} has to be > the Full Load Current, rounded off to the practically available rating. 120% FLC is an accepted norm that takes care of design contingencies, future expansions etc.

CT secondary current

Secondary ampere ratings of 5A or 1A are both common. IEC 60041-1 prefers 5A rated CTs. However this will suit for short runs of cables. Long runs for 5A CTs impose a higher burden on the CT and use of 1A CTs is therefore more prevalent.

Metering & Protection CTs

Metering CTs need to saturate early to save the meters while protection CTs should NOT saturate even at high fault currents to ensure proper operation of the protection relays.

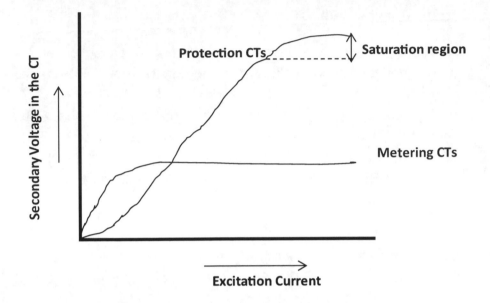

Correct CTs will therefore have to be selected by the Application Engineer in consultation with the Protection relay vendor in particular. A few guidelines given below might be useful.

Accuracy

Metering CTs are either tariff class (more accurate) or normal class.

Metering CTs need to be accurate upto say 120% of FLC while Protection CTs need to be accurate even during flow of fault currents that can be of the order of a few kA.

Typically metering CTs require accuracy classes of 5P or 10P, the numbers indicating the % accuracy

Different accuracy classes are required for different applications for protection relays.

Typically as follows:

Differential, REF protection   -   Class X
Other protections at MV   -   5P20
LV Main Incomer protection   -   5P20

LV Outgoing feeders	-	5P10
Neutral O/C protection		
In resistance grounded system	-	5P10
In solidy grounded system	-	5P20

Modern digital relays used for protection have low VA burden and so usually a 10VA rated burden should suffice.

The System short circuit levels decide size, cost and short time factor while the burden is decided by the secondary rating, lead lengths and connected meters/relays.

The Application Engineer needs to specify:

> The rated burden at rated current
> Accuracy Class
> Accuracy Limit Factor (ALF) particularly for protection CTs since beyond ALF the accuracy is not guaranteed.

Short circuit level

The system SC levels play a very important role in selecting the ALF values that is a multiple of the FLC values. For low FLC values with high SC levels the CT has to be accurate for the SC values but the normal rated primary current will be low making it difficult to procure such CTs in the market. Solution is to use higher rated CTs without sacrificing the protection settings for over current operations.

Voltage Transformers

VTs are used for

> Metering
> Protection
> Indication
> Providing Synchronising signals

VT rated voltage

General Industrial standard is a 'safe' 110V

Accuracy

Metering Class: Accuracy is needed in the 80~120% range of rated voltage.

Protection Class: Accuracy has to be there even beyond the above range

It is therefore common practice to have two secondary cores. One for metering and another for protection applications.

Sometimes a 3rd core is needed for formation of an open Delta that provides a residual connection depending on what is the protection relay we are using. These need separate error limits.

VT ratios:
Typically

For Metering & Protection: $\dfrac{xxx\ kV}{\sqrt{3}}$ / $\dfrac{110\ V}{\sqrt{3}}$ / $\dfrac{110\ V}{\sqrt{3}}$

For open Delta: $\dfrac{xxx\ kV}{\sqrt{3}}$ / $\dfrac{110\ V}{\sqrt{3}}$

VTs are protected on the primary side with Fuses with auxiliary contacts to provide alarm in case they are blown off. Use of MCBs is also acceptable.

EHV VTs

It is common practice to use Capacitive Voltage Transformers (CVTs) for economic reasons.

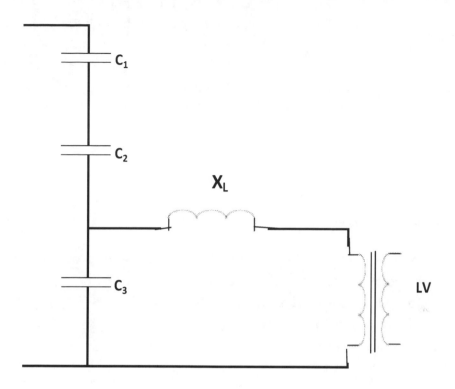

VT Connections

Usually the following connection is common. Note that both neutrals are grounded.

Bus Bars

All Factory Built Assemblies are provided with bus bars.

Bus bars are made of Copper, Aluminium alloy and are either sleeved or left bare. Sleeved bars in HV buses prevent arcing but proponents of bare buses cite that they are more congenial to arc travel upto the end of the board rather than causing a flash over within the section.

The cross section is obviously dependant on the full load current rating and the short circuit current rating.

The support spacing is dictated by the dynamic forces that are likely to be encountered under short circuit.

Modern LV boards have sandwich type copper bus bars that are compact.

Bus bar connections are usually silver plated to avoid hot spots in the connections.

Factory Built Assemblies (FBAs)

We have until now discussed various components & devices that constitutes a 'feeder' in a switchgear.

The "feeder" could be feeding another '"board"

Or feeding a motor with various ratings

Or feeding a valve motor with various ratings

Or feeding a heater

Etc.

Thus each feeder feeding a 'load' is tailor made to suit the purpose with various types & ratings of devices we discussed will be a combination of Switch/Fuse/Contactor/CB/CT/VT etc. Imagine a number of 'loads' fed from a common location. ALL the components have to be put together in an FBA. *This in our parlance is called a switchgear.*

Naturally the switchgear will be feeding all loads whose 'voltages' are identical for optimizing the bus bar design & component insulation ratings and also as a matter of Industrial practice.

Thus we have

> ➤ LV switchgear : 380V, 415V,480V,690V (upto 1000V)

> ➤ MV switchgear : 3.3kV, 4.16kV, 6.9kV, 12kV, 13.8kV, 34.5kV, 69kV, (upto 100kV)

> ➤ HV switchgear : 115kV, 132kV, 220kV, 400kV Gas
> & Even EHV switchgears Insulated Switchgears

While generally they are meant for locating indoor, they are available for outdoor duty too.

We thus bring the concept of 'enclosures' for discussions.

Metal Clad & Metal Enclosed switchgears

In BOTH the executions the earthing of METAL enclosure and protection against direct lightning strike is a must.

In **Metal Clad** execution segregation of specified internal parts (such as control compartment, bus bar chamber, cable chamber) are again by earthed metal barriers.

In **Metal Enclosed** execution segregation of specified internal parts are non metallic barriers.

Thus essentially "Metal clad" is a subsect of "metal enclosed" execution.

Typical designs to convey the 'application driven requirements' are elaborated below:

LV Power switchgear : With ACBs/MCCBs
LV MCC : With motor feeders using switch, fuse, contactors, TOL relays and sometimes ACBs
LV DBs : With switch Fuse/MCCBs/MCBs
HV switchgears : With CBs—VCBs/SF_6 types and/or with Vacuum contactors

Abbreviations are deliberately used since by now you are expected to be in familiar territory.

You can have 'draw-out' design, withdrawable breaker trucks etc.

All draw out modules of identical ratings are similar in construction since they are mass produced in a factory with advanced tooling. Draw out designs help in removing the module and replace with a similar spare module and keep the process going without significant interruption.

The basic aspects of a switchgear that you need to be aware of as an Application Engineer:

For LV switchgear	For MV/HV switchgear
Enclosure type—metal clad or metal enclosed. Usually metal enclosed	Enclosure type—metal clad or metal enclosed. Usually metal enclosed
Bus bar continuous current rating	Bus bar continuous current rating
Bus bar short time current rating for 1 sec	Bus bar short time current rating for 1 sec & 3 sec
Cable entry—top or bottom	Cable entry—top or bottom
Fixed or Draw out type execution	Usually Draw out type execution
Single Front or Double Front	Usually Single Front
Module sizes for various ratings	Panel sizes for various ratings. Sometimes MV switchgears allow two tier formations.
Equipped spares	Equipped spares
Empty spares	Empty spares
CTs	CTs/CBCTs
VTs—draw out or fixed	VTs—draw out or fixed
DC control supply. Is it redundant?	DC control supply. Usually it is redundant
Local indication—ON/OFF TRIP—a must	Local indication—ON/OFF/ TRIP—a must

For LV switchgear	For MV/HV switchgear
Any selector switches?	Any selector switches?
Earthing arrangement	Earthing arrangement

Foot Note:

If you have a good hang of this topic, you have arrived!

I have seen challenges in using VCBs in the late 70s due to reservations about an undetected vacuum failure in the bottles essentialy due to bad handling during transportaton. Cases of switching surges damaging motors were also faced. This experience caused a realisation to look for reliability numbers of contemporary VCB bottles—and these are quite satisfactory. Also the VCBs come with surge suppressers built into the carriage to smother the effect of voltage surges at start. Why I mention this is, were it not for those failures encountered we might not have learnt the applications better.

In another case, I had a situation where the lumpsum contractor for an LV distribution installation had decided—out of cost considerations—to supply a board with MCCBs, that was delivered to site delightfully in time. Later the contractor merely sized the cables as per the full load ratings of the connected loads and when the design was reviewed for correctness, he ended up with the need to provide higher sizes for the outgoing cables, that were not meeting his budgeted cost.

8

EHV switchyards

Outdoor EHV switchyard is an outdoor open Air Insulated HV switchgear (AIS) comprising of Disconnect Switches, CBs, CTs, VTs, Surge Arresters etc connected to bare rigid or flexible conductors/bus bars.

Usually switchyards have 'Gantry Structures' that are basically lattice type steel structures or towers connected often in H-frame arrangement to support/anchor the flexible conductors.

Switchyards also have ALL electrical equipment mounted on 'equipment structures' to provide necessary clearances.

Each complete line-up of all equipment in one circuit is called as a 'bay'.

Switchyards are completely fenced all round with chain link fences/brick walls upto 2.5m high. Usually top of fencing/brick wall are provided with barbed wire protection to ward off unauthorized intrusion considering human safety.

Location of an outdoor switchyard is based on various layout considerations, important being that it is located upwind to prevent plant gases/dust blowing into it causing potential insulation break downs.

Phase sequence convention

R, Y, B Left to Right when facing the front of the switchyard
R, Y, B Behind to Front when facing the front of the switchyard

What then is a 'front' of the switchyard?

It is the side where the overhead line enters the yard.

To achieve the above, at times, it may be necessary to install phase 'cross-over' arrangement at the incoming gantry point.

Bus/Conductor Material

Tubular Aluminium alloy conductors sized 2" to 4" IPS depending on current rating and short circuit rating is common. Unlike in other cases here Aluminium has a preference to copper because of oxidation corrosion faced by use of copper.

The Application Engineer needs to check the spans of the main bus bar supports for adequacy in meeting the deflection and 'aeolean vibration' limits apart from SC levels.

In case 'flexible' buses are used, the material chosen is either AAAC or ACSR.

The final temperature of the bus should not be $> 85^0C$. Due considerations of site ambient temperature (sometimes as high as 50^0C in desert vicinities) will result is selection of large sizes.

Sometimes large current ratings coupled with high ambient conditions may result in selection of multiple bars or 'bundled' conductors that needs appropriate 'spacers' in place.

Shield wires run on top of the yard structures provide protection against lightning and can be of ACSR or stranded GI wires.

Earth wires run atop the structures shall however be of stranded copper conductors

Design Considerations

➢ Should ensure safety of operating & maintenance personnel.
➢ Should ensure safety of Equipment
➢ Should be reliable
➢ Should conform to all statutory codes & standards
➢ Should be expandable in future—safely—without need to take a shut down

Equipment & Systems used commonly

Equipment		Function
Bus Bar(s)	:	All incoming & outgoing circuits are connected off the bus bars
Circuit Breaker (CB)	:	Normally used for switching ON & switching OFF the connected loads or Incomers. They also interrupt the fault currents and help isolate the faulty part of the system in a reliable way. Usually operated from the control room or even remotely from the yard. Local operation will still be made possible with the disconnects isolating the equipment to enable testing.
Disconnect Switches (DS)	:	They are isolation devices, motor operated from remote operating under no-load to enable isolation of the device under maintenance in a safe manner. They can be of single break, centre break or pantograph types depending on the needs. Disconnect switches can also be operated locally and locked in the open position for safety purpose to prevent accidental closure of the same from elsewhere when the associated system/equipment are under maintenance.
Earthing Switches (ES)	:	Outdoor device usually operating in tandem with the line disconnects to Discharge isolated part of the system—dead parts—to earth in order to ensure that there is no potential of the equipment under maintenance, thus ensuring safety of personnel. Generally the ES have interlocks with closure of main isolators
Lightning Arresters or Surge Arresters	:	Since switchyard is connected to long transmission lines the probability of lightning surges that hit the OHLs further travelling into the yard is quite high. Also the line may experience switching surges from

elsewhere and the over voltage surges that 'travel' into the first available external connection i.e., the yard equipment. It is for this reason that the first equipment that is provided at the line entry is a Surge Arrester. These can be of various types, Plate type spark gaps, magnetically blown gaps with silicon carbide resistors in series or of the more modern variety viz, Gapless Metal Oxide (MO) type—all commercially available. The last one has extremely non linear V vs I characteristics. Surge counters below the device provide the number of times the line has been hit by lightning. Sometimes additional SAs are provided close to transformer EHV connections designed to additionally protect the transformer insulation.

Coupling Capacitors	:	These are often provided for connection from the EHV lines for Power Line Carrier Communication (PLCC) needs
Line Traps	:	These are provided at the line entries in order to filter out unwanted high frequency signals from entering the yard equipment.
Current Transformers (CTs)	:	As the name implies, these are wound type stand alone devices in each phase but with all the three transformer tanks mounted on insulators on a common structure and EHV connections taken atop for line-in-line out connections using bushings. Usually they have multiple secondaries as per the SLD needs and the output terminals from each phase are taken through rigid steel conduits to a 'common' cable termination box for further connection. The CT terminals have shorting link arrangement that automatically drops down on removal of the connecting cables as a matter of abundant safety. It is a good practice to earth the CT common points in the three phases in the yard

73

itself rather than in the protection panel where relays are located in the Control Building nearby.

Voltage Transformers (VTs) or Capacitor Coupled Voltage Transformers (CCVT)	:	As the name implies, these are wound type stand alone devices in each phase but with all the three transformer tanks mounted on insulators on a common structure and EHV connections taken atop for line-in connections using bushings. Usually they have multiple secondaries as per the SLD needs and the output terminals from each phase are taken through rigid steel conduits to a 'common' cable termination box for further connection. The VT/CCVTs are also provided with fuses/MCBs on the secondary side. It is a good practice to earth the VT neutral points in the three phases in the yard itself rather than in the protection panel where relays are located in the Control Building nearby. VT output signals are used for Control, Synchronising, Metering & Protection and hence the VT fuses need to be monitored for healthiness in the Control Room Alarm panels as appropriate. These fuses are to be removed during pre-commisioning checks to prevent back feed to the line when 110V 'Test' voltages are injected in the control circuitry for field checks
Shunt Capacitors	:	Sometimes these are provided as per Transmission system design needs to compensate for the reactive lagging loads
Series Capacitors	:	Sometimes these are provided as per Transmission system design needs for compensation of long lines
Shunt Reactors	:	Sometimes these are provided as per Transmission system design needs to control over voltages by providing reactive power compensation
Transformers	:	These are not elaborated any further here
Neutral Earthing Equipment	:	These are not elaborated any further here

Other Systems & Auxiliaries

Protection Relay panels	:	All the protection relays are housed in an enclosed panel and located in a climate controlled room in the switchyard building. Modern relays are 'intelligent' 'self diagnostic' types that communicates with remote yards connected by OHLs and can also be 'set' from a centralized location.
Control & Alarm Panels	:	As the name implies these are either equipment or consoles located in the Control Room from where all the control operations normally needed for the yard devices can be performed. Abnormal conditions throw up alarms here from where 'grouped' alarms and indications are also routed elsewhere for remote monitoring of the switchyard switching status & alarms.

PLCC equipment : Power Line Carrier Communication system
➢ Line traps (in the yard) utilises the EHV OHL to communicate voice and telemetry signals at different frequencies
➢ Coupling Capacitors (in the yard) to remote locations. Though these are still in use, modern Fibre Optic systems substitute the same in a more effective manner utilising
➢ PLCC panels Fibre Optic wires that are run as part of the Ground wires atop OHLs—called OPGWs.

Fire Fighting system : As the name implies these constitute an
➢ Sensors & fire detection system important part of modern switchyards
➢ Water system
➢ Water tanks
➢ Pressuring equipment
➢ Sprinklers
➢ Fire Alarm panels

Hot line washing system	:	In polluted environments the insulators in the switchyard are washed in 'hot' condition using finely atomized water spray under high pressure.
Telephone, Microwave communication systems, Fibre optic linkages	:	These devices are in usage in modern switchyards and adds teeth to the protection & operating systems
Emergency Diesel Generators ➢ Generators ➢ Fuel day tanks ➢ Associated switchgears ➢ Start up batteries	:	These are invariably required in all EHV switchyards to provide stand by power in case there is an outage of the main lines and the switch yard has 'blacked out' completely.

Bus Arrangement

Single Bus	Merits	Demerits	Remarks
	Low cost	Bus faults will cause full outage	Used for upto 33kV switch yards
	Simplicity in operation	Maintenance will be difficult	
	Protections are simple	Future extensions will need shut down	
	Will be more flexible by adding a BC	Not suitable for large switch yards	

Man & Transfer Bus	Merits	Demerits	Remarks
	Low CAPEX & Life cycle cost	Needs an additional BC CB	Popular in 110kV & 132kV switchyards, driven by cost
	Ease of CB maintenance	Complex switching needed for maintaining a CB	
		Bus faults will cause full outage	

Double Bus Bar with 1 CB	Merits	Demerits	Remarks
	Flexbility in operation	More CAPEX since additional bus is required	Widely used for EHV switchyards at all voltage levels
	We can connect 50% of the feeders to each bus	Bus length is twice of a single bus and hence chances of lightning strokes double	Recommended for all MV switchgears that are the 'main feed' for the plant
		CB failure means total loss of the circuit. Total outage if incoming CB fails	

Double Bus Bar with 2 CBs	Merits	Demerits	Remarks
	Each feeder has 2 CBs	High CAPEX.	Not usually found in view of high cost
	Even more flexible since any feeder can be connected to any bus	Note additional isolators needed even on the load side	
	Any CB can be taken out for maintenance		Sometimes used for important utility EHV yards
	Good reliability		

Double Main & Transfer Bus Bar	Merits	Demerits	Remarks
	Most reliable	High CAPEX due to 3 buses	Common in utilities for 220kV & 400kV switchyards
	Highly flexible in operation		
	Both buses can be taken out for maintenance		
	Isolators need not be normally operated. CB operation would do		
	CB failure causes outage of only that circuit		

One-and-a-half Breaker scheme	Merits	Demerits	Remarks
	Flexible operations & maintenance	Protection for Middle CB Is a bit complex for certain schemes since it covers 2 feeders	Used widely for 220kV& 400kV switchyards
	Required 3 CBs for 2 feeders ensuring each feeder is fed by 2 CBs		
	Selective tripping	CAPEX is high	Is a recommended option
	All operations are by CBs		

Ring Bus scheme	Merits	Demerits	Remarks
	Great operational flexibility	A bus fault will separate ring bus into two	Used by large utilities having a number of incoming & outgoing feeders involving different needs for power transfer
		Protection arrangement is complicated	
		All circuits need a VT for synchronising	

81

Minimum Clearances & other parameters related to insulation selection

			132kV	220kV	400kV
Ph to E	:		1070mm	2100mm	3500mm
Ph to Ph	:		1220mm	2100mm	4200mm
SECTION CLEARANCE (SC)*	:		3500mm	4300mm	6400mm
Full wave impulse withstand voltage	:		550~650 kVp	950~1050 kVp	1300~1550kVp
I min Power frequency withstand voltage (dry)			230~275kV	460kV	520~680kV

* SC indicates minimum clearance from an equipment where a person may be required to stand as measured from the feet of the person

Insulators & Bushings

Selection of Insulators & Bushings are dictated by the system voltage and environmental factors that decide the creepage needed.

Thus Creepage values vary to meet needs of

- ➢ System voltage
- ➢ BIL humidity, pollution levels,
- ➢ UV radiations and
- ➢ Rain

Typically the values range from 25mm/kV to 40mm/kV of nominal (or sometimes maximum) system voltage.

Following types of Insulators are typically needed:

> Post insulators—of porcelain or Si rubber polymer. Important to check on the cantilever strength of such insulators to suit spacing provided in the design.
> Tension insulators—of porcelain or Si rubber polymer assemblies. Important to check on the electro mechanical strength with a FOS considered. All metallic parts of such assemblies are usually of heavy duty hot dip galvanized steel.
> Suspension insulators—of porcelain or Si rubber polymer assemblies. Similar to tension insulators, but simpler in construction. Rain shades are a matter of careful choice The assembly will have turn buckles, eye bolts and clamps.
> Wall seal bushings—these are needed when connection to an indoor equipment is to be achieved such as a transformer or a GIS. These are usually rigid assemblies almost like post insulators, but with conductor connections threaded through.

Insulation co-ordination

Determination of proper insulation levels are very important to have all the equipment in a switchyard compatible with each other so that there is no 'weak link' in the chain when we look at the ability of the system as a whole to withstand high voltages. Factors specified include:

> Power Frequency withstand voltage
> Switching impulse voltage withstand values
> Clearance in Air
> Creepage distances

All the above decides on the Basic Insulation Level (BIL) needs.

Design of Gantry structures & spacer spans

The minimum, maximum and everyday temperatures in combination with various wind speeds expected at the site has to be considered along with some Factor of Safety in order to ensure good engineering practices. Typically the combinations are spelt out below to give you an idea of the impact on the design process. These are not prescriptive:

> T_{MIN} & no wind speed to determine limits of tension with an FOS of 2.5
> T_{MAX} & no wind speed to determine the adequacy of clearances
> $T_{EVERYDAY}$ & no wind to determine limiting tensions with an FOS of 4.5
> $T_{EVERYDAY}$ & maximum wind speed to determine limiting tensions with an FOS of 1.4

The Electrodynamic forces on the structures during & after the SC event are calculated to check for adequacy of the structures. FOS considered are typically 1.5 during short circuit and 2.0 during normal conditions.

Spacer span calculations during occurrence of short circuit are also required.

Design of Lighting

A proper lighting design is necessary for safe operation and maintenance of the switchyard. Detailed procedures are discussed in a separate chapter.

The Lux level needs are indicated below to provide a general idea:

Switchyard Equipment vicinities	50 Lux
Switchyard general area including roads	20 Lux
Control Room	350 ~ 500 Lux

Switchgear Room	250 Lux
Battery Room	100 ~ 150 Lux

Switchyard being a critical area on which the entire power supply to the plant is dependant is therefore usually with a small DG set to cater to some part of the lighting.

Apart from the above the 110V DC UPS system provided for control & protection is utilised for some minimal indoor lighting with a caution that too many will unnecessarily expose the dc system to faults in relatively unimportant circuits.

Small power outlets powered by the DG system is distributed at critical locations in the yard for use by maintenance personnel

Design of Earthing

Basic aspects of grounding design is covered in a separate chapter. Specific 'good engineering practices' applicable for switchyard design are discussed below.

It is common practice to provide a bare buried mat under the entire switchyard extending one metre beyond the fencing all round.

The spacings between the conductors in the mat are dictated by 'step' & 'touch' voltage considerations for safety of personnel standing within the switchyard and in contact with the fence/gate even while standing outside.

Over and above the general mat, the operating fronts of circuit breakers & isolators are provided with more closely spaced mats as an abundant caution.

Sufficient earth rods are driven at various locations, in particular at the corners where the mesh voltages due to fault current are usually higher.

The overall length of the buried mat together with benefits of having a number of well spaced ground rods ultimately lower the 'resistance to earth' of the mat. That provides a low resistance equipotential surface.

The buried conductors forming the mat are laid well coordinated with the foundation locations of various equipment in the switchyard. And further connections overground are achieved by copper conductors or Galvanised Steel flats depending on the material chosen for the grid below that could be stranded copper conductor or MS rods with due allowances provided for the latter in the diameter for corrosion for the life of the switchyard typically 40 years.

All the equipment metals, structures, surge arresters, lightning protection shield wires etc are connected to the mat with duplicate connections for redundancy.

The size of the conductor used for the ground mat is based on the highest system single line to ground fault current, usually as high as 40kA for large EHV switchyard. The fault withstand duration is considered not less than the E/F protection relay operating time and the back up time and a duration of 0.5 seconds is normal.

All external services like water pipes for hydrants, hot system washing equipment etc are bonded to the mat to eliminate transfer potentials.

The Application Engineer viz . . . , YOU will be the one carrying out the detailed design that will be quite an involved exercise. IEEE STANDARD 80, CBIP standards and IS 3043 are good references.

Design of Lightning Protection

Switchyard has a huge concentration of vital equipment required for the supply of power to the associated plant and its availability is therefore very important.

Since switchyard is connected to long transmission lines the probability of lightning surges that hit the OHLs further travelling into the yard is quite high. It is for this reason that the first equipment that is provided at the line entry is a Surge Arrester as discussed earlier.

The lightning protection practices presented here is for protection against lightning that could strike the switchyard directly.

Normally switchyard houses a few gantries needed to string-in the OHL connections, tap offs etc. Also a few supporting structures for the bus that runs in two or three levels are also present. A judicious selection of a few structures to extend their heights to string overhead 'shielding wires' is ideal for the bare conductors strung for this purpose to result in a 'zone' below that gets protection coverage.

In the case of large power plants the Generator Transformers, Station transformers and Unit transformers are located in the transformer yard close to the power house to minimize MV Bus Duct/ Cable lengths. So they tend to be little away from the yard. However EHV OHLs and shield wires are strung from the Power House building upto the first gantry in the yard and conductors drop off to the Generator transformers to achieve the connection.

The resultant zone offered by the tall power house and the shield wires mentioned above normally provide enough protection for all the equipment in the transformer yard.

Needless to add here that the shield wire requires to be properly connected to the earth mat below.

The methodology for working out the zone of protection varies and are discussed in the separate chapter on lightning protection.

Switchyard Hardware

Clamps & Connectors properly tooled to avoid/minimise corona around at the tap off/connection points is important in an outdoor EHV switchyard apart from need to avoid hot spots in the connections.

The bus to PI connections are either fixed or sliding or flexible type depending on the application needs.

For all equipment connections it is important to ensure Electro Chemical (EC) compatibility to minimise bi metallic corrosion seen when dissimilar metals are in contact in an outdoor environment. Special bimetallic formed pads or liners need to be used as required.

Control Building

Switchyard Control Building is the nerve centre of all operations connected with the yard. Even if normally the operations are from a remote control centre through SCADA, a local control room shall always be there for manual mode of operation.

The building shall typically accommodate the following in a modern switchyard:

> ➢ Control & Relay Panel (CRP)
> ➢ Bus Zone protection Panel (BZP)
> ➢ LV switchboard
> ➢ 110V DC UPS
> ➢ 48V DC UPS for telecom needs
> ➢ Transformer Remote Tap Changer Control (RTCC) Panels
> ➢ SCADA system Panels alongwith its RTU & Isolation panels
> ➢ Tele protection Panels
> ➢ Fibre Optic Patch panels
> ➢ Power Line Carrier Communication (PLCC) panels
> ➢ Battery Room
> ➢ Auxiliary building Fire & Gas panels
> ➢ Lighting & small power panels
> ➢ Miscellaneous O&M equipment
> ➢ Office

Control Room

The Control Room located in the above building is where the human interface with other equipment takes place under normal operation. The building has to be therefore located to withstand blasts in the adjacent plant that the yard caters to. Separate entry & egress facilities should be provided.

Usually the entire Control Building or at least the Control room is elevated well above the grade level to facilitate cabling below.

Related Engineering Drawings

Basic Engineering Drawings

- ➢ SLDs
- ➢ General Arrangement (GA) Drawing
- ➢ Electrical Layout—Plan & Sectional views
- ➢ Control Room Architectural Drawings

Detailed Engineering Drawings

These will be discussed separately in a general sense for all plants.

Foot Note:

Design of AIS yards are not so much 'routine' as you might tend to think.

I had the rewarding experience of designing a 132kV AIS execution located indoor. The reason was, it was for a coastal based fertilizer plant in a corrosive and cyclone prone region and at that time it was not customary to go for a GIS due to commercial availabillty and cost considerations. Note that even nuclear power plants in India in the 70s and even early 80s had 220kV "indoor' conventional AIS and not GIS!

9

Overhead Lines

Overhead lines in the context of our discussions imply use of bare conductors suspended from structures using insulators to transmit/ distribute power. This is the most economic way of distributing power since the major cost of extruded insulation needed for cables and construction of underground trenches for the same are avoided.

However the limitation is in finding the 'Right Of Way' (ROW), safe clearances etc. for construction of the lines in a densely populated area or within plant premises.

Many urban areas still have overhead power distribution at Low Voltage (LV) using insulated cables run overground and these are not considered as OHL for purposes of our discussions.

Some of the aspects of OHL engineering that fall under the following broad categories will be briefly discussed.

- ➢ Electrical aspects
- ➢ Mechanical aspects
- ➢ Structural aspects
- ➢ Miscellaneous aspects

Selection of Voltage levels

Usually OHLs in the following voltages are common.

11kV, 33 kV, 66 kV, 132 kV, 220 kV, 380 kV & 400 kV

In the rural power distribution system 11kV & 33kV OHLs are common.

In the oil & gas sector widespread use of 33kV OHLs to remotely located oil field clusters are common particularly in Gulf countries.

Voltages at and beyond132kV are selected for long run of OHLs to transmit power from generating stations for long distances.

As a "rule of thumb" assume that the voltage should be xx kV if the distance in kms to distribute the power is xx, assuming that the line is loaded to its capacity. Simply put—

> ➤ A 33kV line is good for a distance of 33kms.
> ➤ A 132kV line would be required for longer distances upto 132kms beyond which it might be uneconomic necessitating selection of even higher voltages.

Conductor

Material

Aluminium and Copper are the preferred material. Aluminium and its alloys have superior strength to weight ratio and is preferred because of the impact of this property on other hardwares & spacings of supporting structures needed.

Use of the following Aluminium conductors are common:

AAC	-	All Aluminium Conductor, Stranded
AAAC	-	All Aluminium Alloy Conductor (Al-Mg-Si alloy), stranded
AACSR	-	Aluminium Alloy Conductor, Steel Reinforced
ACSR	-	Aluminium Conductor Steel Reinforced

In general, the conductor external surfaces are preferred smooth so that the ice & wind loading encountered in severe weather, in certain parts of the world, are reduced thus benefiting by requiring reduced number of poles or allowing longer spans.

Towards this the whole assembly extruded is 'compacted'. In compacting process the conductors are compacted by using 'compacting dies' in the manufacturing process. The process results in reduction of OD by circa 6%.

Use of Trapezoidal Wires (TW) is a relatively new concept. Here trapezoidal strands are used. On a like-to-like area basis conductors using TW results in 20~25% more Al area, reduction in AC resistance by 15~20% and increase current carrying capacity by 8~10%.

Vibration Resistant conductor (VR conductor) is another new development. There will be two identical conductors twisted together in "Fig 8" shape that provided superior characteristics in sites having turbulent wind flow eliminating conductor 'galloping'.

Specially designed ACSR conductors have good resistance to 'Aeolean Vibrations' due to wind due to their inherent self damping properties.

Bundled Conductor

Frequently use of 'bundled conductors' where two or more conductors are used in parallel are resorted to in order to ensure operation at lower temperature & lower losses since they offer lower resistance and superior cooling.

Typical conductor spacing in a bundled conductor;

Along the line for twin ELM/YEW AAAC	-	400mm for 132kV lines
		450mm for 220kV lines
Jumpers for above are used at	-	every 200mm for 132kV lines
		every 250mm for 220kV lines

Bundled conductors resultant in lower line reactances and in voltages in the 220kV and above category results in a reduced corona and radio noise.

Insulators

Insulators are vital in OHLs to insulate the electrical line from the supporting structures/Poles. Usually the OHLs have a 'string' of insulators depending on the type & application. Higher the line voltage, more are the insulator units in a string.

Types of Insulators

Different types of insulators are used, depending on the Voltage and mechanical strain (tension) needs. You are encouraged to look from the internet, how various types of insulators look like.

Insulators in general, whatever be the type, need to have good electrical and mechanical strength.

Creepage Distances

As the name implies this is the length measured along the surface of the insulator and the requirements are dependant on the pollution level classifications of an installation.

'Water shed' fins provides better 'creepage'. More the 'creepage' less is the 'leakage path'.

Sharp radii of curvature is avoided in any insulator to reduce voltage caused stresses. They are glazed and free from rough particles or unevenness or voids within. Glass insulators are ideal from this point of view.

More creepage distances are required (from the standard 25mm/kV value) in environments that have sea salts, icing possibilities, bird droppings, chemical deposits or simply dust.

	33kV	132kV	220kV
Minimum creepage distance required	1440mm	5800mm	9800mm
Arcing horn spacing	—	1150mm	1900mm
Power frequency withstand voltage	70kV	275kV	395kV
Lightning Impulse withstand voltage	170kV	650kV	950kV

IEC standard 60815 provides concise guidelines for selecting the appropriate insulators applicable for OHL systems.

Various types of insulators commonly used in OHL are as follows:

Disc type

Here the insulation discs (or insulation units) are strung together. Each disc is typically rated for 10~12kV with a capacitance of 30~40pF. The number of units strung together depends on the rated Voltage of the OHL. The units are strung with each other via their *caps & pins.* Locking mechanism is usually by *ball-socket* or *clevis-tongue.* The cap is insulated from the pin by the porcelain or Glass disc using adhesive cement. These are commonly used in suspension or tension applications.

Long rod type

These use assembles strung together with longer stacks, using manufacturing techniques similar to above. Their longer lengths makes them ideal for phase to phase insulation and reduce line galloping during strong winds. These are commonly used in suspension or tension applications.

Pin type

Pin types, as the name implies are screwed onto a bolt shank secured on the cross arm of a transmission pole. The pin type does not take strain (tension) and functions as a jumper line insulator.

Shackle type

Usually these are applied to take the strain (tension) of the OHL where there is a change in direction of run.

Post type

They have thicker insulation and more discs than pin types and can be mounted by vertical cantilever support to take the OHL/bus dead weight. They usually have a maximum design cantilever load (MDCL) rating. These are never used as a suspension insulator

Hewlett type

This is a variation of the disc type, but can take more strain (tension) due to its internally insulated steel bolt interlocks that holds the discs together instead of cement. Again these have higher internal stresses due to the internal steel bolts rather than cement.

Materials of Insulators

OHL insulators are commonly made of:

Porcelain

This is the most widely used material

Glass

These may be used as disc or pin types. Has superior thermal stability.

<u>Composite synthetics</u>

These are a combination of plastics, resins and fibre glass. More commonly used for long rod and post type insulators. Have superior water resistant properties and tensile strengths

<u>Grading and String efficiency</u>

The voltage stress falls off linearly from the line end disc with the number of insulator discs used. There is also some capacitance coupling of each disc with the pylon and neigbouring structures.

$$\text{String Efficiency} = \frac{\text{Total Votage insulated}}{no.of\ discs\ x\ voltage\ on\ line\ end\ unit}$$

Grading devices in the form of channelizing external flash-overs away from insulators prevent surface damage to insulators.

Typically,

132kV lines have 10~14 11kV insulator discs
220kV lines have 16~20 11kV insulator discs

Insulator surfaces and hence the insulator itself are affected by:

Voltage stresses

Caused by change in surface resistance due to chemical changes and variations on the surface or due to polluting films covering the surface—all increasing the risk of the insulator 'tracking', a phenomenon where a physical scar is caused as a semiconducting track on the surface. Over time with more discharges on the surface, the track may worsen. Arcing horn installed on line insulators reduce the risk of tracking by providing a discharge path further away from the insulator

Mechanical stresses

Caused by bending, tension, compression or torsion loads that could be static or dynamic.

Environmental effects

Caused by end-fitting moisture ingress, surface area contamination, salt water ingress and extreme wind loading.

Vandalism

Caused by the susceptibility of the suspended insulators as a target for shot projectiles or objects thrown by vandals that cause shattering. Problem is acute in case of Porcelain & Glass insulators and lesser in case of polymer types.

Sag and Tension

Before we discuss Sag & Tension, some definitions on the terminology in OHL engineering viz., "Span" is mentioned below:

Basic Span

Basic span indicates distance between centres of adjacent supports on level ground with specified clearances to ground in still air at maximum conductor temperature.

Wind span

Wind span is half the sum of adjacent horizontal span lengths supported by any one support. The maximum wind span of an OHL is therefore a function of the strength of the pole to resist the bending moment caused by wind at right angles to the OHL (the conductors, FO cables, ground wires & insulators) and the support itself.

Weight Span

Weight span is the horizontal distance between the lowest points of conductor on either side of a support at minimum temperature.

Equivalent Span

Equivalent span is used as a representative value of span for a section of OHL for calculation purpose. This is also known as the Ruling Span. A set of different spans within a section of the OHL will be subject to the same horizontal tension. Its equivalent span is given by

$$[(S_1^3 + S_2^3 + S_3^3 \ldots\ldots)/(S_1 + S_2 + S_3 \ldots\ldots)]^{0.5}$$

Where $S_1, S_2, S_3 \ldots\ldots$ spans between various supports 1,2,3 . . . .

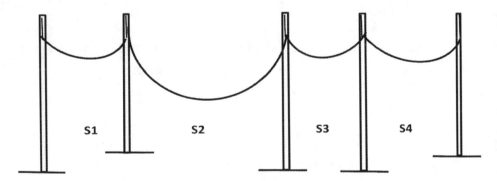

Sag & Tension

Sag at the middle point of the span for poles at equal height is given by the following equation since the conductor forms a catenary

$$\text{Sag} = T_h/W_c * \{\text{Cosh } (W_c * S/2T_h) - 1\} \text{ —(A)}$$

The above value is at a distance of S/2 from the pole. The notations used are;

T_h = Horizontal Tension applied on the conductor
W_c = Weight of conductor per unit length
S = Span between two adjacent supports

The formula can be approximated as follows by a simple "parabola method" for spans below 300m or where the sag is less than 5% of the span length.

$$\text{Sag} = W_c S^2 / 8T_h \text{ —(B)}$$

For unequal heights of adjacent structures the sag does not occur at the mid point between them, but at a point closer to the shorter structure. The "equivalent" span for equal heights will then be more than S and will be twice the distance at which the maxmum sag occurs from the taller pole. This is given by the equation (parabolic method).

$$x = (S/2) - \{T(H_2 - H_1)/W_c S\} \text{ —(C)}$$

where x = distance from the taller support at which there is maximum sag

Value (2x) will now provide the theoretical equivalent span to calculate from Equation (B) above, the value of sag relative to the taller structure.

In OHL stringing we need to meet the following three fundamental considerations:

1) At a conductor temperature of $90^\circ C$, the minimum ground clearances are met
2) Tension at minimum ambient temperature and maximum wind speed does not exceed UTS/FOS specified, usually 2.5.
3) Tension at Every Day Temperature (EDT) and wind speed does not exceed UTS/FOS specified, usually 6.

For this discussion we will denote the T & W values by appropriate suffices 1, 2 & 3 for the three conditions.

If we know the tension of the OHL conductor (or for that matter the FO cable above) at any particular set of conditions of effective weight and temperature we can calculate the tension at any other set of conditions by solving the following equation:

$$T_1 W_1 \sinh(S*W_1/T_1/2)*((1+\alpha)*(t_2-t_1) + (T_2-T_1)/A/E) = T_2/W_2*\sinh(S*W_2/T_2/2)$$

where

T_1 & T_2	=	Horizontal Tension (kgf)
W_1 & W_2	=	Unit weight (kg/m)
t_1 & t_2	=	Temperature (^{0}C)
S	=	Span Length (m)
A	=	Cross sectional area of conductor (mm^2)
A	=	Temp. coeff. of expansion of conductor material (/^{0}C)
E	=	Modulus of Elasticity (Young's modulus) in (kgf/mm^2)

Conductor Spacing

Typically applicable values are given below:

Minimum clearances recommended	33kV	132kV	220kV
Electrical clearance to Earth	320mm	1570mm	2320mm
Spatial clearance	2.5m	2.5m	3.0m
Ph-Ph	2.5m	2.5m	3.0m
Ph—earth wire	320mm	5.0m	6.0m
Clearance to Ground & other facilities			
Normal Ground	6.3m	6.7m	7.0m
Roads with level surface	16.0m	16.0m	16.0m
Buildings/structures/walls	4.6m	4.6m	5.2m

Other lines upto 33kV	2.7m	2.7m	2.7m

For all vertical clearances an allowance of 0.6m should be added as an adhoc value to account for long term conductor creep, the computation of which is otherwise through rigorous empirical methods.

Conductor Hardware

Transmission line hardware are needed to perform long term, not corrode, damage or degrade in strength and be visually aesthetic when in contact with OHLs or with each other. They should also be compatible. You are encouraged to see how the hardwares look like from the internet. The hardware will fall under two broad requirements:

➤ Conductor related hardware

These have significant influence on the operation & maintenance of the line. Such as

- Suspension clamps
- Clamp top clamps
- Tied supports
- Dead end clamps
- Splices
- Strain yokes
- Insulators
- Fittings

➤ Structure related hardware

These affect the required framing of the structure, the requisite clearances and common guying needs such as

- Armour rods
- Cushioned suspension units

- Dampers
- Bundling spacers
- Disc weights/ball weights
- Fasteners (for wooden poles)
- Framing fittings (for wooden poles)
- Swing angle bracket (for wooden poles)
- Guy attachment
- Corrosion hardware

Conductor Motion

Galloping

Conductor "Galloping" sometimes called dancing, is a phenomenon where the transmission line conductors vibrate with very large amplitudes. It usually occurs only when a steady, moderate wind of 10~85kmph blows over a conductor covered by a layer of ice deposited by freezing rain, mist or sleet. The coating may vary from a very thin glaze on one side to solid 75mm cover resulting in the conductor presenting a slightly out-of-round, elliptical, or quasi aero-foil shape. The wind blowing over such irregular shape causes aerodynamic lift.

During galloping the conductor oscillate elliptically at frequencies circa 1Hz or less with amplitudes of several metres. Sometimes the movement is in two loops super imposed on a basic loop.

Such movement may result in hazards such as

- ➢ Ph-to-ph, ph-to-Earth short circuits causing outages/burn outs
- ➢ Violent stresses at supports that may cause conductor failure
- ➢ Structural damages—termed "racking" of structures
- ➢ Mechanical damage at supports
- ➢ Excessive sags due to over stressing of conductors

Galloping however is a concern only when it is historically known to occur or is expected such as in icy areas with cold wind conditions.

The remedy is to graphically check the 'lissajous" ellipses and ensure that none of the ellipses touch each other by providing the required clearances at the supports

Aeolean vibrations

The phenomenon of "Aeolean vibratons" are produced by wind. It is a high frequency low-amplitude oscillation generated by a low velocity with steady wind blowing across the OHL conductors. Steady wind causes air vortices or eddies on the lee side of the conductor. Such vortices will detach at regular intervals from the top & bottom of conductor creating force on the conductor acting from bottom and top alternately. If this frequency resonates with the natural frequency of the span aeolean vibrations are caused whose peak to peak amplitudes may cause bending stresses on the conductor strands and induce fatigue at the attachments to the structure.

Mitigation is by the following:

> Reduced tension
> Use armour rods at support points to cause damping
> Provide cushioned support along with armour rod
> Use stockbridge damper and other types of proven devices. Application techniques in placing these are a highly specialised activity.

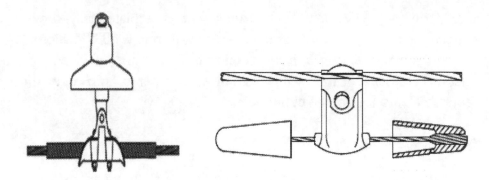

Conductor creep

Prediction of the long term creep characteristics of the OHL conductor and shield wire are an in-depth exercise to be learnt by a practising OHL engineer. Creep compensation regimes are applied at the time of stringing, typically involving prior pre-stressing of the conductors with higher initial tensions over and above the design tension. This will usually work effectively for the initial 10 years service life.

Selecton of type of structures

The purpose of the structure is very basic. It has to safely hold the bare OHL at a prescribed height, with proper spacing between the conductors and withstand the loading of conductors, insulators and other hardware under all design conditions of environment.

Usually the type of structures are decided by Owner companies based on their historical experience, dictated by prevailing practices. Commercial considerations dictate though of late environmental issues are also being addressed.

Usually in the Gulf and in European as well as American environment wooden poles are extensively used for voltage levels of 33kV and 132kV.

Lattice steel structures are widely used for voltages beyond the above.

Types of structures are spelt out by their functionality. For a given section length, comprising of a number of a section of spans, the *intermediate* structures are meant to just support the conductors at the required elevation while the *terminal structures* at the ends of a section carry the tension loads of the entire section and provides an integrated stability of the entire strung section viewed as an assembly. Thus the intermediate structures will carry the conductors on suspension or post insulators while the terminal structures will have the conductors clamped in tension insulators or a combination of tension & suspension insulators or a combination of tension & suspension/post insulators to let the conductor pass through to the next section and so on.

The design/configuration of the above structures are usually standardized to achieve economy in fabrication/procurement/replacement, but by no means an Application Engineer for OHL should stop from seizing more economical options.

Loadings

Loadings "requirements" are passed on to Structural Engineer designing the OHL support structures. Typically as follows:

> - Unequal wind load and/or differential ice conditions on equal/unequal spans
> - A broken conductor
> - Stringing loads
> - Change in the ruling span
> - Construction & maintenance activities that might cause load

It is customary—for economic reasons—not to design the intermediate wooden pole supports for "broken" conductor longitudinal loadings. The restraining capacity of the dead ends are relied upon thus not ruling out cascading failure of poles within a section.

Design Climatic conditions

These form a very important consideration. Typically in brief as follows;

- ➢ Design Temperatures   -   Minimum, Maximum, Every day
- ➢ Design Wind Pressure   -   At minimum temp
- ➢ Wind force coeff   -   for conductors, for shield wires etc.
- ➢ Shape factor   -   for conductors, for shield wires etc.

Recommended Factor Of Safety (FOS) in the design.

Typically in brief as follows:

Conductors, Shield wire etc., for min temp & maximum wind pressure	: 2.5
Conductors, Shield wire etc., for still EDT	: 5.0

Supports & Foundations

Intermediate supports	: 2.0
Angle/Section Dead End supports	: 2.5
Under maximum unbalanced loads	: 1.5
Under maximum construction & maintenance loads	: 1.75

Insulator strings & shield wire fittings	: 3.0

Foundations

For steel towers

Following types are common

- ➢ Pad & chimney foundations
- ➢ Rock anchor foundations
- ➢ Pile foundations

> Drilled shaft foundations
> Raft & special foundations for submerged conditions

For wooden poles

Wooden Poles are usually laid in excavations carried out by machine driven augurs to suit pole base sizes and mechanical tamping of the back fill around the poles. Depths are normally more than 1.75m. Unreinforced concrete is poured inside the interspace.

Guys & Anchors

For terminal wooden poles stay wires are used for terminal and angled structures, sections, road crossing structures.

Lattice steel structures normally do not require stays.

Stay wire designs should factor-in the following;

> Strength of stay wire
> Strength of anchor point
> Crippling strength of wooden pole
> Bending strength of wooden pole
> Mechanical strength of connecting insulators

After installation all stay wires are adjusted using turn buckle arrangements.

Miscellaneous aspects in OHL engineering

Line Routing

A thorough investigation of the line route is called for; to begin with a Preliminary route to ensure availability of space, safe clearances, right of way, impact on adjacent facilities construction costs, maintenance cost, engineering issues and aesthetics.

To start off line routes are now a days selected using photogrammetry, further improved with high attitude satellite imagery. Modern GIS tools provide an automated route identification process taking into account Roads, highways, streams, rivers, lakes, river beds, rail roads, air strips, other OHLs in the area, pipelines, UG cables, buildings etc.

Right Of Way Preliminary surveying

The entire route of the OHL is physically mapped.

A basic route is chosen to avoid/minimise need for in line joints. The maximum section length is usually chosen as 2000m for 33kV OHL on wooden poles, 5000m for 132kV OHL on wooden poles/steel towers.

Line Survey

A ground based level survey is done apart from the route survey. The plan and profile drawings in scale 1:100 horizontally and 1:20 vertically are prepared showing vicinity details, ROW etc.

Pole/Tower spotting

Poles/Towers are then spotted at vantage locations—such as change in directions, elevations, high points, river banks, sides of road crossings etc. The intermediate poles are then located as per span needs and to suit section lengths.

Thus a preliminary spotting is done for all types of structures that will be provided.

Intermediate structures normally tolerate a deviation of 5^0 beyond which a section tower might be needed.

Sag calculations would reveal adequacy of ground clearances and help decide which poles are to be more closely spaced.

Coupling aspects

In an oil & gas environment the influence of EHV OHLs on pipelines in the vicinity carrying hydrocarbons becomes important. The metal pipelines are in reality conductors insulated from earth. The OHL can have three types of coupling with it viz., Capacitive, Inductive and conductive.

Under normal conditions induced voltages may be reasonably low, but under faut conditions with inadequate protective measures, the induced voltages on pipelines could reach several hundred volts to a few kilo volts.

Capacitive couplings are possible only if pipelines are above ground, but in realty almost all pipelines are buried.

Inductive couplings happen if pipeline runs are in parallel with the OHL for long stretches. The voltage magnitudes depend on the separation distance, transmission voltage levels, pipeline coating resistance and soil resistivity. It is good engineering practice to restrict the voltage under normal condition to not more than 50V. Assessment of the induced voltages under fault conditions calls for good expertise. Some practical go-bys in the separation distances are as follows for various values of parallel run of OHL & Pipelines:

- Upto 4.5kms   -   500m
- 4.5 to 6.0kms   -   1 km
- 6.5 to 10.0kms   -   1.75kms
- > 10kms   -   specialized study is called for

Other mitigation measures as an abundant caution are providing low resistance pipeline coating, grounding mat near the pipelines, crushed rock/limestone on the surface near pipelines etc. for persons to safely stand and work.

Conductive coupling is dominant if the above two is absent. The potential of the pipeline will be close to that of the reference potential of the "remote" earth. Faults in adjacent towers will therefore cause a potential rise with respect to above at times causing puncturing of the pipeline coating. Mitigation practices include maintaining a separation of at least 50m between the OHL and the pipeline, maintain crossing angle of the OHL and pipeline to more than 45^0 and increase thickness of pipeline die electric coating.

Communication

Present day practice is to run fibre optic cable along OHLs for Protection & Control functions. Aerial All Dielectric Short Span (ADSS) FO cables are usually used for OHLs on wood poles. Composite Overhead Optical Fibre Ground Wire (OPGW) are usually common in case of OHLs on steel towers. The OPGW is a combination of AAA wires, Aluminium clad steel wires and stranded FO unit. These also come with its requirement of hardware similar to the OHLs.

Aviation Warning Systems

All towers in the flight path vicinities are painted red & white in accordance with ICAO Recommended practice.

Orange coloured aircraft warning spheres of 600mm dia are installed on the conductors in runway/landing approaches, near helipads etc.

Aircraft Induction warning lights of the neon type are also installed as required by ICAO.

Tower peaks are provided with aircraft low intensity beacons—usually in pairs with solar cell back-ups, batteries and photocell operated.

Those near aircraft landing areas should have high intensity beacons backed up from DG sources.

Earthing System

All pole/tower top devices are interconnected and earthed for safety by connecting them to the earth provided below. Earth provided below is as per the usual earthing practice. Each tower will have a dedicated earth rod adjacent to the diagonally opposite legs. During dry weather the tower footing resistance to earth should not be more than 10 ohms. Otherwise sufficient lengths of bare wires buried underground are to be connected in combination with treated earth pits and multiple earth rods.

Bird Risk mitigation

Birds have a tendency to perch on top of the support arm of wood poles and their droppings could cause insulation tracking. A safe bird nesting platform is at times constructed below at a safe level rather than risk birds to do so on the pole top.

Access Roads

Vehicular access roads of at least 4m width is normally laid using appropriate back fill along the entire stretch of the OHL for construction & maintenance purpose.

Foot Note:

However much you think engineering of OHL is a science, it still tends to be an art.

A good OHL design engineer can always look for cost saving opportunities by deviating from the much beaten track and look for optimizing the location of poles, configuration of poles etc. This field is open to a lot of engineering gymnastics that you should enjoy doing!

10

Insulated Cables

Insulated Power, Control & Instrument cables constitute a substantial part of the Capital Expenditure (CAPEX) involved in a large Industrial plant. In one large Process plant receiving power at 132kV the cost of insulated cables alone was as high as about 30% of the Total Electrical Cost

YOU as an Application Engineer can thus understand the importance of selecting and buying the cables right. An awareness of the different types of cables and their construction etc. will help.

Cable Construction

Conductor : This could be of Aluminium or Copper.
Flexible stranded or even solid.
Shaped round or 'shaped' and/or compacted

Conductor Screen : This is a semiconducting wrap around the conductor to provide an equipotential surface to the insulation above. This is not provided for cables in the low voltage range.

Insulation : This is mostly of extruded material and could be of Poly Vinyl Chloride (PVC) or Cross Linked Polyethylene (XLPE) or Ethylene Propylene Rubber (EPR). The thickness depends on the voltage grade requirement.

Insulation screen : This is a must for cables whose voltage grade is > 3.3kV. It comprises of an extruded/wrapped semi conducting screen above which there is a metallic screen. The latter is usually a wrapped tape, normally of copper. In addition to this often some drain wires of copper strands are also provided.

Binders/Fillers : These are needed in a multi core cable to keep the overall shape round for ease of extrusion. Usually the fillers/binders are of non hygroscopic material.

Inner Sheath : The extruded sheath holds the multi cores inside 'together' and provide some protection to the insulation within. Usually this is of PVC.

Armour : This is a metallic protection above the inner sheath (of multi core cables) made of Galvanised steel 'wires'—either Flat or round and in case of single core cables it is made of Aluminium round wires. For specific applications the armour is made of GI wire braiding to render better flexibility to the cable.

Outer Sheath : This is extruded above the armour and makes the cable have a tough exterior so that it becomes suitable for direct burial with uncontrolled back fill with chances of even flooding. This is usually made of PVC or PE.

Lead Sheath : A layer of lead sheath above makes the cable impervious to oil and hydro carbons around and therefore often used in refinery applications.

Obviously there are many variants to the above depending on the application needs.

Application Issues

Choice of Conductor is driven by essentially cost. Aluminium cables are usually cheaper than copper. Conductivity of Aluminium is about 60% that of copper So for the same ampere rating you need a larger conductor which in turn means larger amount of all other items needed above the conductor like insulation, inner sheath, armour, outer sheath etc leading to higher overall diameter (OD).

Cross section of conductor is dictated by the current rating requirements as follows:

> ➤ The Full Load Current (FLC) of the connected equipment
> ➤ The Short Circuit (SC) Current of the system it has to carry in kA for . . . sec.

Flow of FLC & SC current causes shooting up of the conductor temperature under steady state and for short time respectively and hence the property of the insulation could dictate the maximum temperature (T_{MAX}) allowed.

For PVC insulation it is 70^0C and 160^0C whereas for XLPE insulation it is 90^0C and 250^0C.

Thus for the same SC level in the circuit we can have a cable with lower cross section in case of XLPE insulation and thus use of XLPE cables are widespread.

$$I_{SC} = \frac{0.0927}{\sqrt{t}} \text{ A for copper conductor XLPE cables}$$

$$OR \quad \frac{0.141}{\sqrt{t}} \text{ A for aluminium conductor XLPE cables where}$$

I_{SC} = Short Circuit Current in kA

A = Conductor cross section in mm^2

t = duration of short circuit current in seconds

It assumes an initial conductor temperature of 90°C and a final short time temperature limit of 250°C, typical for XLPE cables.

The formulae is derived from fundamental material constants/properties that can be found in any text book. Note that for PVC insulated cables the values corresponding to above are 70°C and 160°C and hence the formulae is DIFFERENT.

Another important criterion that dictates the conductor size is therefore the 't' to be considered.

t = 0.2 seconds in case the outgoing circuit where it is used is backed up by an HRC fuse that can clear the SC downstream in even lesser time.

t = 1.0 seconds or even higher in case of Incomer cables to switchboards to allow for downstream clearing tme + relaying time + breaker operating time + some design margin.

Note that choice of t alters the cost significantly and is an important aspect in designing a safe plant.

Voltage Drop

An important issue we did not discuss till now is that the choice of conductor cross section will affect the voltage drop in the cable even if it were selected to meet the current rating criteria discussed earlier.

You should be familiar with the typical vectorial representation of voltage and current in an AC system that you should remember forever.

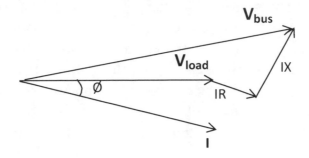

This is a very usual scenario in practical power distribution.

The notations are explained below:

V_{bus} is the supply voltage at the bus,
V_{load} is the voltage at the load terminals,
I is the current considered to be flowing through the cable
cosØ is the lagging power factor.
R is the resistance of the cable/m
X is the Reactance of the cable/m
L is the length of the cable in metres.

With reasonable accuracy within acceptable norms, we have voltage drop

$$(V_{bus} - V_{load}) = \sqrt{3}I(Rcos\emptyset + Xsin\emptyset)L$$

How much this drop is allowed depends on the application needs and there can be a lot of engineering gymnastics on this.

The supply voltage usually has a variation of ± 10% thus implying that if the motor is already running, the bus voltage can fall to 90% of its rated value due to supply variation. The motors are specified to run satisfactorily upto 90% rated voltage at its terminals. Hence there can be very little drop allowed in the cables during running condition.

Therefore during running condition of a typical load, including a motor load this 'drop' should not be more than 2.5% of the rated voltage of the connected equipment.

The value of Resistance R is to be computed at 90°C from the catalogue value of ac resistance at 20°C as per the formulae

$R_{90} = R_{20} * (1 + \alpha(90 - 20))$ where α is the coefficient of resistivity of the conductor.

During starting condition of a motor, the I_{START} is typically 6 times I_{FLC} with a 20% tolerance.

Thus the I_{START} of the motor can be upto $7.2 I_{FLC}$. This is the value of current that should be used to determine the voltage drop in the cable at starting of the motor unless the application calls for use of specially designed motors that are designed for much lower starting current, ofcourse at a cost.

The voltage drop at start is thus given by

$$(V_{bus} - V_{motor}) = 7.2 * \sqrt{3} I (R cos \emptyset s + X sin \emptyset s) L \text{ where}$$

the new notation $\emptyset_s$ indicates the pf angle at start. Typical starting pf values are 0.4 against a running value of 0.85 and this results in a larger influence of reactance X in the calculation.

The voltage drop at start is typically allowed as 15% of the rated terminal voltage. Since normally motors are specified for suitability to start at even 80% rated voltage a 5% cushion is kept to account for bus voltage already lower from the rated voltage due to the other running loads and the incoming cables would have been designed for a 2.5% drop with the remaining 2.5% being a slight cushion in the distribution design.

Remember if the bus voltage itself is lower, say 90% of the rated value due to the fluctuation of ± 10% allowed, the starting current also will be proportionally lower and hence need not be factored-in in our calculation of voltage drop in the cable at start.

Current Rating of Cables

The current carrying capacity of cables in Amperes or 'Ampacities' are also affected by the way the cables are laid.

"Catalogue" values are for a particular ambient temperature and a "single cable" laid in 'free' air. So the influence of the laying parameters on the cable ampacity should be clearly understood.

1) Air temperature variation

Ambient air temperature (^{0}C)	20	25	30	35	**40**	45	50
Rating Factor	1.18	1.14	1.10	1.05	**1**	0.95	0.9

2) Ground temperature variation

Ground temperature (^{0}C)	10	15	20	**25**	30	35	40	45
Rating Factor	1.11	1.08	1.04	**1**	0.98	0.91	0.87	0.83

3) Thermal resistivity of Ground

Thermal resistivity of soil (^{0}Cm/W)	0.7	**1**	1.2	15	2	2.5	3	3.5
Rating Factor	1.14	**1.0**	0.93	0.84	0.74	0.67	0.61	0.55

4) Depth of laying

Depth of laying (m)	0.50 ~ 0.70	0.71 ~ 0.90	0.91 ~ 1.10	1.11 ~ 1.30	**1.31 ~ 1.50**
Rating Factor	1.09	1.05	1.03	1.01	**1**

5) <u>Group rating factors for multi core cables **in flat formation in ground**</u> (typlcal for 1~33kV cables)

Spacing	No. of cables in the same trench						
	2	3	4	5	6	8	10
Touching	0.79	0.69	0.63	0.58	0.55	0.50	0.46
70 cms	0.85	0.75	0.68	0.64	0.60	0.56	0.53
250 cms	0.87	0.79	0.75	0.72	0.69	0.66	0.64

6) <u>Cables in pipes</u>

Spacing		No. of cables in pipes						
	1	2	3	4	5	6	8	10
Touching	0.80	0.75	0.65	0.60	0.60	0.55	0.55	0.50
70 cms		0.70	0.70	0.65	0.60	0.60	0.55	0.55
250 cms		0.70	0.70	0.70	0.70	0.65	0.65	0.65

7) Cables in metal trays			Rating Factor		
			No. of cables		
			1	2	3
Touching	⊙⊙⊙⊙⊙⊙⊙⊙	1 tray	0.97	0.85	0.74
		≥ 2 trays	0.97	0.83	0.71
With spacing	⊙ ⊙ ⊙	1 tray	0.97	0.96	0.93
	≥30mm for d ≥ 30mm	≥ 2 trays	0.97	0.94	0.90

Cables in metal ladders			Rating Factor		
			No. of cables		
1		2	3		
Touching	●●●●●●●	1 tray	1	0.87	0.74
		≥ 2 trays	1	0.85	0.71
1	● ● ●	1 tray	1	1	1
1	≥ 30mm for d ≥ 30mm	≥ 2 trays	1	1	1

Note that derating factors occur cumulatively.

Overall derating factor = that in (2) x (3) x (4) x (5)

Or = that in (1) x (7)

The above is usually always < 1 even as low as 0.4!!

Thus where apparently a single run might look adequate, even two runs per phase might be needed to meet the ampacity needs.

Take this into account—in our favour—while computing the voltage drops.

This has no role in short circuit rating—easy to guess?

Choice of insulation

Use of Paper insulated cables is now virtually obsolete.

Insulation of Poly Vinyl Chloride (PVC) is very common in low voltage applications. The mechanical properties of PVC are also superior as an ideal outer sheath for the cables. PVC can tolerate a continuous temperature of 70°C while for a short duration a temperature as high as 160°C. The conductor cross sections are dictated by the above for the ampacities they have to carry. PVC—though not inflammable—burns in the presence of air (oxygen) and releases Hydrogen and Chlorine that poses limitations in its uses in large plants.

Cross Linked Polyethylene (XLPE) insulated cables are very popular. XLPE can tolerate higher continuous temperature of 90^0C and for short time as high as 250^0C. The conductor ampacities are therefore superior to PVC. XLPE however is inflammable and burns easily but does not liberate Hydrogen and Chlorine. Hence XLPE cables with inner & outer sheathing of PVC are almost the Industry standard.

Ethylene Propylene Rubber (EPR) is another insulation material that has even better properties than XLPE is widely used in the US. EPR is particularly suitable in nuclear environments and extreme low temperature environments where PVC & XLPE are found to dis integrate fast.

Voltage Grade

Apart from the 'physical' properties of the insulation the Application Engineer needs to understand the Electrical property called **Voltage Grade** of the insulation that decides the thickness of insulation that contributes to a significant cost component of the cable.

For Earthed system, the voltage grade of the cable is (U_0/U) indicated as 'earthed grade cables' while for unearthed system it is (U/U) indicated as 'unearthed grade cables'. The insulation thickness is dictated by the 'phase' voltage in the former and the line-to-line voltage in the case of latter.

In the event of Single Line to Ground Fault in the cable, in "Earthed System" the voltage/phase will never reach the line-to-line value whereas in 'Unearthed System" it will. The insulation thicknesses are therefore different for "Earthed Grade" and "Unearthed Grade" cables for the same line-to-line system voltages.

Cable Capacitance

Capacitance of cables are dictated by the type of insulation and dimensional configuration of the conductors. The capacitance governs the di-electric losses in the cables This is highest for Paper Insulated (PILCA) cables and quite low for XLPE cables.

Choice of Armour

"Armour" of a cable—as the name implies—provides mechanical protection to the cable. This is very important since the reliability of an electrical installation can only be as good as that of the cable.

Armour can be of

> - Single Round Wire (GI wire)—for multi core cables
> - Single/Multiple Flat Wire (GI flat)—for multi core cables
> - Single Round Aluminium Wire—for 1c cables
> - Braided GI wire cables—for multicore flexible cables

Flat wire armour provides better protection compared to round wire since the latter has only a 'line' contact with the sheathing below. However flat wire often 'bites into' the inner sheath/outer sheath with which its surface is in contact due to its relatively sharp edges. This particularly manifests when cables are laid with a lot of bends with small radius that stresses the armour and pushes it off from its original position. Round GI wire armours are therefore superior in this respect.

Braiding provides greater flexibility to the cables when compared to the other types of armour but its relative strength is lesser since it is made of thinner wires.

Armour has its electrical functions too. It provides a good 'return' path to the SLG fault currents. Often the current ratings of armour is checked for the SLGF current capability for the duration by which time the Electrical Ground Fault protection relays come into operation.

For single core cables armour has to be of non magnetic material since there is always an induced current in the armour that causes significant eddy current heating in case of current flow through earthing at either end. This substantially influences the current ratings. For armours earthed at both ends, the circulation of current in the armour causes derating of the cable. For armour earthed at only one end there is a potential rise at the other end with respect to the 'earthing' of armour that can cause insulation break downs depending on the cable length involved.

Submersible cables

Cables for submersible duty are called for in the offshore industry and such cables have added constructional features that make them totally impervious to water under pressure.

Fire resistance/Fire proof cables

Fire resistant/Fire proof cables are used for applications where survival of the circuit is vital for working of the electrical system even under fire. E.g., cables supplying Fire water pump motor or Fire & Gas alarm systems. The standards prescribe special tests for such cables to ascertain the 'oxygen index' of the PVC outer sheath. More the number, more oxygen is required to ignite the PVC sheath and less vulnerable it is to burn.

For continuous high temperature environments, Mineral Insulated (MI) cables are used.

Solar Radiation

Constant exposure to sun may suffer degradation of the outer sheath that is off-set by adding carbon compounds in the sheathing material. Still it is usual practice to provide covers in the cable trays for protection against direct sun, with provision for air circulation so that there is no compromise on the derating factors for current ratings.

Rodent & Termite attack

Many Installations in tropical countries in particular are susceptible to rodent & termite attacks. For such applications the cable outer sheath is provided with some chemical additives that repels such attacks. However the effect on the environment should there be direct burial of such cables needs to be carefully ascertained.

Control Cables

Usually multi core PVC insulated, sheathed, armoured and PVC outer sheathed cables are used for purposes of Electrical Control, Interlocks, Metering & Protection circuits.

Conductor is always of copper and the sizes are typically 1.5, 2.5 or 4 mm^2.

The no. of cores are from 2C to even 37C. The requirement is selected by the Application Engineer based on control wiring needs depending on the application and segregation of circuitry desired. Normally a few unused 'spare' cores are provided for future contingency.

Instrumentation Cables

Cables used for Instrumentation or telecommunications are required to carry either Digital signals (on-off), High level analogue signals (4 to 20mA) or low level analogue signals (in milli volts) depending on the applications. The conductors come in 'pairs' or 'triads' each provided with its insulation, sheathing and braided shielding to render them immune to external electrical noises and the whole cable has such multi pairs/triads, with overall shielding and armouring.

Cable Drums

Cables are packed in wooden or steel drums and the lengths in a drum are continuous called the 'Drum Length'. Drum lengths are dictated by manufacturing constraints and supplies are usually not very precise, but a certain ±% of what is ordered. Power cables usually come in lengths of 500m, lesser in case of large sized cables. Sometimes drum lengths of even 1000m are specified to avoid joints in critical installations.

Joints in Control cables are usually avoided and so large drum lengths are common.

Most of the large users require embossing of running lengths on the outer sheath to facilitate ease of cable cutting and quantity reconciliation at site.

Transport and site handling constraints dictate sizes of cable drums and hence the drum length it can hold.

Handling and storage of cable drums at site need special attention. Since cables lie unused at site yards for a long time until all other civil works and equipment installation is completed, proper storage of drums at site becomes important.

Foot Note:

If anyone thinks he knows enough about cables he will be surprised to know that he doesn't. The manufacturers constantly come up with improvements that could provide more economic solutions.

Selecting the right cable to just meet the need calls for rigorous, systematic design efforts.

I have come across a case where a coal handling plant contractor had most of his LV motors of the conveyors not able to start since while engineering, the designer had overlooked the actual route lengths of the rather long LV cables usual in a coal handling system. By then the cables have already been installed & terminated at site. Imagine the extra cost and the upset schedule.

11

Bus Ducts

Bus Duct is an effective alternative to cable connection where a large number of cables are involved particularly for short runs—such as Incomer to switchgear from a transformer, connection between two sections of a switchgear etc. By its very nature of construction they are much more reliable than a cable connection, and look neat and compact.

Conductor material in a bus duct is either copper or Aluminum. They are usually bare and hence have good ampacity per sq mm of material used. Conductors are usually separated from each other by air with spacing dependant on the service voltage.

Enclosures render the bus duct totally enclosed, impervious to moisture and ingress of dust and also prevent mechanical damage to the conductor. Enclosures are usually of steel or Aluminium or stainless steel depending on the application.

Bus ducts broadly are categorized as follows:

➢ Non segregated bus ducts—usual for all LV applications and even for some MV applications too.
➢ Segregated phase bus ducts—here a barrier exist between the phase conductors that are usually laid in flat formation for the three phases. These are common for MV & HV applications.
➢ Isolated Phase bus duct—here the conductors of the three phases are separately executed with individual enclosures. Such bus ducts are common for high ampacities such as for a Generator connection. The isolated execution necessitates

use of non magnetic material (Aluminium) as the enclosure to minimise eddy losses in the enclosure and consequent heating.

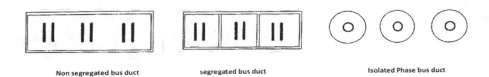

Non segregated bus duct   segregated bus duct   Isolated Phase bus duct

Some Application Engineering considerations are discussed below:

Conductor

Conductors that are of Copper or Aluminum come in various shapes and sizes to provide an optimal geometry. Rectangular bars are common in low ratings since providing a similar additional bar can cater to higher ratings, thus standardizing the manufacturing process. Providing supports for such bar shaped conductors are usually achieved using pre moulded insulated support pieces.

Larger ratings call for use of channel shaped conductors or even two channels placed face-to-face to almost form a box. This arrangement provide better cooling and also can be easily supported since the 'assembly' of the conductor is quite rigid for this shape.

Very large isolated phase bus ducts have unique geometrical shapes such as open C shaped or bars drawn with annular shapes to minimize corona effect by avoiding sharp contours. Also equidistant spacing is provided between the conductor and the circular enclosure. Invariably the conductor is supported at 120^0 spacing along the insides of the enclosure for maximum stability.

Non segregated bus duct conductors have their ampacities from 600A to even 6000A.

Ampacities are normally based on 40°C ambient temperature where conductors have silver-plated joints, and the allowable temperature rise of the conductor is 65°C. For non-current carrying parts that can be readily touched, it is common to allow a 40°C rise.

Ambient temperature range limits are usually −30°C to +40°C, and altitude is up to 1000 metres. Other ambient conditions need special consideration and may need de-rating.

Conductor ratings for isolated phase bus ducts go from 1200 to even 24000A.

Conductor Joints

Conductors are normally connected up using fish plates that are tin plated in case of copper and silver plated in case of Aluminium conductors. The fish plates ensure use of standard length of conductor sections and also are required near where the CTs are mounted so as to facilitate their removal and replacement.

Conductors should also have expansion joints to allow for the movement in conductors due to thermal expansion.

Insulators/Conductor supports

As the name implies the insulators provide required separation of conductors from the enclosure and at the same time ensure appropriate mechanical support. The spacing along the run of the conductor is dictated by flexural deflections of the conductor, even though they are reasonably rigid. Conductors are mounted on custom moulded FRP blocks or on post insulators

Conductor to conductor spacing between two adjacent phases are dictated by electrodynamic forces between them and the same is ultimately withstood by the insulators that are checked for their cantilever strength. It is usual to mount the insulators on resilient pads before bolting the bottom frames to the enclosure so that the pads can provide adequate damping to the forces acting on the conductors.

Enclosures

Enclosures are the most important component of the bus duct since this is what causes bus duct to achieve the connection as a single entity, impervious to moisture ingress and also provide necessary air space inside to achieve the required steady state ampacity without temperature rise in the conductor exceeding the pre determined limits.

Enclosure insides are often coated black for maximizing absorption of heat radiated from the conductor inside.

Enclosure has to be sufficiently thick to have adequate rigidity, should not rust both inside as well as outside. Besides the outdoor portion of the bus duct run should have enclosures with sloping tops to ensure that rain water flows off and do not collect into a puddle between the flanges, access hatches etc.

Enclosures need to have access hatches for the insulators and insulator supports so that they can be removed and replaced if required later. It is important to design the hatches covers with suitable gaskets in order to ensure that the hatches when closed are weather proof.

Drain points are provided at strategic locations to ensure that condensed water, if any drains off appropriately.

Bus Duct supports

Supports provided externally to the bus duct run ultimately provide a stable and rigid arrangement for the entire bus duct run to stay in place as per the layout. These supports are usually of pre fabricated galvanized steel and are readily installed at site as per properly engineered drawings for installation.

Support intervals are dictated by layout considerations and are design checked for short circuit forces that may occur. An independent self standing support is usually the norm. Advantage is taken of existing structures of the buildings nearby rather than unnecessarily investing in dedicated structures, also to minimize interferences with roof beams, bracings, air con ducts, lightings, roof/wall openings etc.

For critical runs such as generator bus ducts or even the runs used in the main substations, it is now a days customary to model in 3D the entire structural support along with the bus duct to check for feasibility of the routing as also for clashes and take remedial measures since later on at site it will be very difficult to incorporate any changes in the fabricated items.

Terminations of bus duct

Termination of bus ducts at the switchgear or transformer terminals need careful dimensional matching. Also the phase sequences are to be kept in mind. Usually conductor connections at both ends make use of tin plated copper braids/Aluminium flexible that will allow good heat dissipation and also lend itself well to slight adjustments due to dimensional tolerances, level mis matches etc.

The hot spots are invariably at the terminations Therefore use of silver/tin plated Aluminum/Copper reduces contact resistance and thereby remove possibility of local hot spots.

Bellowed enclosure at transformer end

Transformer foundations tend to sink if the transformers are large and this may lead to enormous stresses in the connections between the enclosures of bus duct at transformer end with the flanges at transformer terminals. While the flexible connections take care of stresses in the conductors a bellow like arrangement at the enclosure release the stresses on the enclosure.

Elbows/bends

Bus duct connections are not flexible and will have to follow pre engineered routes. Therefore it is required to make use of Horizontal/ Vertical elbows, bends etc to achieve a smooth layout. These are usually stand alone sections—meaning, it will have its own set of insulators supporting the conductors, minimum two per phase.

Wall entries

Entries of bus duct from the outside to inside a room such as a switchgear room are usually through a wall opening. If the entire run is taken in through a cut out, chances are that the outside moist air might enter the switchgear and cause insulation break down. To prevent this specially made wall seal sections are used in the bus duct run. These house sealed bushings to which the bus duct conductors are connected at either end for electrical continuity but at the same time isolates the air from the two sides.

CTs

Usually window/ring type of CTs are used with large ratios since the current ratings are normally high which is why a bus duct is used in the first place.

Provision exist in the enclosure for inspection and access to the CTs and also access hatches are provided for removal of the CT if required.

Space Heaters

Space heaters are distributed throughout the length of the bus duct and are in service when the circuit connections are OFF. This is to prevent condensation on the support insulators that might track on re-energisation.

Breathers

Since the bus ducts hold a huge volume of air inside it is desirable to allow the hot air to escape out, but at the same time ensure that the normal convectional inflow of outside air are taken through Silica gel dessicators to absorb moisture if any rather than it settling on the insulators inside that may result in tracking.

The breathers are usually made of glass so that change in colour of the siica gel inside would indicate ingress of moisture.

Hot Air blowing equipment

Provision of connections for attaching a hot air bowing equipment is a simple mechanism to blow a stream of hot air inside prior to energizing a large bus duct after a prolonged shut down so as to drive away any moisture entrapped within.

Cable Bus ducts

Cable bus ducts are compact versions of bus ducts and consist of a metal enclosure containing copper conductors that are fully insulated. Support bocks for the cables keep them inside at prescribes spacings > 2D. Cable buses are available at voltages upto 38kV and currents upto 5000A. These are used in applications involved in connections between transformers & switchgears, tie between switchgears etc.

Bus Trunking System using "sandwich" type bus ducts

The busbar trunking system is another compact version of air enclosed bus ducts. Use of these are prevalent in workshops etc where power feeders are taken to a large number of users. These offer a high short-circuit rating and is particularly suited for the connection of transformers to low-voltage main distribution boards and sub-distribution boards. The system offers optimal power distribution for both horizontal and vertical bus bar runs and facilitates a neat layout.

Foot Note:

Use of bus ducts provides a neat/compact layout and a reliable installation. However in many situations, I have seen this is not so much encouraged in a project to 'avoid' the so called co-ordination issues.

Isolated phase generator bus ducts of the MV variety for large utility generators on the other hand, call for a great deal of care in designing and ingenuity in working out the finer points. Even simple things like locating the hot air blowing equipment, providing expansion bellows, flexibles, elliptical holes in flanges etc. need good eye for details.

12

Lighting

Lighting constitutes a very important requirement in any Industrial installation and hence a very significant 'load'. Thus, a properly engineered lighting installation will render the installation

- ➢ Safe
- ➢ Aesthetic
- ➢ Optimal from power consumption point of view
- ➢ Reliable

Unlike in residential premises, almost all plants need a significant illumination even during the day time and adequate importance in illumination Engineering is called for that addresses these aspects of Uniformity, colour and Glare.

Terminologies used

It is important to be aware of a few essential terminologies, relevant for this discussion, that are commonly used in illumination engineering. Instead of 'bland' definitions, explanatory notes are provided for clarity.

Candle Power	:	Intensity of light given off by a light source in a particular direction. Also known as Candela
Lumens or Luminous Flux	:	The unit is Lumens. It is a measure of the amount of light that 'flows out' of the lamp.

Luminous intensity	:	It is the solid angular luminous flux density in Candelas.
Lux levels	:	It is the density of luminous flux incident on the surface considered.
Lamp Lumen Depreciation	:	Light loss takes place in a lamp due to gradual decay in lumen output over a particular period of burning time. This is given by the ratio of total lumen output at any time to the Total lumen output initially. Catalogue Norms of providing lumen output values are usually those after 100 burning hrs.
Ceiling reflectance	:	This is a number that indicates how reflective the ceiling surface is. Maximum value is 1.
Wall reflectance	:	This is a number that indicates how reflective the wall surface is. Maximum value is 1. Normally walls are less reflective than the ceiling.
Floor reflectance	:	This is a number that indicates how reflective the Floor surface is. Normally floors are less reflective than the ceiling and wall.
Working plane	:	It is the height above which the general or task illumination is considered. Typically the value is 0.7 metres from the floor.
Room Index (RI)	:	$RI = LW/(H_m*(L+W))$ where L & W indicates the length and width of the room considered and H_m is the 'mounting height' above the working plane considered i.e., the distance from the 'bottom of the fixture' to the 'working plane'
Coefficient of Utilisation	:	This gives a measure of the amount of useful light that reaches the working plane from all the luminaires. It is a function of the type of fixture, its mounting height, room proportions and reflectances of wall, ceiling and working plane.

Cut off angle : The photometric data of a lighting fixture is given in Cd/1000 lumens plotted against the angle from the vertical axis. The value of the angle (say θ on either side) where the output is 10% of the maximum value Is termed as the cut off angle. Cut off angle of the lighting fixtures or beam spread will then be indicated as $2 \times \theta$. Lumens outside the cut-off angle are not considered useful for practical purposes.

Beam Lumens : The 'lumens' contained within the beam spread of a flood light. Beam spread is the angle between the two directions in which the candle power of the flood light is 10% of the maximum candle power.

Glare & Glare Index : Glare is a feel of 'excessive brightness' either direct or indirect. Glare Index (GI) is an analytically computed measure of the same.

Colour rendition : Different lamps produce different colour renditions perceptible to the human eye since they are in the visible spectrum.

Luminous efficiency : It provides a ratio of the total luminous flux emitted by the light source to the total power input to the source. Unit is lumens/watt. Naturally, higher the lumens/watt, better is the light source. Trade-off is the cost and other practical factors Like "is it desirable to have just a few sources? What happens if one of them conks out?'

Louver : Louver is a series of baffles placed around the lamp to shield the lamps in the fixture to prevent direct viewing at a certain angle to prevent unwanted light.

Maintenance Factor

This factor allows for the decline in the effectiveness of the lighting fixture. It factors-in the light loss due to accumulation of dirt or foreign particulates or coating due to pollutants on all the reflecting and transmitting surfaces of the fixtures, lamps and the room.

Lamps

Lamps available in the market are of various types. The Application Engineer needs to have a clear understanding of the various types of light sources commonly available and the application intricacies involved.

Incandescent lamps

This is the most basic and common light source. Passage of current through a tungsten filament located in a glass bulb filled with inert gas (to prevent burning off of the filament) causes heating of the filament due to the I^2R losses to the point of incandescence (glowing white light), bulk of the energy lost as heat. Typically the lamps emanate 20 lumens/watts and have on an average a life of 1000 burning hours depending on the number of times they are switched on and the degree of voltage fluctuations beyond their rated voltage.

Discharge lamps

Two types of Discharge lamps are common—Fluorescent and High Intensity Discharge (HID) lamps.

Fluorescent lamps

These are commonly seen. Discharge between end filaments inside a fluorescent coated tube filled with inert gas produces the illumination seen as predominantly "white light". The light colour has several variants such as 'cool day light', 'warm white' etc. Typically they emanate 75 to 80 lumens/watt.

High Intensity Discharge (HID) Lamps

HID lamps have many varieties of light sources described below.

High Pressure Mercury Vapour (HPMV) lamps
These use mercury vapour and argon and comes with a slight violet tinge of lighting. However they are usually colour corrected.
Starting time is 3~5 minutes
Re-starting time is 3~6 minutes.

High Pressure Sodium Vapour (HPSV) Lamps
These use mercury, xenon and sodium and the colour rendered in the lighting is almost like sunlight.
Starting time is 3~4 minutes
Re-starting time is 0~1 minute.

Low Pressure Sodium Vapour (LPSV) Lamps
These use low pressure sodium and have a very high luminous efficiency of 133~183 lumens/watt. However their colour rendition is highly mono chromatic in the yellow band. Everything under this light appear yellow or grey and therefore not suitable for indoor or task lighting.

Metal Halide lamps
These use Mercury, Argon and Iodine components. The colour rendition is 'cool white'.
Starting time is 3~5 minutes
Re-starting time is 8~20 minutes.
Some of the HID lamps are sensitive to 'burning position'.

Lamp choice is dictated by

> ➢ Lumen rating
> ➢ Life expectancy
> ➢ Colour rendition and
> ➢ Price

Lumen rating can vary from catalogue values after the lamp has burned for 100hrs. This needs to be ascertained correctly. Fluorescent lamp outputs are affected by the ambient temperature.

Lamp life decides the 'total life cycle' cost of an installation. It is difficult to indicate the life in exact terms. It depends on the burning hours and burning cycles/start.

Colour rendition is an aesthetic issue. It is judged based on the colour of the light source itself and the colour rendition on the seeing task. Fluorescent lamps alone are available in 13 colours—all so called 'white'. Colours are controlled by addition of phosphors to the insides of the lamp envelope as part of the manufacturing process.

Ballasts

All discharge lamps have ballasts. They provide the L 'start-up' voltage. Other than being a single choke, they are basically transformers with Primary & Secondary sides. Sometimes they are common for more than one lamp. They protect the lamp from excessive thermal conditions. Some ballasts come with a built-in capacitor to have an overall improved pf (0.9 or greater). For distribution circuit engineering we should be aware of the ballast power also. Manufacturers provide this data. Ballasts also cause some noise.

Lighting Fixtures

The Lighting Fixtures broadly fall under the category of Decorative fixtures and Industrial fixtures.

Some of the essential requirements of Lighting fixtures in large plants are:

- ➢ Need to be dust tight.
- ➢ The enclosure must be properly gasketed.
- ➢ In some cases the fixture has to be "explosion proof" conforming to the hazardous area classification.
- ➢ In case of flood lights, should have a feature to enable lamp replacement without disturbing the fitting from its position so as not to disturb the setting of the aiming angle

In a plant illumination context **Decorative fixtures** are more for indoor use such as lighting for Control room, offices, canteens and in case for outdoor use for street lighting, etc.

Industrial Fixtures cover the following:

Fluorescent lighting fixtures for general purpose lighting that comes with Industrial reflectors that are used without louvers for outdoor duty.

Those for indoor duty come with a louvre to minimise glare for use in switchgear rooms, corridors etc. and with recess mounting features for mounting on false ceilings such as in control rooms, office rooms etc.

Special corrosion proof housing is required for fixtures used in battery rooms apart from suitability for the hazardous area.

Almost all fixtures have twin lamps connected in such a way that stroboscopic effect is minimized.

The fixtures have gear trays provided with ballasts and pf correction capacitors all located behind a protective cover and are normally not visible.

Sometimes the fittings are provided with a built-in battery to back up power supplied to the fitting for an autonomy time of 30 minutes to an hour.

High bay/Medium bay fittings are used along with HPMV/HPSV/ Metal Halide lamps in workshops, pump houses etc where the ceiling is at a considerable height.

Flood lights with HPSV lamps are common for yard/general area lighting while those with

LPSV are occasionally used for large areas such as material stock yard or Coal storage area where colour rendition is not important, but minimal energy cost is the criteria.The fixtures come with a variety of beam spreads—wide beams (even $> 120^0$), medium spread beams ($20{\sim}45^0$), narrow beams ($10{\sim}18^0$) etc and sometimes even with asymmetrical beam spreads.

Street Lighting fittings with HPSV lamps are also common. The uniqueness is in terms of the photometry design that ensures good distribution on the street side and very minimal on the kerb side.

Compact General purpose bulk head fittings/well glass fittings for use in platforms, walk ways etc. using low powered HPMV lamps.

Safety Lighting

Exit Lighting
These are needed for safety of personnel to ensure safe movement when the general lights suffer a power supply outage. The fixtures come with a back up battery having an autonomy time as required.

Signage Lighting
These are mandatory needs for EXITS needed in control room exits, cable cellars, substation rooms etc.

Aviation warning lights
These are placed on tall structures/equipment as per the heights prescribed in codes. The lights are usually in pairs and powered from sources backed up from DGs.

Illumination levels recommended for various areas

Human eye adapts itself to view a task irrespective of the Lux level in the environment. Typically on a sunny day the illumination level outside is over 10,000 lux and the human eye can 'see' comfortably.

However what is sought to be achieved by artificial lighting is much below the above, more for reasons economic.

"Seeing" at low lux levels are strenuous for the eye, induces fatigue and possibly accidents in industrial establishments. What we need to 'see' varies from area to area. E.g., in a Control room the need to see graduation on the panel meter warrants a high illumination level, whereas in a coal yard a mere visibility of what is there is good enough.

The Table below recommends the Lux levels needed in various areas commonly encountered in an industrial plant—widely adapted from IES Lighting Handbook—that brings out an extensive listing of all areas.

What is normally required is to maintain "average" illumination levels in line with the above and at the same time ensure that the min:max lux levels are also as per prescribed norms to ensure minimal discomfort due to contrast.

Indoor operational area	Average Lux level	Working Plane
Control Room (General lighting)	300 ~ 500	1 m
Rear of Panels	150 ~ 250	1 m
Switchgear Room	150 ~ 250	1 m
Battery Room	150 ~ 250	1 m
Plant Room	150 ~ 250	1 m
Near entrances	100 ~ 150	0 (grade level)
Plant Area		
Pump Rooms	50 ~ 150	1 m
Outdoor—operational area	50	0

Indoor operational area	Average Lux level	Working Plane
Outdoor—non operational area	< 5	0
Platforms & walk ways	30 ~ 50	0
Non Plant area		
Offices (Design)	500 ~ 750	1 m
General Offices	350 ~ 500	1 m
Corridors	100	1 m
Canteens	350 ~ 500	1 m
Conference rooms	500 ~ 750	1 m
Toilets	100 ~ 150	1 m
Streets	< 5	0
Storage—Buk materials	100 ~ 150	1 m
Yard (material)	5 ~ 10	0

Determination of no. of lighting fixtures by COU method

No. of fittings needed N $= \dfrac{A * E}{\left(\frac{Lumens}{fitting}\right) * LDF * MF * COU}$ where,

A	=	Area to be lit in m^2
E	=	Average illumination level needed
Lumens/fitting	=	Light output from a fixture
	=	lamp lumens x efficiency of fixture
LDF	=	Lamp Depreciation Factor (< 1)
MF	=	Maintenance Factor (<1)
		Clean area—0.7
		Dirty area—0.3
COU	=	Coefficient of Utilisation

The above is prescribed by a table; is a function of the room geometry, mounting height etc and is <1.

144

Better for square areas, poorer if it is a narrow corridor

For indoor LIghting COU is determined more easily by computing the Room Index (RI) given

$$\text{by RI} = \frac{LW}{Hm\,(L+W)} \quad \text{where,}$$

L is the length in m,
W is the width in m and
H_m is the total height—height of working plane—mounting length of suspension

For various values of ceiling, wall & floor reflectances RI is read-off from standard tables provided by manufacturers.

<u>Method for determination of illumination level by point-by-point method</u>

By inverse square law illumination level on plane A-A = I_θ/d^2 where

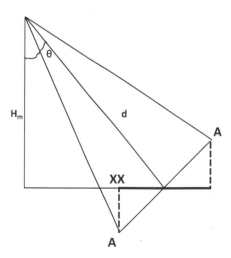

I_θ = Candelas of output of fixture that is read-off from the photometric data of the manufacturer

d = orthogonal distance to plane A---A

MF = Maintenance Factor

Illumination on Plane X---X = (Illumination on Pane A---A) x (cosθ) x (MF)

$$= (I_\theta/d^2)*(\cos\theta)*(MF)$$
$$= (I_\theta/H_m^2)*(\cos^3\theta)*(MF)$$

For a number of fittings located at various points in the area, the 'contribution' of each fixture can be computed for a particular point and by experience (trial & error) the Lux levels at various critical points can be examined.

The whole area can be divided into 1m x 1m grid and the lux level at the mid point of each grid can then be worked out.

The curve joining points having equal lux values provide an isolux diagram for the area.

The above features are integrated into a software that manufacturers now provide—e.g. CalcuLux by PHILIPS—where rigorous trial & error exercises can be done and optimal results obtained.

Flood Lighting/Street Lighting

A practical way to start off the exercise, is by first locating the fittings at vantage points in an intuitive layout using vendor's recommended spacing to mounting ratio and then iterate the results till optimal lux values are obtained.

Power Distribution for Lighting & Small Power

The power distribution for lighting & small power should be carefully engineered to cover

a) Normal Lighting
   These are for the lighting system installed for normal permanent use and supplied from the MAIN power source.

b) Essential Lighting

These are for maintaining enough lights to facilitate a 'safe' shut down and/or minimal operation of the plant in the event of failure of the normal mains supply. During normal times, the above will be fed from the normal source. On outage of the same, the power is drawn from a distribution board that has a back-up of Essential Services Generator (in practical jargon an "emergency" generator).

Typically this constitutes 20~30% of the total Light & SP fittings.

c) Emergency/Escape Lighting

These are required to ensure that some lighting is available for facilitating emergency evacuation/escape of personnel when (a) & (b) are lost due to power outage, even for a short while that otherwise are fed continuously from (b). The duration of this requirement various from industry to industry.

In oil & gas plants the practice is to feed from plant AC UPS all such fittings or/and have fittings with integral battery back-up that can feed it for an 'autonomy' time of say 30 minutes. Higher autonomy times are not unusual in some projects. For certain unmanned electrical rooms a delayed start is also engineered to ensure that the batteries do not drain off just about the time maintenance crew starts arriving.

The % of such essential fittings vary for plant areas. Typically

30% for Control Room & substations

20% for Plant rooms & utility areas

10% for offices & administration areas or Process areas.

Circuiting for Lighting

A great deal of attention is required while grouping the lights for control & distribution from a local lighting panel. This comes with diligent practice and eye for detailing.

147

> Cluster of lights should be in different phases in a particular area so that loss of one phase will still not result in total darkness.
> MCB rating shall take into account the starting in rush current for discharge lamps.
> Adequate margin shall be kept in the rating of MCB and the actual load it feeds.
> Two pole MCBs are desirable for total isolation.
> Three phase power outlets if any, are fed from TPN feeders with MCB.
> An ELCB at the incomer will be required.
> Outgoing wire sizes from the MCB to the first junction box feeding a cluster of light shall be adequately sized considering the voltage drop criteria. Rest of the wire sizes for loop-in-loop-out connections can be standardized.
> Total load on each phase for a lighting panel shall be calculated, balance between phases ensured and the corresponding rating of Incomer Isolator shall be checked.
> Incoming cable sizing shall be checked for adequacy.
> Adequate spare MCBs shall be provided in the lighting panel for contingency.
> Generally for large projects the lighting panels are standardized for no. of outgoing MCBs to facilitate procurement.

Foot Note:

I started off my career as a lighting engineer for a nuclear power plant where early decision was required to provide steel embedded plates on the reactor containment wall for the lighting fixtures and the conduit wiring installation since the nature of the crack free containment structure prohibited any drilling of holes later. This required completing the detailed design upto the last detail even as the civil works were in progress—requiring tremendous amount of detailing so that the embedment plates are located at the right place. This taught me to have patience and focus on a systematic development of detailed design.

In the early seventies and even in the eighties no softwares were in use for lighting design. A lot of calculations were done by the point by point method even for designing an optimal flood lighting layout for a coal storage yard or for plant street lighting. So much so that my first paper in a symposium was titled "Dilemma of a Lighting Engineer" calling upon more lighting fixture manufacturers to provide photometric data, Coeff of Utilisation tables etc. to aid the Application Engineer.

Fortunately present day lighting engineer invariably will have access to vendor's softwares to make the design process much less tedious, but still a careful eye for aesthetics and details are required to arrive at a good design.

13

Batteries

Various types of batteries using different technologies continue to emerge in the market as follows:

> Lead Acid cells   - Proven, currently in widespread use

> Nickel Cadmium Cells   - Proven, currently in widespread use

> Nickel Iron cells   - Being commercially developed

> Nickel Metal Hydride cells - Being commercially developed

> Nickel Zinc cells   - Being commercially developed

> Sodium Sulphur Cells   - Being commercially developed

> Lithium Ion Cells   - Under Research & Development

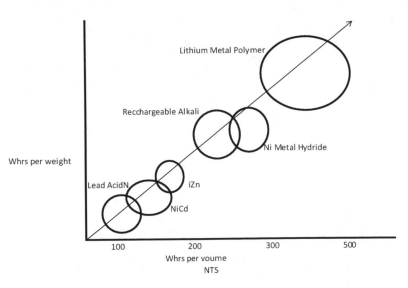

Energy Storage Capabilities of rechargeable Batteries' Technology evolution

Out of the above our interest for these discussions will be the first two types and their variants. Those are:

1) Vented/Flooded Lead Acid Batteries
2) Sealed Maintenance Free Batteries (VRLA type)—Popular in UPS due to their compactness. Has limited usage in the oil & gas industry.
3) Vented/Flooded Nickel Cadmium Batteries

Our discussions will broadly cover BATTERIES used for back-up power applications in the form of AC & DC Uninterruptible Power Supply System (UPS) and Solar Power applications for the following:

- Sub Station Control & Protection power supply applications   -   110V DC
- SCADA applications   -   48V DC
- Telecom system   -   24V DC
- Fire & Gas Alarm system   -   24V DC
- Solar Power System Back-up   -   12V DC
- DG/EDG System start up   -
- AC UPS   -   110V DC
- Turbine emergency Lube Oil pump   -   110V DC

These three types of batteries and related auxiliaries and requirements cover most of the applications in large facilities:

How are Batteries rated?

Batteries are rated in Ampere Hours (Ahr)

Broadly we can say that the discharge capability in amps is inversely proportional to the duration for which the discharge happens. However this linearity is not valid for very small durations where the batteries can discharge a huge Amperes for very short durations.

The discharge again will cause the voltage to sink and hence the 'duration' is relevant as long as the voltage is not less than a particular lower limit.

The industry practice is to provide C10 ratings in Ahrs. That means the battery can discharge a particular Amperes for 10 hrs with the cell end voltage not less than a particular voltage. If we allow lower end voltage the C10 rating will be obviously higher. As a typical example, a Lead Acid battery by a manufacturer has indicated in their catalogues the following discharge figures for their batteries:

Battery Rating (C10 rating)	Nominal Voltage	Ampere-hour rating for a duration of (Hours)			
		20	10	5	1
250 Ahr	2.0 V	262.5	250	213.8	150
400 Ahr	2.0 V	420	400	342	240

Note the significance of the C10 rating. The above discharge amperes are for tolerating an end of discharge cell voltage of V. The discharge amperes will be more if a lower end of discharge voltage is tolerated and less if we are more stringent about the voltage requirements.

The Peukert Equation

In general terms the above is brought about by the equation

C   = $I^n T$ where

C   =   the capacity of the battery in amp hours,

I   =   the current,

T   =   discharge time in hours, and

n   =   the Peukert Number, a constant for the given battery.

As per the equation at higher currents, there is less available energy in the battery.

The Peukert Number is directly related to the internal resistance of the battery. Higher currents mean more losses and less available capacity.

The value of the Peukert number gives an idea as to how well a battery performs under continuous heavy currents. A value close to 1 indicates that the battery performs well; the higher the number, more capacity is lost when the battery is discharged at high currents.

The Peukert number of a battery is an empirical number. For Lead acid batteries the number is typically 1.3 ~ 1.4.

We shall now discuss some of the salient features of the three* types of batteries commonly used in the industry. (*) Sealed NiCd is very expensive and is rarely used.

Key aspects	Vented/Flooded Lead Acid batteries	Valve Regulated Lead Acid batteries (sealed)*	Vented/Flooded Nickel Cadmium batteries
What is inside?	Tubular or Flat plate type of cells	Some call it 'maintenance free', a misnomer since it vents when overcharged. Comes in a sealed execution. Usually flat plates or spiral rolled plates.	Pocket plate technology is used.
➤ Electrodes		Pure lead (–)ve, & Lead dioxide(+)ve.	
➤ Electrolyte	Solution of sulphuric acid & water. Specific gravity indicates state of charge	Same as in flooded LA, but very little quantity entrapped as either gel type or absorbent micro porous glass mat type	Potassium hydroxide solution in water. Specific gravity do not change during charging/ discharging process

Key aspects	Vented/Flooded Lead Acid batteries	Valve Regulated Lead Acid batteries (sealed)*	Vented/Flooded Nickel Cadmium batteries
Voltage per Cell	2V/Cell	2V/Cell	1.2V/Cell
Aging	25%	25%	10%
Life	Tubular: 8~10 yrs Flat plate: 15~20 yrs	3 ~5 yrs .	> 20 years
Maintenance needs	Frequent	Nil	Low. Topping up is required at long intervals.
If dry, what happens?	Causes sulphation		
Cyclic discharging/ charging	Tubular: good for cyclic & frequent Flat plate: for standby loads	Rectifier needs additional provision of float charging	During discharge the voltage is practically flat
Full discharging			Can fully discharge without jeopardising its life or recharge capability. Voltage drops abruptly at the end of discharge duration
Full charging	55 ~ 90 hrs Charge for first charge should give 2.6~2.7 V/ Cell	2.25 ~ 2.3V/Cell Rapid charging will result in evolution of excess gas that is over & above recombination within causing the pressure valve to open.	Fast recharge feature is a useful parameter. Voltage rises rapidly on charging and hence charging circuit is simple.

Key aspects	Vented/Flooded Lead Acid batteries	Valve Regulated Lead Acid batteries (sealed)*	Vented/Flooded Nickel Cadmium batteries
Weights on a like-to-like basis	Highest	Lowest	
Transportation	In charged condition	Withstands good amount of vibration since electrolyte is virtually immobile and the batteries can take any position	Can be in charged condition
Storage		Shelf life: 4~6 weeks. Prolonged storage stratifies electrolyte in the micro porous glass mat	many years when dry. even for a year when filled. Hence can be dispatched 'site ready'.
Room requirement	Locate indoors in a controlled temperature	Not required since it is in a sealed execution	similar to vented lead acid batteries.
Ventilation needs	Well ventilated since hydrogen discharge is possible	Minimal since it is a sealed execution	
Other accessories	Acid proof tiling Eye wash Drains PPE More civil loads Heavier lifting equipment needs		

Key aspects	Vented/Flooded Lead Acid batteries	Valve Regulated Lead Acid batteries (sealed)*	Vented/Flooded Nickel Cadmium batteries
Impact of ambient temperature	Life decreases if temperature is > 25^0C. For every 8.3^0 rise, life halves	Impact is more severe since it can cause dry out leading to open circuit. So always operate in parallel. At > 25^0C decrease by 3mV/cell/^{0}C. At < 25^0C increase by the same amount. Water in electrolyte is susceptible to freezing at low temperatures	Can tolerate temperature range of (–) 20^0C to (+) 50^0C With special electrolytes can tolerate even extreme ranges of (–) 40^0C to (+) 70^0C
Horizontal mounting		Possible, hence needs less space	
General			Can take a lot of mechanical & electrical abuse.

Battery sizing

Battery size is a function of maximum & minimum variation of dc voltage. Higher window will result in more cells and recharge Ahr rating.

Input needs for the Application Engineer is a Battery load curve or discharge profile in Amps or watts or kW for the required autonomy time.

Application softwares provided by vendors are useful in readily arriving at the required ratings but the ratings arrived at is only as good as the accuracy of the load curve provided as inputs and this is precisely the area where the Application Engineer need to sharpen his pencils.

Battery type based on discharge

Low discharge type (infrequent discharge)	-	say every 3 hrs
Medium discharge type	-	every 0.5 to 3 hrs
High discharge type	-	every 30 minutes

Temperature de-rating factors

Since batteries are located indoors in a controlled ambient, Site minimum ambient temperature need not be considered while sizing. We need to talk to HVAC team and take the HVAC provided room minimum temperature—typically 22~25^{0}C.

Battery protection/interface needs

On short circuit an MCCB or Fuse is provided. The device has to be located close to the batteries within the room that is usually categorized as Zone 2 or even higher.

Auto ignition temperature of Hydrogen is 560^{0}C. Hence Gas group IIC & Temperature class T1 is needed. Hence an Exd enclosure is required for the above.

A low cost solution is to keep this outside but with minimal cable run.

Battery Cables

Normally single core cables are used that avoid risks of short circuit. These are run on separate trays. Short runs of cable, that are usually large sized, can be a bit unwieldy in termination at the battery terminals. So use of flexible cables with braid could be a better solution. A good application practice is to go for fire resistant cables.

Usually a drop of only 1V is considered between the battery and the UPS terminals.

Battery Racks

These are usually of acid resistant wood.
Mountings need to consider anti seismic needs.

Battery Monitoring System

On line monitoring & testing is required. Alarms for abnormal conditions are usual to alert maintenance personnel. Just the Voltage and current for each cell is monitored. Monitoring can be more complex in case of temperature of each cell, discharge cycle etc. Modern installations come with serial communication capability.

Foot Note:

I realised the importance of sizing up the batteries adequately only after I happened to visit a running chemical producing plant that encountered a pitch dark main receiving substation that was almost on a crisis state and when they felt relieved to get the substation re-energised, it was found that the batteries have conked off.

How big the batteries should be is an eternal challenge. Like I stated in the foot note of the first chapter on load list, your role in a particular organization might dictate playing it tight, but still be a pessimist and generously get the required Ampere Hours right. You never know.

14

DC UPS

A DC Uninterrupted Power Supply System (DC UPS) is one where there is a DC supply always available to the identified loads fed from a DC Distribution board that is normally fed from the AC mains via a rectifier and in the event of its outage the source is seamlessly transferred to the Batteries that otherwise always remain on line drawing its charge from the mains.

These are required mainly for the Electrical Control & Protection system loads apart from a few other loads in certain plants. The following are the Loads to be considered:

Switchgear closing/Tripping operation on loss of power supply. At times even the spring charging motor should be accounted for. The types of loads will be discussed in more detail later.

SLD of a typical 2 x 100% redundant DCUPS is shown below to identify the key equipment. The practices in locating the same are explained by depicting them within a box shown by dotted lines to understand the practical significance of the same.

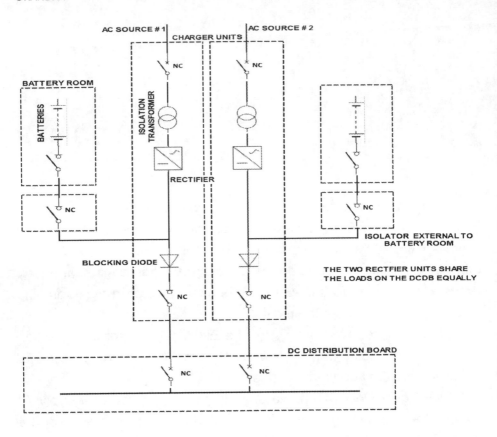

Nomenclatures

Before we proceed to discuss further let us get familiar with a few jargons used in DC UPS Application Engineering terminology.

Autonomy time of UPS	:	Duration for which the UPS supported by the Batteries can deliver its rated kW.
Rated output of UPS	:	Continuous rating of UPS in kW or Amps that can be delivered to the loads over the entire range.
Battery Duty Cycle	:	Loads to be supplied for the specified time periods

End-of-discharge voltage	:	Minimum voltage discharged by the batteries beyond which support to the load is terminated.
Equalising charge	:	Normally such charging improves battery life. A charge is applied periodically at > normal float voltage for a duration usually recommended by the manufacturer.
Float charging	:	Battery needs to be in a state of charge. A constant voltage charging from a source helps compensating for internal losses.
Full float operation	:	DC UPS operating by charger supplying full load charging current for the batteries
High rate charging	:	If in a limited time span—after prolongued discharge—the batteries have to be restored to a predetermined state of charge, constant current charging at controlled voltage is resorted to. This is NOT recommended for sealed VRLA batteries.

The DC UPS shown above has the following operations for one set:

1) Normal operation

AC supply (three phase or single phase depending on the UPS load) from two independent sources. The "rectifier charger" will feed the DC loads and maintain the batteries in "float charge" mode. The rectifier units are sized for 2 x 100% capacity. There is no need of synchronizing on the DC side.

2) Loss of normal power

Loss of one source ensures that the DCDB will still be able to support the DC loads from the other AC source.

3) Total loss of normal power

In the event of a complete loss of AC source, the batteries will take over the feeding of the loads for the autonomy time they are designed for and maintain the output voltage within the limited period.

4) Resumption of normal power

The operation goes back to what it was in (1) with an additional load that the batteries will now undergo charging.

Configuration

The rectifiers and/or batteries could be a single unit or 2 x 100% or 2 x 100% for the chargers & 2 x 50% for the batteries depending on the back-up philosophy. In the oil & gas industry the dual redundant system is preferred due to the criticality of loads that hinges on availability of the UPS.

Each bank of batteries is charged by its rectifier unit. Also the batteries are kept under float charge mode during normal operation from AC source.

Note that the two isolation facilities are kept for the batteries—one in the battery room while the other outside the room. The one within the room has to conform to the hazardous area classification of the room as we discussed earlier.

The above philosophy is commonly adopted for centralised DC UPS or even when they are decentralized, say kept within the HV switchgear itself. In that case the two units are housed at the two ends of the switchgear and the batteries are of VRLA type so that they can be mounted within the switchgear panel itself.

Rating of UPS

The rating depends on the DC power requirements that has three components

<u>Momentary loads</u> — This is the beginning of the discharge cycle of the batteries. Usually trip coils of circuit breakers. Load typically lasts for a minute.

<u>Continuous loads</u> — These loads exist throughout the autonomy period. Loads such as indication amps, relays, quiescent loads of RTUs, SCADA, PLC and Intelligent Motor control devices.

<u>Momentary loads</u> — loads again appear during end-of-discharge cycle, such as closing coils of breakers, spring charging motors that can last for quite sometime, but usually after the closing coil loads and typically all such loads last for a minute again.

<u>Random loads</u> — These appear any time during the load cycle. The autonomy period of the batteries depend on the plant requirements.

It is important to take into account inrush currents of all the loads while sizing.

For large generators, compressors etc, the emergency lube oil pump may have to be considered until coasting down of the main equipment and hence such load might last for the full autonomy time.

A typical shape of the duty cycle needs of a DC system is shown below that must be understood in the context of the discussions above.

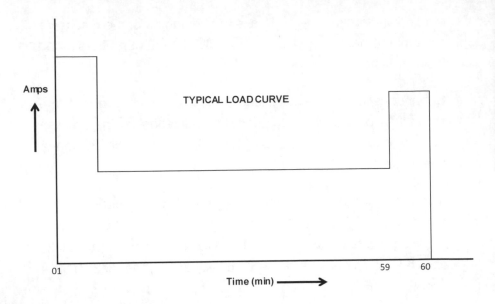

Rectifier unit sizes

Upto around 1.8kW size the input is usually single phase ac beyond which it is from three phase. Inputs are usually taken from a DG backed source for obvious reasons.

Output voltage ratings are usually 24V/48V/110V/125V/220V.

Larger voltages are preferred if we have lube oil pump motors to cater to. Lower voltages will need cable drops to be accounted for carefully.

The output ratings should cater to the loads and the charging needs with some cushion of 20~25% to cater for the unknown at the Application Engineering stage.

DC UPS units emanate noise and the application engineer needs to ensure that they are $\leq$ 70dBA. Also EMC compatibility with other equipment is important.

Foot Note:

Like the back-up batteries, DC UPS sizing usually carries a lot of design margin.

However I had once encountered issues relating to long run of low voltage DC cables that was routed upto a critical solenoid valve. Note that the voltage drops need to be looked at critically since if the DC power is there, but not available at the right voltage at the critical equipment terminals, it will be a calamity.

Provide spare feeders liberally in the board.

Another favourite concept was not to distribute DC power all over the power plant unnecessarily for lighting etc. since somewhere an earth fault might happen that would expose the availability of the entire system when it is most needed. Keep the DC distribution as much as possible within the confines of the switchgear, control room and control equipment rooms.

Yet another issue—the maintenance needs of the DC board that once cropped up in an old running plant under power outage when it was realised that the rear of the board needed access that wasn't available.

15

AC UPS

AC UPS power is required to feed power **without any interruption** to critical consumers in a facility on loss of normal power.

AC UPS derives its power from batteries. It also provides stabilized quality power even if it is from normal sources.

UPS configuration varies widely. IEC 60441 defines them.

The importance of UPS supply is to be well appreciated by the Application Engineer as markedly different from that from an "'Emergency" Diesel Generator system in the sense that the latter has some minimum time required for the DG to start and being a mechanical device it may fail to start—also at times—fail to start for even non equipment related causes such as an empty day tank, or a clogged line or simply a drained starter battery. There are critical plants that may not tolerate such black outs even for the small duration. Blow Down Systems have to come on line to shed inventories that are always building up in the pipes & equipment. Gases have to be flared. Several safety measures have to come into play automatically and it might be a massive safety hazard for the environment should there be no back up power available for such durations. The same is true in case of nuclear plants where a lot of safe shut down measures have to be in place post power failure—before a DG set eventually gets whirring.

Nomenclatures

Before we proceed to discuss further let us get familiar with a few jargons used in AC UPS Application Engineering terminology.

Rated output of AC UPS	:	Continuous rated output of AC UPS in kVA that can be delivered to the loads under the entire range of service conditions
Autonomy time of UPS	:	Duration for which the AC UPS can deliver rated output (kW), at specified condition when normal plant power has an outage with UPS supported by its batteries.
By pass supply	:	In case inverter fails or is out-of-limit an alternative source is connected to the load through isolation transformer/ static stabiliser/directly. This is called "by pass" supply.
Inverter	:	A device with SCR/Transistorised circuit that converts DC supply to synthetically produced AC sinusoidal supply.
Maintenance by pass switch	:	A Manually operated switch in the UPS used during maintenance to bypass the entire UPS (completely isolating the batteries/charger/ inverter) and supplies the load directly.
Static Transfer Switch (STS)	:	Static Transfer Switch—An automated SCR controlled switch that automatically transfers the load from one source to another (that was automatically pre-synchronised), without significant interruption in the load.
THD	:	Total Harmonic Distortion

Basics

Most commonly used configurations applicable for oil & gas facilities are described below:

Single Static UPS

The Automatic Static Transfer Switch usually comes as part of the inverter equipment and the transfer power can be drawn from the same source too. The purpose of STS is to ensure that the loads are fed continuously even if the inverter unit develops some problems.

The By pass source is manually brought in should there be a failure of the normal source and or need for maintenance of the UPS unit including its STS unit.

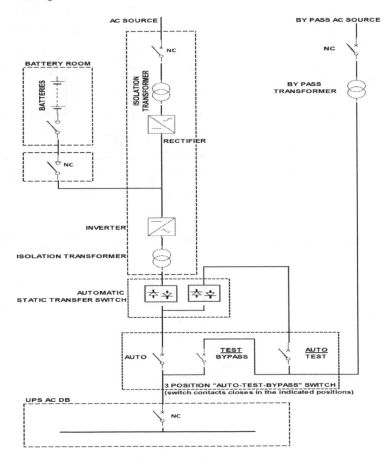

Advantages	:	Low cost
Disadvantages	:	➢ Remember: more the 'single point failure mode possibility' more the unreliability. ➢ This option has restricted availability of plant in case the UPS fails. This can be overcome by using static stabilisers in the by pass circuit. ➢ If module is under maintenance, the maintenance bypass will feed unregulated supply to some loads. Not recommended for critical plants such as oil & gas plants

Duplicate Static UPS (isolated operation)

Here 2 UPS modules operate independently and feed their respective DBs. Outputs are NOT synchronized.

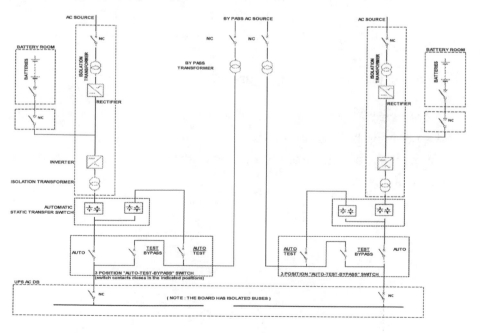

Advantages	:	➢ Configuration offers isolated operation, so no concern of 'common mode' failure. ➢ The 2 modules with its AC DB can be located in different places maintaining good distances avoiding 'common mode failure' due to risk of fire in the room. Sometimes they are even kept in two independent blast proof rooms to ensure availability for the critical blow down system, F&G system, Plant flare system etc during a blast in the plant. ➢ The 2 bypasses can be from different sources
Disadvantages	:	➢ Since outputs are not synchronized it is not possible to provide redundant power supply to each consumer. So some of the consumers, even if they have redundant supplies will need an interruption. ➢ Equal load sharing by the 2 UPS is not possible. ➢ Costly since separate ACDBs are needed.

Duplicate Static UPS (parallel operation)

Here two UPS modules are configured to operate in parallel and feed a common bus bar of an AC DB.

By pass is required from the same source so that the outputs are synchronised.

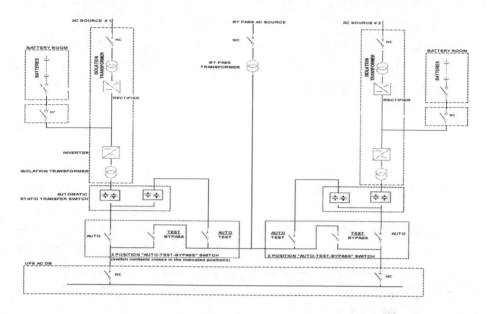

Advantages	:	➢ There is no risk of inadvertent paralleling of two supplies at the consumers' end.
		➢ Loads shared equally between the two UPS.
Disadvantages	:	➢ One danger is the ACDB can be a cause for common mode failure
		➢ Local equipment room failure can cause Loss of both UPS.

This configuration is usually adopted in oil & gas plants.

UPS Rating

The list of consumers is usually provided by the Instruments & Telecom groups.

The Application Engineer should guard himself against the 'easy route' of just adding up all the loads and decide on the sizing. Remember: for autonomy time > 1 hr every additional VA counts, because of its impact on the cost of batteries, resultant HVAC needs for the room and so on.

Second important thing is to pay attention to the power factor of all the loads. Wild assumptions may impact the kW since for a given kVA in the list assuming a Lower pf will result in assessing a lower kW and hence an erroneous lower battery size.

All UPS need to have a 150% design overload capability for a short time of one minute to support instantaneous peak currents of a few loads.

Autonomy Time

Typical design considerations in assessing the autonomy time of the AC UPS is discussed below. These are by no means prescriptive and are intended to make the Application Engineer aware of some good engineering practices adopted in a few process plants.

Consider the following:

30 minutes	:	Time required for the plant automaton system to bring plant to safe shut down in the event of failure of the main supply system and if there is back up DG system that has more than 1 set.
30 min ~ 1 hr	:	Time required for the plant automaton system to bring plant to safe shut down in the event of failure of the main supply system without considering Emergency DG to come on line during this period.

4 ~ 8 hrs, even 24 hrs at times	:	Time needed to maintain the Fire & Gas (F&G) system and Emergency Shut Down (ESD) system
4 ~ 6 hrs	:	Time for complete plant blow down—staggered blow down
Travel time	:	Allow for the travel time of the O&M personnel to reach an unmanned plant to commence shut down operations.
External communication		Allow for time needed for the pant O&M personnel to communicate with external agencies who manage the main power supply.

Thus the autonomy requirements vary from plant to plant. The Application Engineer should closely look at

- Plant automation & Control systems
- Analyser & Metering skids
- ESD system
- F&G system
- Telecom system
- ENMCS/PMS system (Electrical Network Monitoring System/ Power Management System)

If a single UPS has to feed all the systems then you need to go for a properly defined load shedding system.

Outputs of AC UPS

The output voltage is usually 110V or 220/230V $\pm$ 2%

Since all consumers can usually tolerate ±10% voltage, restrict Voltage drop in the cables to 5%.

All consumers are usually single phase loads, the AC UPS may be single or three phase equipment depending on the capacity. For capacities > 30 kVA, three phase units are cheaper by about 5~7%. Three phase units are designed for 100% load unbalance, so ensure that the neutral conductor is of the same size as the phase conductor.

Harmonics

Usually these are of no concern if all the down stream devices are IEC compliant with requisite pf corrections built into them. UPS itself is a non linear load and the corrective measures built into the UPS are by ether a series inductor, or a 12 pulse double wound transformer rectifier or by passive filters.

UPS equipment is better located in a separate room since there will be some noise emissions of the order of not > 70dBA at 1m distance.

UPS AC Distribution Board

UPS ACDB shall be separate from the other panels in the AC UPS. All the outgoing & Incoming MCBs/MCCBs shall be well coordinated to ensure no untoward tripping of the incomers for down the line equipment faults that may throw the entire UPS out of gear.

Using ELCBs are best avoided so that there is no nuisance tripping. Exception could be power supply sockets in critical areas fed from the board, and long feeder cables, if any. In such cases a verification of the earth loop impedance is required to ensure that the MCB/MCCB/Fuse trips on a remote earth fault.

Foot Note:

Sizing the AC UPS right is an age old challenge, the high cost being a major driver.

I have often noticed that the information available from Process, Instrumentation and Safety departments tend to be inaccurate when the system is sized and even if available tend to be the 'catalogue' name plate values that if we add up will result in a huge size that is seldom required. A good understanding of the diversity of the loads that will come into play under "UPS alone" conditions is needed.

A good grasp of "common mode" failures in the distribution tree will help design a reliable system.

I have heard from my colleagues about a near catastrophic gas release in a gas processing plant abroad where a post scenario analysis revealed that a major root cause was the an earth fault down the line that resulted in the tripping of the main feeder MCB rather than that of down the line feeder MCB due to poor relay coordination in the AC UPS DB.

Like in DC cables, cable sizing based on voltage drop considerations are important since the feeding cables to consumers are single phase runs that needs to have the voltage drops assessed right, considering both the conductors in the circuit.

16

Electrical Protections

The Arts & Science of Protection Relays is one of the most interesting topics in Application Engineering.

Protection relays are provided to protect the Equipment, System and Personnel against all dangers in the event of any abnormal occurrence in the feeder or equipment or due to mal operation of the system causing Ground Faults, Phase Faults or Overloads.

Months of study is required to understand the subject well. The present chapter is to lead the engineer to delve into the topic further and make them aware so that they are not overwhelmed by the vastness of the subject.

Contrary to the earlier prevalent electro mechanical relays, present day DIGITAL RELAYS provide extremely reliable protection with a lot of other Multi Function like metering & integrated communication between the relays in a comprehensive manner offering sophisticated setting, automatic setting protective ware, remote logging, fault diagnostics and self supervisory features.

All said, an understanding of the basics will help.

Standard Device Numbers (Ref. ANSI/IEEE Std C37.2)

The standard device numbers that have been in use for almost a hundred years in the Electrical Engineering field are selectively listed below:

2	:	Time Delay Relay	21	:	Distance Relay
25	:	Synchronising or Syn Check Relay	27	:	Under Voltage Relay

29	:	Isolating Device		:	
30	:	Annunciator Relay	32	:	Directional Power Relay
33	:	Position Switch	37	:	Undercurrent/Under power Relay
40	:	Field Relay	41	·	Field Circuit Breaker
42	:	Power Contactor	43	:	Selector Switch
46	:	(−)ve sequence/Phase unbalance current Relay	49	:	Thermal Relay
50	:	Instantaneous over current or Rate-of-Rise Relay	51	:	AC Time overcurrent Relay
52	:	AC Circuit Breaker	55	:	Power Factor Relay
59	:	Over Voltage Relay			
60	:	Voltage or Current unbalance Relay	64	:	Ground Protection Relay
67	:	AC Directional Over current Relay	68	:	Blocking Relay
74	:	Alarm Relay			
81	:	Frequency Relay	86	:	Lock-out Relay

Auxiliary Devices (selectively listed)

C	:	Closing Relay/Contactor	CL	:	Auxiliary Relay
CS	:	Control Switch	PB	:	Push Button
R	:	Raising Relay	L	:	Lowering Relay
X	:	Auxiliary Relays	Y	:	Auxiliary Relays
Z	:	Auxiliary Relays			

Fuses

Fuses are one of the most basic protections against short circuits (Not overloads) as we had discussed earlier. Use of fuse—of the HRC variety—is very much prevalent n the industry in LV distribution and as a back-up in the MV & HV distribution. Never in EHV though.

Typical Operating Characteristics:

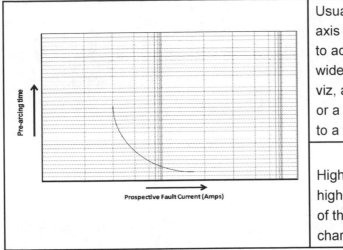

Usually both X & Y axis is in log-log scale to accommodate a wide range of values viz, a few amps to kA or a few milli seconds to a few seconds	
Higher the fuse rating, higher is the position of the curve in the characteristics	

The concept of pre-arcing time, arcing time and total operating time vis-à-vis discriminatory needs were discussed earlier. The curve area provides the Energy let through or the I^2t value of the fuse. For proper discrimination I^2t of the major fuse has to be > I^2t of the minor fuse.

Thermal Overload Relays (TOL) (49)

TOLs are extensively used to protect motors. The relay has a bi-metallic operated contact that operates as soon as temperature increases above a set value. Each phase of the relay has a bi metal element that gets heated due to flow of the current in the phase.

TOL relays protect motor against

➤ Overload
➤ Single phasing

The relays are usually ambient temperature compensated from (–) 25°C to (+) 55°C to ensure that the temperature at which the contact operates is accurate.

The relay setting scale is in Amps. For higher amps of motors CTs are used to feed TOL relays. Industry & International standard practice is to SET the relay in "motor nominal current" and not the "tripping current". The characteristic has a 'cold' & 'hot' curve.

Standard 'tripping' classes are 10, 20 & 30.

No tripping at 1.05 I_e

Tripping at 1.20I_e within 2 hours.

Tripping class = maximum tripping time (in seconds) at 7.2 times the setting current and various tripping times between 1.5 & 7.2 times setting current. Carries tolerance of ±20% on the tripping time.

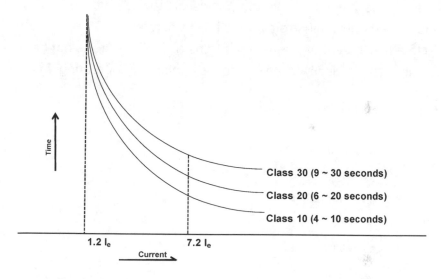

As per IEC 60947-4-1 there are 2 types of coordination—Type 1 & Type 2.

Type-1:

Under short circuit condition starter does not endanger person or installation but *may not* be suitable for further service without repairs or replacement of parts.

Type-2:

Under short circuit condition starter does not endanger person or installation but *WILL* be suitable for further service without repairs or replacement of parts.

Basic Characteristic of a over current relay (50) & (51)

As the fault current (as a multiple of set current) increases the relay's operating time gets lesser—means it operates "faster".

Note it is asymptotic in the Y-axis signifying that very close to values of set current the relay does NOT operate.

Note therefore that the X-axis begins at 1. Y-axis does not begin at zero since theoretically there has to be a minimum operating time.

The universal equation is [Ref. IEC 60255/BS 142]

$$t = (k*\beta)/\{(I/I>)^{\alpha} - 1\} \text{ where}$$

t = operating time in seconds

k = time multiplier

I = current value

$I>$ = set value of current

	Normally inverse	Very inverse	Extremely inverse	Long Time inverse
α	0.02	1.00	2.00	1.00
β	0.14	13.50	80.00	120.00

Modern micro processor based relays make use of above constants in its algorithm to arrive at the characteristics from the fed value of current and/or voltages measured.

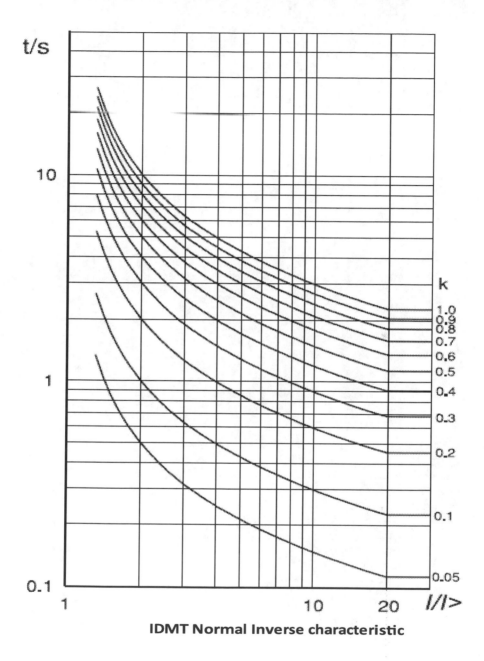

IDMT Normal Inverse characteristic

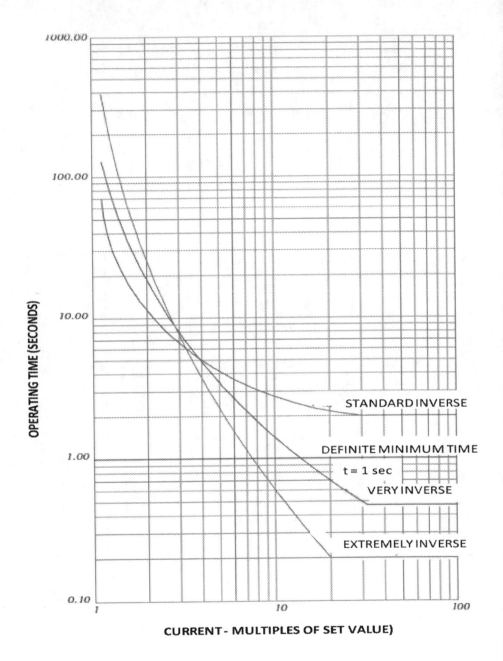

Thus a typical need of protection as we saw earlier is to protect against currents caused by

> ➢ Overload and
> ➢ Short circuit

Typically the former allows operating time in seconds while the latter in milli seconds. Hence the desired characteristic has to be as shown below:

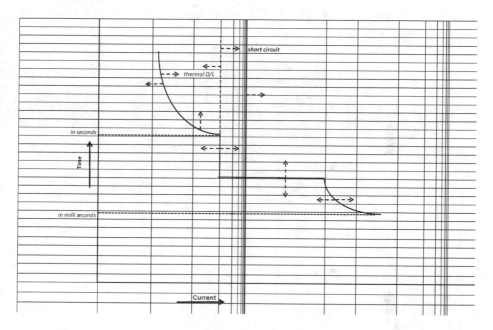

You are advised to clearly understand the significance of movement of the curve in the direction indicated by the arrows and understand its impact on the protection provided by the protection relay.

The characteristic needs are essentially the same—be it overcurrent protection or Earth Fault protection. Only the value of current & time are different. Both the axis are usually in logarithmic scale, though not shown above for the time scale.

Basic needs of O/C coordination

In the typical radial distribution shown below, try to figure out the coordination needs in the protection.

Fault at A

It is an "Incomer Fault". CB-1 should trip. In view of the transformer, the current seen on the HV side will be low even if there is a short relay circuit at A. Hence an overcurrent protection relay is adequate for relay R1.

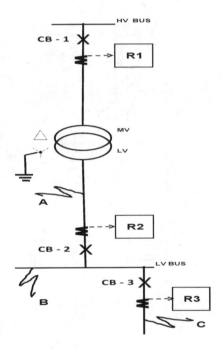

Fault at B

It is a "Bus Fault". We need to quickly trip CB-2. Hence we need to have a short circuit protection relay for R2 as a minimum.

We shall shortly see that an O/C element is also needed in R2 as a back-up for R3 should R3 fail to pick up/CB-3 fails to trip after R3 picks up.

Fault at C

It is a "Feeder Fault". Ideally only CB-3 should operate so as to maintain availability of the rest of the system. Hence we should have both O/C and SC protection for R3. As we discussed earlier R2 provides a back-up protection for R3 and therefore R2 needs to operate after a considered time delay.

Delayed operation of R2 therefore brings in its own limitations. Fault at B is tolerated for that much more time. Therefore the short time rating of the bus bar has to be adequate for that much duration.

In general terms, you should now be able to construct the "desired" characteristics of Relays R3, R2 and R3. If you are able to do that yourself you have UNDERSTOOD "DISCRIMINATION" in Protection Engineer's parlance

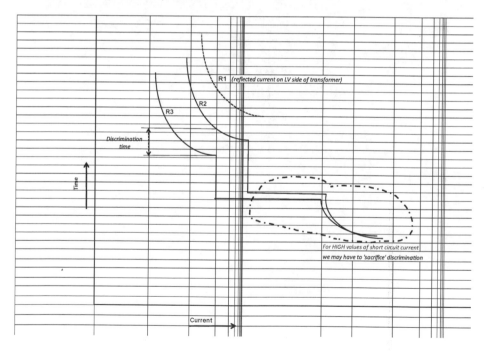

The "discrimination time" allows for Relaying time + operating time of CB2 + some margin. Typically this is 0.3 seconds in industry practice.

Note the impact on short time ratings of upstream equipment for same values of short circuit current.

Differential Protection (87)

Basically the 'Merz Principle' used checks that the current that goes in equals the current that comes out thus implying that no "internal faults" are there in the equipment or connecting cables that feed.

For fault at A the relay 87 operates since I_{in} is not equal to I_{out}.

For fault at B the relay 87 should not operate since $I_{in} = I_{out}$.

For no fault anywhere the relay 87 should not operate too since $I_{in} = I_{out}$ under this condition also.

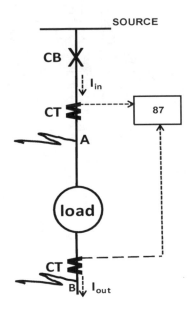

The above principle is used to protect large transformers, Generators, Motors, Bus Bar protection for EHV switchyards and even long run of cables. The last one is called "Pilot Wire Protection for cables".

Earth Fault Protection (51N), (50N)

The Earth Fault relay's current settings are applied for the SLG fault current values (duly taking into account the CT ratios) and coordinated on similar lines.

There is one important difference.

For relay R1, no E/F on the down stream side from transformer LV winding onwards will reflect on the HV Line side since the transformer is Delta/Wye connected.

Hence R1 can be set for minimum operating time values to protect the HV side (by CB-1) against SLG faults there and WILL NOT BE AFFECTED BY DOWN STREAM EARTH FAULTS.

This is why Delta/Wye connected transformers are used in distribution.

If it were a Y/y Transformer (that can still be used for certain other advantages that we discussed in the chapter on transformers), the grading needs will throw up a huge requirement of tolerating SLG faults in the system OR cause unnecessary tripping of HV side CB (here CB-1) for E/F in the feeder fed by CB-3.

Typical Protection needs for various Equipment

Motor Feeders
LV Motors

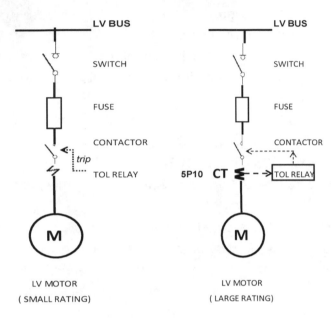

LV MOTOR
(SMALL RATING)

LV MOTOR
(LARGE RATING)

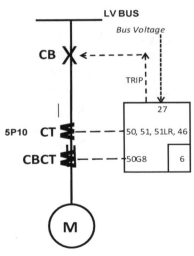

LV MOTOR
(VERY LARGE RATING)

MV Motors

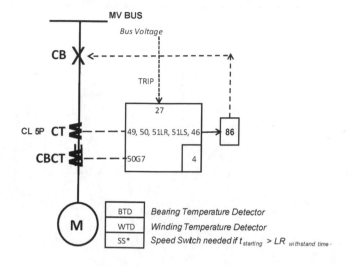

MV MOTOR
(WITHOUT DIFFERENTIAL PROTECTION)

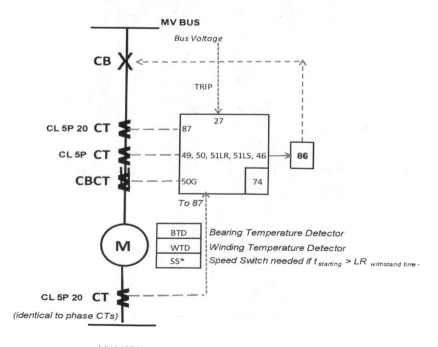

MV MOTOR
(WITH DIFFERENTIAL PROTECTION)

Transformer Feeders

MV/LV

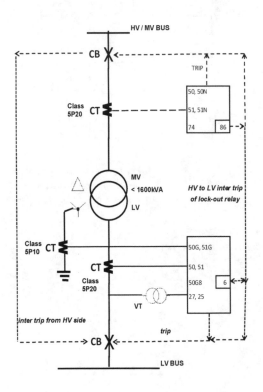

MV/LV (Larger ratings)

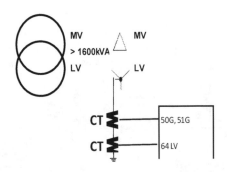

HV/MV

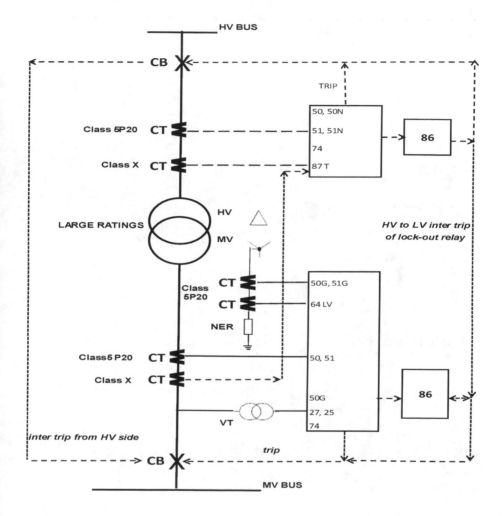

Outgoing Power Feeders

MV

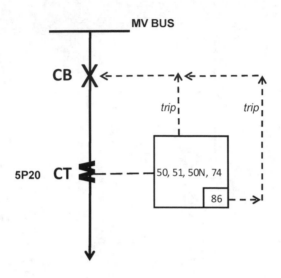

Bus Tie (MV or LV)

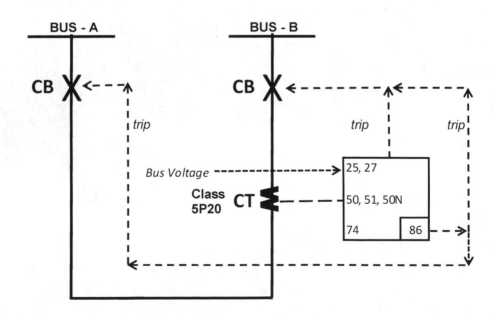

HV Capacitor Bank

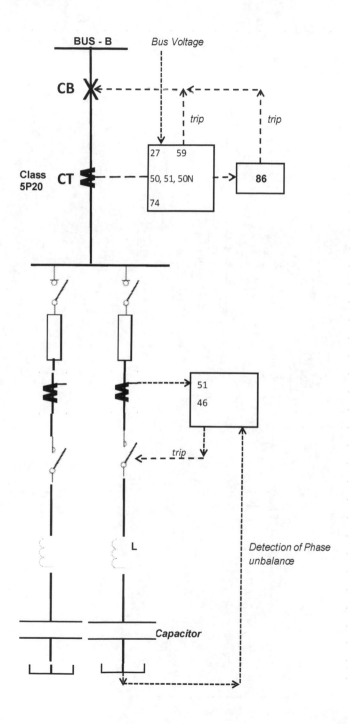

Generators

LV Generators

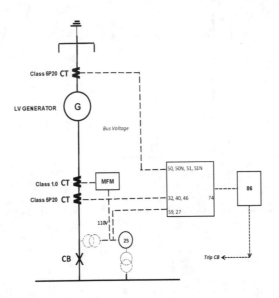

Large MV Generators

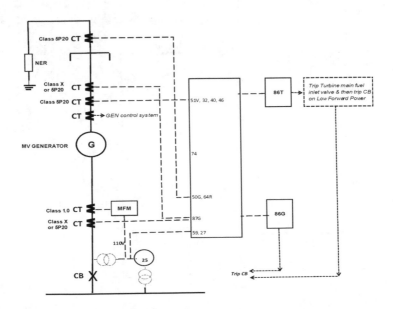

High Impedance Bus Bar Protection

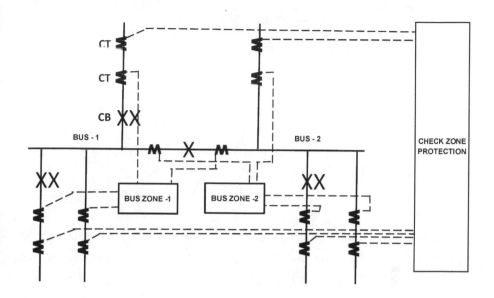

Pilot Wire Protection

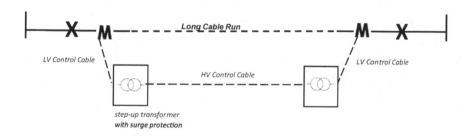

Overhead Line Feeders

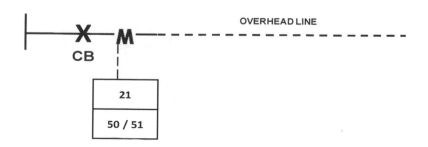

Distance Relay (21) (impedance relay or mho-relay) has three zones of protection. Zone-1 covers 80% of the line, Zone-2 covers 120% of the line while Zone-3 has a 50% back reach.

Foot Note:

As an Application Engineer it is very important for you to get the Electrical Protection Relaying concepts right, before you get drowned in advanced details of a proprietary nature usually provided by manufacturers.

This field is a continuously developing field where more and more sophisticated protections are developed to ensure that the assets are protected to the hilt. Modern relays come with self diagnostic features, advanced communication features where a mal functioning triggers an upstream protection.

The trend now a days is to have a very closely monitored and safeguarded 'relay setting' regime where only skilled hands can access modification to the settings. Relays also come with post tripping analysis features that sheds light on what exactly had gone wrong that caused the protection relay to operate in the first place.

17

Control of Power Distribution

This chapter will cover some basic discussions on how power circuits are switched ON & OFF, how they are supervised for proper functioning and its resultant safety. The discussions can be by no means exhaustive and therefore is intended to make you aware of the 'complexities' involved in the "Control" aspects of Power Distribution.

An awareness of the following will be very useful:

- ➢ Controlling Devices and related terminology
- ➢ Basic circuitry

Once you are aware you will be able to "read through" any control schematic, understand the logic involved and ultimately as an Application Engineer you can review Electrical Control Schematics and with more practice can even design one.

Controlling Devices and related terminology

Switching Relay   :   Usually a basic attracted armature type of relay, coil wound on a low retentivity, high permeability core. The armature closes the magnetic circuit and in doing so operates a set of electrically isolated contacts. Relays that are rugged and suitable for a long service life are commercially available.

NO, NC Contacts	:	These specify If an electrically isolated contact is 'normally open' or 'normally closed' in the de-energised state of the relay (i.e., in a condition as it is available in the shop). It is a universal convention that ALL control schematics depict the contacts under such conditions only.
Pick-up voltage	:	Relays used in practical applications are usually suitable to pick up even when the control supply voltage drops to low values so as to ensure integrity of the circuitry. The minimum voltage at which the relay can pick up is called the pick up voltage.
Drop-off voltage	:	As above, Relays used in practical applications are usually suitable to stay picked up even when the control supply voltage drops to low values so as to ensure integrity of the circuitry. The minimum voltage at which the relay will drop-off is called the drop off voltage.
Time Delay on Pick-up	:	As the name implies these relays pick up after allowing for a specified (can be set) time delay.
Time Delay on Drop-off	:	As the name implies these relays drop off after allowing for a specified (can be set) time delay.
Make-before-break contacts	:	Relays/auxiliary stacks of contacts normally have NO & NC contacts that change state when the relay/switch operate to cause Closed & open contacts respectively. Some of the applications might need contacts that make before the other set of contacts break
Break-before-make contacts	:	Similar to above with a difference that some of the contacts break before the rest make

198

| Power Contactors | : | These are the contacts used in the MAIN POWER CIRCUIT. They are usually 3 pole or 4 pole version for AC applications. ANSI device no. is 42. |

In LV range the commonly available ratings are 16, 25, 32, 40, 63, 100, 125, 170, 300 and even as high as 400A.

Its auxiliary contacts are denoted as 42a for the NO contacts and 42b for NC contacts and are used for critically important part of the circuitry since the number of such contacts available with the power contactor is usually limited. Otherwise the 42a & 42b are 'multiplied' using additional auxiliary contactors for use in indication circuits etc.

| Auxiliary Contactors | : | These are auxiliary contactors used in the control circuitry for non power applications as explained above. Contactors that consume less VA and are very reliable are commercially available. The only aspect that needs to be checked is its suitability to make/break the inductive currents of various devices used in the control circuits. |

| Lock out relay | : | This is the 'master trip' relay (ANSI Device no. 86) that gets operated by any other protection relay and even if the protection relay operates for a fleeting moment this relay will pick up and will lock out further energizing of the circuit until it is 'reset', various types of which are described below. |

| Self reset relay | : | This relay will reset itself once the cause is gone. |

| Hand reset relay | : | This relay will not reset itself once the cause is gone and needs an operator to physically reset it by hand. |

Electrical reset relay	:	This relay will not reset Itself once the cause is gone and needs an operator to physically reset it that in this case can be done electrically from another location instead of physically accessing the relay.
Under voltage relay	:	This relay drops off once the voltage across it falls below a set value and picks up again once the voltage is restored above the drop off value.
Over voltage relay	:	This relay picks up once the voltage across it rises above a set value and drops off again once the voltage is restored below the pick up value.
Push Button (PB)	:	As an electrical engineer you are already aware of this. The device can be either 'push to make' or be 'push to break' a contact that returns to its original state on release of the mechanical push. The advantage of a simple PB is its ability to momentarily cause an impulse that will no more be there once the hand is withdrawn unless it is a 'stay put' PB
Control Switch (CS)	:	Control Switch, unlike a PB may remain in the operated position of say "ON or OFF" or equivalents. It can be an AUTO—STANDBY selection a LOCAL—REMOTE selection, a MANUAL—OFF—AUTO selection, an Ammeter selector switch a voltmeter selector switch, or a RAISE-LOWER switch
Control Switch contacts	:	Control Switches are usually multi stacked with each stack electrically isolated from the other and each may have a unique contact configuration like 'contact made in ON' position, contact made in 'OFF' position, contact made in all positions except in OFF position and so on.

Rotary selector switch	:	As the name suggests these are switches with ergonomically designed handle that are distinctly different from other operation switches so that the operator does not make an error while operating when he goes for 'selection' process.
T-N-C Switch (spring return to neutral)	:	A CS that has three positions TRIP-NEUTRAL-CLOSE with the switch always returning to the NEUTRAL position on completion of each operation. These come with an ergonomically convenient 'pistol grip' handle and are very common in operating circuit breakers. The reason it is required to return to the N position is to mechanically avoid 'holding' the closing & trip coils continuously causing a drain on the control DC system.
NAT, NAC features of above	:	NAT indicates normal after TRIP position. The stacks of the switch are so constructed that the switch 'remembers' by cam action that even after it returns to NEUTRAL position, it last performed a TRIP operation. Similar explanation for NAC for CLOSE operation.
Discrepancy lamp	:	These lamps are very useful by being wired for indication for discrepancy in operation—"did the CB TRIP after we wanted it to TRIP?" and so on. Such lamps are often placed within the switch itself to blink on discrepancy condition and glow steadily when the function is performed correctly.

Mechanical lock out feature : Once a CB trips due to any fault the breaker cannot be closed any further since it gets mechanically locked out.

This is a safety feature that needs someone to physically reset the CB after ascertaining that the cause of the tripping has been rectified.

Basic Control Circuitry

The widespread use of Programmable Logic Controllers (PLC) has replaced a lot of complex control circuitry. However a few parts of the circuit are still very much **hard wired**. Some of the elementary principles of hard wiring are described below and are by no means exhaustive.

A relay picked up from an external impulse without and with reset feature

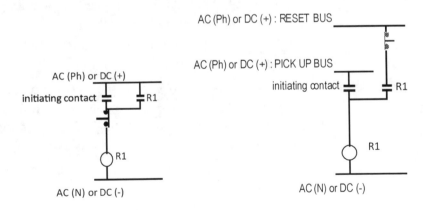

The above circuits are shown to prime you into 'reading' control schematics. Try and understand the concept of 'seal-in' contacts, 'resetting' an alarm condition etc.

Basic ON-OFF schematic wiring for a contactor (42) controlled circuit

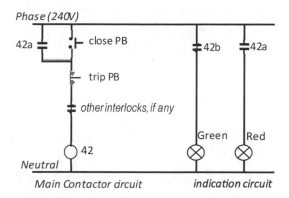

This shows simplistically a contactor energized to close and de energized to open with its auxiliary contacts used for indication purpose. What is not shown is the power circuit from which the control supply is usually drawn and others are features like TOL relays, service/Test positions of the switchgear module.

Note that the source of the control supply is not shown. It is usually taken from the three phase power circuit that feeds the load by tapping any one phase after the main power switch to ensure that the control bus is dead once the power circuit is isolated. In any case the control circuit will have separate HRC fuse in the phase and isolating link in the neutral. The draw back of this practice is the control circuit will have the same fault level as the power circuit that may not be desirable. Also there is no guarantee that the remaining two phases are healthy prior to switching ON.

To ensure that the scheme 'monitors' the healthiness of the phases, an isolation transformer is connected across two phases to provide a 240V output. This also lowers the fault levels of the control circuitry that is likely to be 'felt' by the operator.

Anti pumping circuit

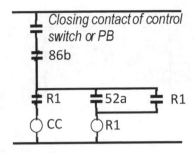

In case a closing command given through a switch that is stuck, or if the operator holds on in that position by mistake and if the CB trips due to an electrical fault we do not want to have a potentially dangerous 'pumping' operation of trip-close-trip-close . . . . operation until the CB contacts weld. The anti pumping circuit is an electrical feature that is a very common safety feature in all CB control schematics. Some vendors achieve this by mechanical means too.

Typical Circuit Breaker (52) control schematic

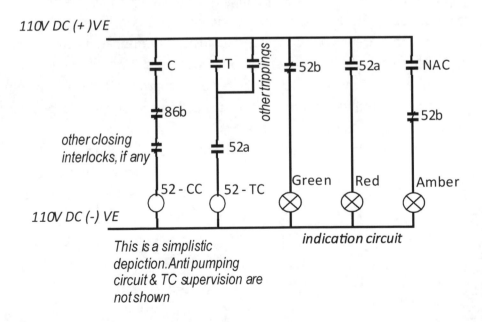

The schematic is presented to explain the separate closing coil & tripping coil in an MV or HV CB. Note how the amber lamp is wired to indicate a discrepancy condition should it occur after a close command is given. The circuit is over simplified because what is not shown are the circuits for spring charging motor, anti pumping, service and test positions of the carriage etc apart from the regular electrical protections.

Schematic for indication lamps with discrepancy features

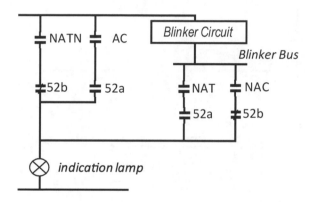

The circuit uses the NAT & NAC contacts of the Control Switch to provide flashing indication in case of discrepancy in what is achieved while closing or tripping the CB. Sometimes the lamp is placed within the switch itself. Common for EHV switchyard applications.

Trip Circuit Supervision schematics

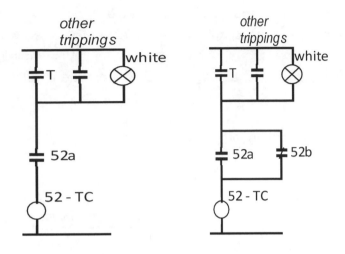

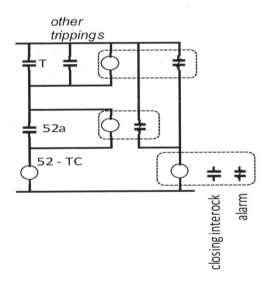

The first figure shows supervision of the trip coil (by an indicating lamp) with the CB in closed position only while the second figure achieves it in both closed & open positions. The third figure shows an application with relays that provides remote alarm and closure lock out features under all faulty situations of the trip circuit in both closed and open conditions of the CB.

Foot Note:

I have seen the trend has been to move from control from the 'front of switchgear' to control from a 'control room panel with hard devices' to 'control from computer screens'—depending on the complexity of the plant. An understanding of all the above will help the Application Engineer to choose the right system required.

The practice abroad, particularly in the Gulf countries is to have totally unmanned EHV substations monitored & operated from a central location.

Even in plant power distribution at the MV and LV level is controlled defacto from the DCS since the operation of the motors are linked to the process devices they run. Control cabling from the switchgear panels are minimized with the application of 'intelligent' Switchgears/MCCs that essentially have other add-on diagnostic features than just ON-OFF controls.

18

Locating Electrical Equipment

Locating the major electrical equipment i.e., to develop a basic electrical layout during Front End Engineering Design (FEED) phase calls for a lot of experience and knowledge. Some major issues that crop up later are averted by putting-in a considered thought process during development of the Electrical layout in the FEED stage itself.

A well planned layout will address

> ➢ Safety
> ➢ Cost
> ➢ Future expandability
> ➢ Convenient safe & controlled access for different operating & maintenance personnel
> ➢ Ease of handling during maintenance

Let us now look at some of the common issues that will address a few of the considerations listed above.

General for Indoor substation

HV switchgears/Equipment are located on one side with adequate segregation from the other equipment.

Separate room for Batteries

Raise floor to get cabling space below.

Extended aprons for handling/lay down space particularly if the floor is elevated

In such cases plan for removable hand rails that will help in handling heavy equipment such as switchgears or batteries from/to a truck.

Provide two exits for each switchgear room

Emergency doors to open outwards with panic bar

Outer apron level shall be slightly lower than the inside floor level to avoid rain water from going in; but not too much lower since it might result in a tripping hazard for personnel moving in & out.

Ensure redundancy in Heating, Ventilation & Air Conditioning (HVAC) equipment.

Air lock for personnel entry will ensure no leakage of HVAC controlled ambient within.

Main Receiving Sub Station (MRSS)

Locate the MRSS to suit incoming cables or Overhead lines.

Future expandability is very important.

Switchgear location and line-up shall suit outgoing cables.

Panel line up within a switchgear shall take into account outgoing cabling needs to minimise criss-crossings of large sized cables.

Other Substations

Locate the substations at "load centres"

Do not locate in Hazardous areas

Locate the transformers properly orienting the S/S layout considering I/C cables.

Elevate S/S for ease of cabling from below in case of large number of cables.

Emergency Diesel Generators

These shall be very near to the load centres

These shall not be located in areas classified as hazardous since it is very expensive to get generators that meet such area classification.

Try and locate these close to Diesel storage area

There are noise issues with the DGs. Locate them considering the impact of such issues on the remaining plant.

Take care of handling issues later. These are heavy equipment.

In Plant Generators

Normally these are located at one end of the plant to allow for tie-up with utility lines if required.

These have to be located outside hazardous areas.

These are very heavy equipment and therefore pay attention to handling issues.

Normally these are located close to MRSS.

Facilitate location of the vent stack in case of Gas turbines.

In case of more than one generator the centre to centre distances between the generators shall be well away for safety reasons.

Outdoor transformers

These are large heat sources and are best located outdoors.

In desert/icy areas they need to be protected by a shade.

In case shading is provided ensure adequate clear space exists from the top for allowing good convection space for hot air.

Adjacent transformers need to have fire walls, height just above the top most part of the transformer. Ensure you don't overdo it since cooling of transformers will get affected.

Transformers of Large Variable Speed Drives (VSD)

These transformers produce a lot of heat and hence they are best located outdoors.

Smaller sized transformers can be with solid dielectric in which case they can be located indoors. However prefer a separate room since its HVAC needs are different.

Ensure that the handling of the transformer is thought through.

LV Transformers feeding switchgears

Locate the transformers close to the switchgears, but outside the room to minimise the cable costs. The cables are usually short runs, but are more in numbers and are large sized.

Plan for removal & handling of the transformer.

Orientation of the transformer should suit bus duct connection & layout.

Locate oil pits sized appropriately below the transformer.

HV Capacitor Banks

These have a certain amount of 'explosion' hazard while switching-in. Hence prefer them located outdoors.

Also the dielectric might occasionally leak and hence a proper disposal arrangement has to be considered.

General for all large transformers

Provide rails for hauling the transformer out.

Soak pit adequately sized for the oil that may leak out or even drain out should be considered.

Supports for sprinkler system pipes should be planned without compromising on the clearances all round.

Facility to remove the transformer without disturbing the cable box is a good engineering practice.

Outdoor switchyard

Locate the switchyard where the OHLs come in so that they can be easily reached & terminated. Locating the yard at one end of the plant is usual. The orientation should be such that the deviation is not more than 30^0 to the gantry structure to which the incoming OHLs are strung.

Allow cabling space for outgoing feeders.

In oil & gas plants the switchyard should be located well away from flare area in a safe area upwind so that the gases are not blown into the yard.

Future bays may be required in the yard and hence space within the fenced area should be planned accordingly.

Plan for access road all round.

Escape gates @ every 50m along the peripheral fencing shall be provided.

Gas Insulated Substation (GIS)

Location should ensure ease of incoming cable/OHL termination. At the same time it should be borne in mind that the outgoing HV cables need a lot of trench space.

Plan for removal, handling and laying down of the GIS individual bays.

Bus Ducts

Plan for shortest run, with minimum bends.

Provide for flexible bellows at equipment ends to allow for level mismatch and future settling of heavy foundations.

Plan for locating the bus duct supports during development of the layout itself.

Plan for entry into the substation. Ensure no fouling is there with structures.

Plan for hot air blowing and CT removal during maintenance.

EHV Cables

Plan for dedicated pre-formed trenching for buried installation. EHV cables occupy a lot of space.

Plan for straight through jointing kits, terminations etc.

Segregation from other cables is a must.

In the trenches plan for future additions too.

Also plan for redundancy in the cable routing.

HV/MV Cables

Plan for segregation from other cables.

Plan for redundancy in cable runs.

LV Power & Control Cables

Plan to segregate all cables from HV cables.

As far as possible plan to install cables in a single layer if they are going to be directly buried.

If power cables are laid touching each other, check the sizing considering the applicable derating factors.

Pan for redundancy in routing.

Cable Trenches—Pre formed

These are usually of RCC.

Allow for chamfer at the ends to facilitate bending of cables of the order of 6 to 12 times their overall diameter.

Top of trench shall be kept slightly above grade level to prevent rain water from draining into it.

Look for possibility of 'water ponds' forming due to too many trenches criss crossing

Allow for access into the trench.

Provide barrier at building entries so that rain water does not enter into the building via the trenches.

Cable Trenches—for directly buried cabling

Consider access for future digging.

Re-look at spacing vis-à-vis sizing calculations. It is important to have consistency.

Plan for buried pipe crossings in the roads and buildings judiciously.

Plan for redundant cable trenches.

Seal building entries against water ingress.

Cable Tray Banks

Need to ensure access to ALL cables.

Keep provision for supports.

Separate trays for HV, LV Power, Control & Instrument cables.

Re-look at spacing vis-à-vis sizing calculations. It is important to have consistency.

Provide 'spare' trays for future use since it will be difficult to install additional trays later once the cables are pulled.

Personnel access between tray banks should be ensured. Use available structures nearby rather than go for dedicated structures for supporting the cables.

Assess cable tray loads well in advance for the structural engineers to factor them in during their design

Lighting Towers

Locate without hindrance to movement of equipment during O&M.

In Oil & Gas plants, locate the towers outside hazardous areas as far as possible.

Security Lighting

These should not be located arbitrarily. Consult security requirements before locating these.

In Oil & Gas plants, locate these outside hazardous areas as far as possible.

Street Lighting

Locate poles so as not to hinder movement of equipment.

Consider distance of pole from the edge of the road and the overhang at the tip of the pole as per which illumination levels should have been worked out.

Locate the Junction Boxes (JBs) away from the road side to avoid the hazard of impact from moving vehicles.

Indoor Lighting/Lighting inside sun shade

Lighting fixtures should NOT be located above equipment since it might hinder lamp replacement/maintenance of fixtures.

Space the fittings as per 0.5x − x − 0.5x norms to have near uniformity in lighting levels.

Have staggered phase distribution so that adequate illumination exists even during loss of a phase.

Consider adequate clearances from the bottom of overhead cranes/mono rails during design stage.

Small Power Outlets

Choose properly classified sockets for the hazardous area in question as applicable.

Locate these spaced judiciously such that any portable equipment with a 25m cord can still reach the desired point in the plant.

Foot Note:

Paying proper attention to location of electrical equipment can save a lot of issues.

The first time I ever did that was for a large Thermal Power Project when I took the initiative and battled through odds to inform a 33kV switchgear vendor—at a rather late stage—to alter the panel line-up just to ensure that we save on the lengths and avoid criss crossings of the expensive 33kV cables that formed the back bone of power distribution for the entire plant.

In another project we had a large number of LV substations throughout the green-field fertiliser plant. I decided to examine each and every case, if a mirror image of the substation would be more economic from cabling point of view. In the process I also realised that changing the orientation of the LV transformers and location of access through the fencing can result in straight run of the LV bus ducts avoiding a few bends—a money saver.

19

Indoor Substation Layout

Designing the layout of a large Indoor substation is both an art as well as a science in probably equal measure.

First of all where do you locate the substation?

A lot of careful thought need to go into that.

Is it a good idea to locate it at the load centre? This will no doubt optimise cable lengths and beat voltage drop issues.

Doesn't the above mean bringing in the "Incoming" supply cable or OHL through a cluttered plant making the cabling less reliable and perhaps expensive to maintain later.

Is the substation building "expandable" in future?

If there is a "Phase II" of the plant—as is usual—can we easily expand the building?

Is there adequate space outside?

Is it constructible? With NIL or minimal shut downs?

Is it located considering less probability of wind blowing into it from the plant—possibly causing hazardous gases swept into it?

Usually a minimum distance of 30m should be maintained from the source of the hazard.

In an Oil &Gas plant, is it close to a "Flare" area that may cause an increase in the ambient temperature in the vicinity?

Once you had located the substation, you need to put more thoughts on how the layouts inside & the immediate vicinity are going to be like.

Fundamental principle behind the design of a building is to house the electrical equipment in a protected environment and disallow outside air to freely flow inside carrying with it dust, gases and particulates apart from causing air at ambient temperature to flow in that may not suit the design needs. Normally these buildings are therefore provided with a lot of internal ventilation achieved by allowing air circulation and air changes as required, at times heated or air conditioned maintaining a slight positive pressure inside.

Thus substation building constructed as an RCC framed structure with RCC roofing and RCC flooring will lend itself well for such housing. Floors usually should have "cut outs" to suit cabling for the equipment located on them. Unused cut outs—for safety reasons—should be closed by chequered plate of minimum 6mm thickness. These should be easily removable and suitable for resizing to locate equipment in future.

Chequered plates are best avoided in front of switchgear panels since this might create difficulty in racking out the panel—note that breaker panels are quite heavy—due to minor mis match in levels between the top of concrete floor and that of the chequered plate.

Sometimes to minimise site based activities the S/S are of pre-fabricated package type. They are disassembled after Factory Acceptance Tests (FAT), despatched to site and re-assembled there.

In certain oil & gas installations codes dictate that these be designed to be "blast proof" so that even if there is an eventual blast in the "plant" outside, the substation will stay intact.

Elevated Building

It is common practice in the oil & gas industry in particular to elevate the floor level of the substation building for ease of cabling. The 'cabling plenum' below will serve as an easily accessible place to lay the cable trays/cables without much clutter and allow for future maintenance of the cables.

How much 'head room' should we have in the cellar?

Ideally from the 'grade level' a clear height of 2m is preferred so that in an emergency, one can easily walk/run through in what is likely to be a poorly illuminated space. By 'clear height' we mean clearance from the grade level to the 'soffit' of the beam above. Naturally this will mean that the floor level of the s/s will be a good 2.5 ~ 2.6m level above the grade if we account for the depth of the beam and thickness of the RCC floor.

Next acceptable (as a cost saver) will be to settle for a clear height of 1.6m. This should be fine for most of the cases.

In some cases the building is even brought down to just have a 1m cellar height with the premise that anyone would need to go there very rarely anyway and entry is possible with a bit of inconvenience. So smaller the floor area of the building more likely will be the temptation to stick for this option since anyone can quickly get out of the constrained space, should there be an urgent need.

Equipment in a substation

Let us now see what are the likely equipment that will be located in a substation.

Distribution Transformer (oil filled)	:	These are located usually in the periphery of the s/s
Emergency DG set	:	Located in a DG room adjacent to the s/s
VSD Transformer (oil filled)	:	Located outside the s/s
'Remote' Tap Changer Cubicle of transformers	:	Located inside
Capacitor banks	:	Located outside the s/s
NERs	:	Located outside the s/s
Dry type transformers	:	Located inside
HV/MV/LV Switchgears	:	Located inside
MCCs/ACDBs/HVAC DBs	:	Located inside
AC UPS, DC UPS	:	Located inside
EDG Control Panel	:	Located inside

Lighting, & Small Power DBs	:	Located inside
LV VSDs	:	Located inside
HV VSDs	:	Located inside, but at times lined up in a separate room to minimize noise and segregate the unusually high heating load for appropriate HVAC design
Electrical Protection Panels	:	Located inside, but sometimes n a separate room
Fire Alarm Panels	:	Located inside
Batteries	:	Located inside but inside a separate room. However in the oil & gas industry there is a practice of doing away with a separate room if the product of Vah is low.
ENMCS Panel, IMCS, RTUs	:	Located inside
Substation maintenance equipment	:	Located inside

How we lay them out?

Having understood 'what' & 'why' we keep the particular equipment inside/outside, let us understand more on 'how' you need to prepare the layouts.

You need to think through the following requirements:

➤ Safety	:	Are the interpanel front, rear, top clearances 'safe'? Do they meet recommendations of vendor? Can they operate at rated capacity?

➢ Operability	:	Can an operator access the ON/OFF switch? Can the operator 'reset' the relays? Can the operator rack-out/rack-in the panels?
➢ Maintainability	:	Can the maintenance personnel access the interiors and do servicing?
➢ Removal & Replacement	:	Can the panel be removed and taken out safely while the rest of the panes are in service? Can the panel pass through the door?
➢ Expandability	:	Can you add one or two panels on either side of the switchgear line-up in future?
➢ Ease of Cabling	:	Battery might be in a separate room, but the charger needs to be close to that. Incoming panels of switchgears can be close to their respective transformers that are usually located outside. This will result in minimal length of cables/Bus ducts and hence low voltage drops. Remember that incoming cables are short runs, but the numbers and cross sections are usually large.

We will now proceed to analyse in a structured manner the important factors in layout considerations for each type of equipment using the above template of Safety/Operability/Maintainability/ Removal & Replacement/Expandability/Ease of cabling

		Layout
➢ Safety	:	Emergency access gate @ 30m in the fence Rooms to have exit doors that opens outwards & provided with panic bars
➢ Operability	:	HVAC should be 2 x 100% designed for achieving an internal temperature of 25^{0}C and RH 50% $\pm$ 10%
➢ Maintainability	:	Provide acid tiling in battery room
➢ Removal & Replacement	:	At least one equipment access door of 2.5m x 3.0m to be provided. This should be separate from another personnel access door that is provided. Raised platform, if any shall have removable hand rails wherever equipment handling is planned. Height of building should factor-in on height of switchgear, whether there is top entry of cables planned, provision of bus ducts, lighting and HVAC ducting.
➢ Expandability	:	Minimum 15% space shall be vacant
➢ Ease of Cabling	:	Top clearance shall be 500 to 1000mm to Bottom of Beam For 50mm deep ladder type of trays top-of-tray to bottom-of-beam shall be minimum 300mm.

		Transformers
➢ Safety	:	On the side that is away from the plant. Provide fire barriers between the transformers
➢ Operability	:	Provide sun shade Keep at Grade level
➢ Maintainability	:	Clearance of 1000mm all round.
➢ Removal & Replacement	:	
➢ Expandability	:	
➢ Ease of Cabling	:	Bus ducts to be routed through wall openings with proper fire rating

		HV/MV/LV Switchgears, MCCs
➢ Safety	:	GIS should be in a separate room For ratings > 52kV need an EOT crane Rear clearance either ≤225mm or ≥ 760mm
➢ Operability	:	
➢ Maintainability	:	HV switchgear—2500mm clear LV switchgear—1500mm clear HV to LV—2500mm LV to LV—1500mm Rear of LV—1000mm Rear of GIS—1500mm
➢ Removal & Replacement	:	
➢ Expandability	:	Minimum 15% spare
➢ Ease of Cabling	:	Seal unused opening in floor with fireproof seals

		Capacitor Banks
➤ Safety	:	Indoor in a separate room or better outdoors
➤ Operability	:	
➤ Maintainability	:	Provide 1000mm clearance all round
➤ Removal & Replacement	:	
➤ Expandability	:	
➤ Ease of Cabling	:	

		AC & DC UPS
➤ Safety	:	
➤ Operability	:	
➤ Maintainability	:	
➤ Removal & Replacement	:	
➤ Expandability	:	
➤ Ease of Cabling	:	As close to batteries as possible

		Batteries
➤ Safety	:	Locate them in a separate room
➤ Operability	:	
➤ Maintainability	:	Provide 1m clearance all round the battery bank
➤ Removal & Replacement	:	
➤ Expandability	:	
➤ Ease of Cabling	:	No cabling inside a battery room. Use single core cables

		Wall mounted DBs
➢ Safety	:	
➢ Operability	:	
➢ Maintainability	:	Rear clearance can be NIL
➢ Removal & Replacement	:	
➢ Expandability	:	
➢ Ease of Cabling	:	

		Substation Location & Orientation
➢ Safety	:	30m from Hazardous sources Away from wind
➢ Operability	:	
➢ Maintainability	:	Provide unhindered access roads
➢ Removal & Replacement	:	
➢ Expandability	:	
➢ Ease of Cabling	:	Cable entry to cellar should not interfere with transformer and vice versa

Cabling Considerations

The Application Engineer should decide in the beginning whether the transformer and switchgear are planned to be connected using bus duct or cables.

Bus duct layout will be neater but may work out costlier and needs a lot of co-ordnation during engineering.

Cables on the other hand occupies more space. Need to check if this will increase cellar height, cluttered layout and still turn out cheaper. Longer the route, cables are preferred.

Cable entries to s/s should bo through cellar, partially on cable trays and partially laid underground or in trenches.

If cellar has walls, seal off the cable entries.

If entry is through built up trench, provide pipe sleeve with 20 to 25% extra as spare. These need to be sealed with cold mastic compound and unused pipes should have end plugs.

If s/s is blast proof then seal the entries with MCT blocks on floors & walls.

Under cable trays in a cellar minimum space need is 1200mm and tray to tray spacing is 300mm for a 50mm deep tray. Same In case of Bottom of Tray (BOT) to Bottom of Beam (BOB).

Foot Note:

If you have a good eye for detail and have a logical thinking, your indoor substation layout will be perfect.

I was once horrified to note on a site visit after a few weeks, out in the desert, a newy constructed indoor substation had water ingress in the entire hall in front of switchgears, because the civil engineers had overlooked the fact that the floor levels inside and the top of concrete on the landing outside were the same. A small adjustment during designing or even during construction would have saved the blushes for the contractor.

In another case doors opening outwards in an unmanned substation—that are normal in any substation—threw up a new set of issues. How do we enter in an emergency when there is foot deep sand build up outside due to 'shamal' (desert storm)?

In yet another case there was a 'level' issue of the floors that caused a major problem in 'drawing out' the heavy MV switchgear trolley. Reason: The switchgear base floor details were provided by vendor very late, so that portion of the floor was decided to be constructed later, while the rest of the floor was completed by the civil contractor to achieve timely progress. Result was a mismatch in levels that took a lot of effort and cost to rectify.

In one project in the oil & gas sector, I had a huge room with two parallel rows of a number of VSD panels one for each well nearby. Each panel complied with the noise level norms, but the issue was the 'combined' noise level that will be felt by an occasional operator on entering the unmanned room. A number of safety experts battled the problem and eventually came up with a workable economic solution: 'Advise the operator, as a standard operational practice to use a pair of safety ear plugs whenever he was needed to enter the room'.

Handling heavy batteries, though once in a few years, should be thought through.

20

Plant Electrical Layout

Apart from locating and orienting the substations, Application Engineers in Electrical discipline have very little role in originating a "Plant Layout" that is usually dictated by Process & Equipment considerations—particularly for oil & gas installations that we will generally focus on since it has a lot of variety. Timely inputs on Electrical aspects would go a long way towards designing a plant layout that addresses all aspects that we discussed earlier viz., Safety/Operability/Maintainability/Removal & Replacement/ Expandability/Ease of cabling.

Easily said that 'as a rule' avoid keeping any Electrical equipment in hazardous areas. This can be by and large followed for all items excepting for motors.

Keep the substation 30m away from hazardous area but near the load centre.

Keep transformers near s/s but away from the "plant".

Pay attention to which way the wind will blow for you to avoid hazardous gas clouds blown into the s/s.

Keep EDGs close to the s/s, but in a separate room. Pay attention to day tank locations.

If VSDs are needed, be aware that VSD transformers for large VSDs liberate a lot of heat. Try to locate them outdoors.

VSDs per se has to be located indoor. Try to keep them in a separate room to duct out the heat. Also they emanate a lot of noise.

Plan for location of Local Control Units (LCU)/Remote Control Unit (RCU)/Safety Switches (SS) of each drive properly close to drive motor in "visible" range plus for ease of cabling & earthing. Make use of sunshade structures as much as possible.

For cooling tower fans, each fan will need separate LCU/RCU/SS. Plan a grouped location for ease of cabling.

Due to height, you may need SS/RCU at two levels. Pay attention to their cabling needs.

While we will discuss Lighting, Earthing, Lightning Protection & Cabling separately, make sure the 'equipment' involved are factored-in while planning layouts.

> Where will be the DB for Lighting & Small power be located?
> Where will be the photo cell located?
> Have you taken into account cable trenching for lighting?

Can we access lights for maintenance?

Plan for cable trenches with redundancy of cabling in mind i.e., dedicated, separate route if the equipment is meant to be a stand by for the other.

For Fire protection system for transformers (sprinkler system) and for the entire plant, have we accounted for all the equipment.

Plan for fire proof cables.

Locate sump pump motors, plan for cabling for them. Sometimes they will be at below grade level.

For transformers what about oil soak pits, collection pits & even recovery pits for large transformers.

Identify hazardous areas properly.

Plan for 'future' hazardous area too since often motors bought may become useless due to process needs when the area is redefined as hazardous.

Look for Cathodic Protection system interfaces and plan to identify the CP transformer and cabling for the same.

All non plant buildings/sheds will still have cabling needs for Lighting, Telecommunication & UPS needs. Plan for these.

Identify cabling needs for all equipment other than for just the motors such as

> Package units on skids
> Flare equipment
> Desalters

Plan cable routing for those.

Foot Note:

Imagine huge cables laid at site but pose difficulty in termination at the cable box of motors because the cables can't be bent at site with such low radius since the bottom of the box was very close to the top of the heavy RCC foundation. You end up repenting as to why no one thought of simply providing a notch at the RCC foundation while it was cast. Eye for detail in a timely manner is the key.

In another location I had seen a set of 2 x 100% load fed from two cables laid in the same overhead tray. What happens if one of the cables catch fire or the entire tray suffers a mechanical damage? The very purpose of investing in redundant equipment would have been lost and the process might suffer an outage that could be expensive and at times even make the plant unsafe.

Preformed RCC trench tops are usually kept 100 to 200mm raised above grade level to prevent ingress of rain water from the surroundings. In one plant we found much to our dismay that a criss crossing of such trench work caused creation of a pond due to stagnation of rain water.

Paying attention to Detail all the way is the key!

21

Equipment Selection for Hazardous Areas

Our objective in the discussion under this chapter will be to become aware of "how to" select Electrical Equipment for use in Hazardous areas.

We are not going to dwell on how "hazardous areas" are identified. This is a science left to "Safety Engineers" who come out with 'Hazardous Area classification' drawings.

As an Application Engineer, later on you need to get familiar with International Standards for this particular topic. The most important one is IEC 60079 series. This standard has a number of parts that will help you understand the REQUIREMENTS for

- ➤ Construction
- ➤ Testing and
- ➤ Marking of the Equipment for each type of "Ex Protection".

Most Owners specify IEC 60079 & IP 15 for hazardous area related applications. Some with US market influence stipulate NEC & API 500.

Understanding a few terminologies listed below might help the Application Engineer.

Flammable atmosphere	:	Mix of vapours/gases with air that will burn IF ignited.
Flash Point	:	Minimum temperature at which vapours on surfaces of hydrocarbons at a particular barometric pressure will ignite on application of ignition source.
Hazardous area	:	3D space in which we can expect flammable atmosphere at such frequencies warranting special precautions in controlling the potential sources of ignition while selecting the electrical equipment for service in those areas
Ignition Energy	:	Spark energy in joules required to ignite gases
Pressurisation	:	Technique used to guard against ingress of external atmosphere into a room or an enclosure by maintaining a protective gas at (+)ve pressure
Protective Gas	:	Air/Inert gas used for purging and over pressuring for dilution of explosive gases in a particular enclosure or area
Purging	:	Involves passing protective gas through enclosures/ducts so that concentration of explosive gas is brought down to a safe level
Source of Release	:	Point from which flammable liquid/vapour/gas may be released into the atmosphere. Three grades of release are

> Continuous
> Primary
> Secondary

Type of Protection class P_x	:	This reduces from Zone-1 to non hazardous area

Type of Protection class P_y	:	This reduces from Zone-1 to Zone-2 area
Type of Protection class P_z	:	This reduces from Zone-2 to non hazardous area
Vapour Density	:	If density < air, vapour accumulates near the roof If density > air, vapour travels to the lowest levels such as pits, trenches etc and can pose dangers long after release.
Zone—0	:	Flammable Gas is always present in these areas. No electrical equipment should located here
Zone—1	:	Flammable Gas is likely to be here in normal operation
Zone—2	:	Flammable gas is unlikely to be here in normal operation, but may exist at times for short periods
ATEX	:	French term for "Atmosphere Explosibles". ATEX—94/9, 95 & 137 are important landmark EC Directives

Selection of Electrical Equipment in Hazardous Areas

Equipment by itself is not hazardous. Where it is located could pose a hazard. Best is do not use any in such areas! That will be cheaper and bear no risk.

However the above is not always possible. Hence selection has to be based on

Hazardous Area Classification drawings & documents

Hazardous Area Classification schedules that deal with:

Whether an area is open (in shelter) or closed area

Category & flash point of fluid handled there

> ➢ Temperature Class
> ➢ Release source
> ➢ Release grade
> ➢ Ventilation type
> ➢ Zone.
> ➢ Hazard radius

Whether Drain vessels are there

Whether Drain pumps are there and whether vertical drain pumps are there that will need to be seen for location with respect to the floor level.

Additional classifications are there for Battery rooms, Analyser houses.

Electrical Equipment used in hazardous areas are specially designed (and certified) to prevent or control ignitions. We need not go into their constructional details at this stage.

Inputs for the Application Engineer are from the Owner/others as follows:

1) **Zone** in which equipment is going to be used
2) Sensitivity for ignition of the vapours/gases there.—called "**Gas Groups**".
3) Sensitivity for ignition by hot surfaces—expressed as "**Temperature Classification**"

Gas Groups

For upstream Oil & Gas installations, generally the Gas Group is IIA. If H_2S is expected in the gas the Gas Group is IIB.

In the industry mostly all the Electrical Equipment are certified for both the above Gas Groups.

For Battery rooms the Gas Group is usually IIC.

Temperature Classification

If nothing is particularly specified, for upstream Oil & Gas facilities, go for Class T_3 (200^0C).

However you need to check with Hazardous Area Classification schedule.

Note that the above temperature classification is usually assigned for $T_{ambient}$ of 40^0C. If ambient temperature is > 40^0C check specifically and mention the corrected Temperature Classification in the name plate.

The above information is specifically needed for Lighting fixtures and Electrical Heat Tracing tapes.

For Battery Room usually T_6 (85^0C) is often specified by a few Owners even though auto ignition temperature of H_2 is 540^0C. So a Class T_1 (450^0C) should suffice instead of Class T_6 that is quite expensive to source.

Material of Enclosure

Exd enclosures come with Copper free Aluminium or are of Cast Iron.

Cast Aluminium corrodes in H_2S/Saline environment and therefore their usage is limited. In such cases it is better to go for Cast Iron that is however costly and not widely available.

GRP/FRP is used as a combination of Exde. Here the enclosure is Exe while the component inside will meet Exd protection.

If enclosure is metallic as an equivalent it should have Exd protection implying that all components inside can then be either normal Industrial type or can be housed in a separate Exe enclosure

Practical Guidelines for the Application Engineer

Equipment	Zone—1	Zone—2	Safe outdoor
MV Induction Motor LV Induction Motor	Exd, Exp IIB T_3 IP 55		IP55

Equipment	Zone—1	Zone—2	Safe outdoor
MCC Power Socket Lighting Switchboard DBs	Exde IIB T_3 IP55		IP55

Equipment	Zone—1	Zone—2	Safe outdoor
Welding Sockets	Exd IIB T_3	Exde IIB T_3	IP55

Equipment	Zone—1	Zone—2	Safe outdoor
JBs	Exd IIB T_3 IP55	Exde IIB T_3 IP55	IP55

Equipment	Zone—1	Zone—2	Safe outdoor
Lighting Fixtures	Exd/de IIB T_3 IP55		IP55

Equipment	Zone—1	Zone—2	Safe outdoor
Cable Glands	Exde IIB T_3 IP55		IP55

In general

In <u>Process Plants</u> as an abundant caution all equipment are selected for Zone-2 so that future extensions/modifications do not cause any issue.

In <u>Utilities & Off site areas</u> all equipment are selected as industrial types suitable for safe areas.

Sometimes a question will arise whether it is acceptable to keep an equipment in a safe area just outside the limits of a hazardous area. The answer should be NO.

For example **transformers** should be kept farther & farther away depending on their kVA ratings since the oil volume will be prorate higher.

For **Motors**, Windings to have Class F insulation but temperatures are limited to Class B. Non sparking motors are required in Zone 2 areas. Motors with VSDs may operate with hotter surfaces and therefore needs specific application checks.

For **Heaters** specific attention need to be paid since they might have hot surfaces.

For **DGs**, a direction check is needed for the combustion air intake.

For **Cables**, generally the outer sheath is of *flame retardant* PVC to IEC 60332-Part 3. For Fire & Gas services, Escape lighting cables and for UPS outgoing cables the outer sheath has to be *fire resistant* to IEC 60332-1, 11 & 21.

For **cable transit systems** more stringent standards apply for gas tightness properties.

Foot Note:

Imagine a huge MV motor of the normal industrial type already installed at site and later, for some reason, the HSE design department required the area to be classified as 'hazardous'. The cost of replacing the motor with a certified one was phenomenal and everyone got busy looking for whom to blame.

22

Electrical Trace Heating

Trace Heating is a system used to *maintain* or *raise* the temperature of fluids in Pipes or Vessels or Valves in the Pipelines among other items—for freeze protection & maintenance of desired temperature.

Usually the pipes/vessels are provided with a blanket of insulation to retain the heat. So the Electrical Heat Tracers are installed in close contact with the entire length of the pipe line or vessel surface while the thermal insulation is wrapped above that.

Note that trace heating is often done by steam where it is available. In process Industries Trace Heating by electrical means is a proven alternative with its own advantages.

In the northern latitudes extreme cold climate demands trace heating in almost everything.

- Snow/ice protection for stairways, ramps, roof
- Under floor heating
- Door frame heating
- Soil warming
- Prevent cavitation of pumps handling viscous fluids etc.

Thermostats controlling the switchgear feeding the heating circuit help maintain the heating at the desired temperature.

In the oil industry—typically the hydrocarbon will have wax—that solidifies well above the ambient temperature and so trace heating becomes a requirement to prevent clogging of pipelines etc.

Transportation of liquid sulphur in pipelines is common, that needs massive heating of the pipe lines.

Constant Power Heaters

Constant Power Heaters comprise of high resistance heating wires, the I^2R losses of which creates the heating.

Advantages:

Cheap
Can cause high temperatures like using MI cable heaters

Disadvantages:

Can overheat and burn
A 'break' anywhere in the line will cause 'failure'.
Therefore this type of heater needs a good control.
Variant of this type of heater is by using smaller elements in 'zoning' mode.
Two insulated parallel wires have many heating elements connected 'across' by soldering to the 'bus' at intervals.
Disadvantages of these are almost very much the same.

Self Regulating Heating or Self Limiting Heating

These are very common in the industry. This has two parallel bus wires that carry current but do not heat. The wires are encased in semiconducting polymer (loaded with carbon). This is 'self regulating' because as it heats, its R increases and it allows less and less current to flow. The whole assembly is enclosed in a common jacket that has a braid at the top (for grounding and mechanical protection) above which an outer jacket of Teflon or rubber is common.

Specific polymer properties decide what can be the maximum temperature that the heater can provide. Therefore the length decides the quantum of heat it can provide.

Like motors, these heaters have 'inrush' current on starting and therefore the associated switchgear needs to be designed suitably.

Distribution of Power

Essentially the individual loads are single phase. Usually the heaters are grouped to suit process needs as well as convenience of feeding.

The supply needs are 'large' warm-up current to start from cold start situation, while smaller loads under 'running' condition is really a function of the thickness of the insulation blanket.

Overheating by process fluid can damage the heater polymer. So a good understanding of the process parameters are required by the Application Engineers.

Refer International standards:

IEEE 515 & 622
BS 6351
IEC 60208

As discussed earlier, the 'running' heating load depends on the amount of insulation provided. Hence there is a trade-off to achieve minimum life cycle cost.

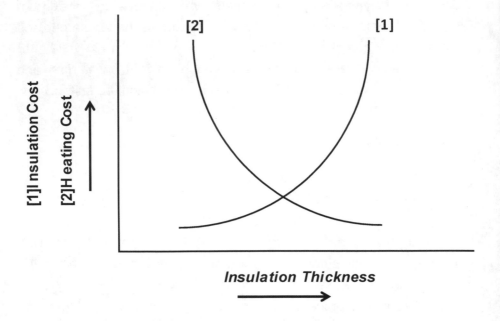

Insulation Thickness

Calculation approach

IEEE 515—1997 Annexure A is a good reference to calculate heat loss from a pipe that is a function of:

> ➢ Desired minimum fluid temperature T_m
> ➢ Minimum Ambient temperature expected T_a
> ➢ Pipe size
> ➢ Thickness of thermal insulation
> ➢ Location—indoor or outdoor
> ➢ Desired safety factor

The following are the recommended steps to bring out the intricacies involved in the calculations:

#1 Determine application ΔT i.e., $T_m - T_a$.

#2 Refer insulation manufacturer's table to determine 'base heat loss' in Watts/m for the insulated pipe. Typical table is shown as Table-1 [courtesy: Heat Trace]

#3 An 'insulation adjustment factor' is selected to apply on heat loss calculated. Typical table is shown below as Table-2 [courtesy: Heat Trace]

#4 For all indoor application use a factor of 0.9 on results of step # 3

#5 Use a safety factor of say 10% on results obtained in step # 4

#6 Valves cause additional heat loss in the line. So use another factor >>1. Typical table is shown below as Table-3 [courtesy: Heat Trace]

#7 Supports used for pipes are a cause for heat loss. Typically heat loss per support is $0.7L(\Delta T)$ where L is the length of the support in feet.

If W/foot of heating cable selected is > Heat loss/foot then use a straight run.

If W/foot of heating cable selected is < Heat loss/foot the options are:

a) Go for a higher wattage heating cable
b) Go for multiple straight runs
c) Go for spiral wrapping of heating cable on the pipe
d) Use higher 'K factor' insulation or go for higher insulation thickness.

(b) causes a little more complication in the installation. The 'wrapping factor' has to be arrived at. Normally should not be >2. Otherwise use parallel heaters.

Normally manufacturers provide detail engineering support for their product.

Table—1

Base Heat Loss for Insulated Pipes for Fibre Glass Insulation with K = 0.25 btu/hr-ft-0F/in and with a 10% safety factor

Ins thk (in)	ΔT (0F)	Nominal Pipe Size								
		0.5	1	1.5	2	2.5	3	6	. . . .	30
		Actual OD								
		0.68	1.32	1.9	2.38	2.88	3.5	6.63	. . . .	30
0.5	50	2.1	3.3	4.4	5.3	6.2	7.3	13.0	. . . .	54.7
	/	/	/	/	/					/
	/	/	/	/						/
	/	/								/
										/
	300	12.3	19.7	26.3	31.5	37	43.9	78	. . . .	328.2
1.0	50	1.4								
	/	/								
	300	8.3								
1.5										
2.0										
2.5										10.4
3.0										62.4

Table—2

Thermal Insulation Adjustment Factors
(with a 10% safety factor)

Insulation Type	Insulation K Factor (BTU/hr-ft^2-F/m)	Adjustment Factor
Polyurethane	0.165	0.66
Polystyrene	0.220	0.88
Fibre Glass	0.250	1.00
Mineral Wool	0.300	1.20
Calcium Siicate	0.375	1.50
Cellular Glass	0.400	1.60

Table—3

Adjustment Factors for Valves

Type of Valve	Heat Loss Factor
Gate Valve	4.3
Ball Valve	2.6
Butterfly Valve	2.3
Globe Valve	3.9
Check Valve	2.0

Termination Kits

In order to maintain integrity of the insulation, termination kits must be used to add leads or splice the heating cables.

Both ends will have to be terminated.

Normally the kits use a general purpose silicone sealant. To summarise the Application Engineer should ensure that the following are procured:

> ➤ Universal kit for connection/termination
> ➤ Splice kit or lead end kit
> ➤ End seal kit

Skin Effect Heat Tracing (SEHT)

So long we have restricted ourselves to trace heating by using specific heaters. Another interesting technology that has been applied for cross country pipe lines is by using the principles of 'skin effect'.

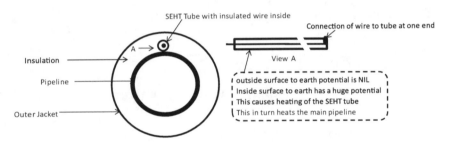

SEHT Tube with insulated wire inside

Connection of wire to tube at one end

View A

Insulation

Pipeline

Outer Jacket

A →

outside surface to earth potential is NIL
Inside surface to earth has a huge potential
This causes heating of the SEHT tube
This in turn heats the main pipeline

Skin Effect Heating System causes generation of heat on the inner surface of a carbon steel 'heat tape' that is welded to the 'pipeline' that is to be heat traced—say a 24" crude oil pipe line.

Inside the carbon steel heat tube you have an insulated, temperature resistance conductor that is connected to the tube at the circuit end.

The tube and conductor are connected to an AC Voltage source in 'series' mode.

Current flows on the inner surface of the tube ($\sim$ 1mm) due to skin effect & proximity effect.

Outside surface remains at ground potential.

The heat generated in the heat tube heats up the crude oil pipe line.

Very long lengths of pipelines can be heated up this way.

A case study of Tyco's work for M/S CAIRN ENERGY as available in the public domain presents an interesting technology.

Foot Note:

At the lowest power distribution level, these can throw up surprises in execution.

Oil & gas plants in the northern latitudes need a lot of trace heating—totalling even 20MW of load—and at a low voltage, that's a huge work.

The challenge is usually late arrival of information from others on what and where and how much to heat—and if the design is not flexible enough finding the source could be a problem.

Aren't Good EHT engineers an asset?

23

Power Factor Improvement

Need for Power Factor Improvement

You all know that in a 3-phase AC system, 'Active' Power consumed is given by

$P_{active} = \sqrt{3}\ V_{L-L}\ I_L\ \cos\emptyset$ where
V_{L-L} is the Line to Line Voltage
I_L is the Line Current & $\cos\emptyset$ is the power factor

Thus $\quad I_L = \dfrac{P}{\sqrt{3}\ V_{L-L}\ \cos\emptyset}$

As a consumer you are likely to have very little 'control' of V_{L-L} and the power consumed P is a given.

Thus increase of p.f. ($\cos\emptyset$) will reduce the current drawn from the line.

That is what your power supplier (viz., Utility) will want. For the same power consumed, if you'll draw lesser current from his system he benefits because,

His "line losses" (I^2R) will reduce.

The voltage he is able to reach to your mains will improve (lower IR drop)

That is why utilities insist on an improved p.f. and so on.

Normally motors constitute 80% of the Plant Load and the p.f. hovers around 0.8. It is therefore usual to go for pf improvement applications to raise it to 0.9 or even 0.95.

Typical pf values of various industrial loads

Load		Cos Ø
Transformers on 'No Load'	:	0.10 to 0.15
3-phase Motors	:	0.70 to 0.85
Welding Loads	:	0.35 to 0.60
Discharge Lamps		
- Compensated	:	0.90
- Un compensated	:	0.40 to 0.60
AC/DC Rectifiers	:	0.60 to 0.90
DC Drives	:	0.40 to 0.75
AC VSDs	:	0.95 to 0.97
Resistive Loads like heaters	:	1.00

In Vectorial Terms

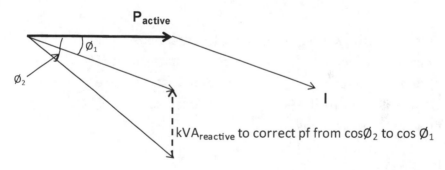

P_{active}

$Ø_1$

$Ø_2$

I

kVA$_{reactive}$ to correct pf from $\cos Ø_2$ to $\cos Ø_1$

gives the kVA$_r$ needed to correct the pf from $\cos Ø_2$ to $\cos Ø_1$.

How to "produce" the kVAr needed for correction?

a) By adding capacitors to the system
b) By generating additional VARs using in-plant generation
c) By using synchronous condensors

We shall dwell on (a) above.

Where to add the Capacitors?

a) Distributed pf correction

Here each motor can have a capacitor installed parallel to it so that it is effective when the motor is on line,
Ideal but expensive

b) Group pf correction

Here each MCC can have a capacitor bank that will provide required correction for its loads.

c) Centralised pf correction

Here the main substation will have capacitors installed taking ALL the loads into account.

Since a process plant has more or less 'steady loads' this type of connection should work fine.

This capacitor will be in 'banks' of various sizes with suitable switching to account for the exact compensation. These are normally automated switching—Automatic Power Factor Compensation (APFC)—and suits best for variable loads, prevents over voltages.

Expensive.

(a) & (b) above will have smaller capacitances in the **LV range** while (c) might result in a need for capacitors in the **MV range** that has its associated higher costs in terms of not only for the Capacitor banks but also for the associated switchgear and installation costs.

What are Capacitors?

Capacitors are essentially passive di-pole devices consisting of two conducting surfaces (plates), isolated from each other by some di-electric material in between. The assembly is made totally leak proof—no ingress of humidity and no entrapped gas pockets.

Classification will be according to the geometry of the plates, as follows:

- Plate Capacitors
- Cylindrical capacitors
- Spherical capacitors

Energy in a capacitor is given by $E_c = \dfrac{1}{2} CU^2$ where

C is the Capacitance & U is the applied Voltage.

LV capacitors have self restoring metalized polypropylene film as di-electric.

Value of capacitance is calculated from $Q_c = V^2C_r$ (C_r stands for Capacitive reactance) or C (in µF) = $Q_c/\omega\, V^2$ where Q_c is the required kVAr

ω is 2 π f

V is the system voltage in Volts

Note that $Q_c \, \alpha \, V^2$. So a small variation in voltage increases kVAr dramatically.

How are Capacitors Connected?

Capacitors are connected either in WYE (grounded or ungrounded) or in DELTA across the loads in parallel. So the voltage rating is same or a little lesser. Designed Voltage ratings are lower if WYE connected.

Is the Capacitor LV or HV?

All industrially used capacitors are heavy duty type implying that they are designed to exceed the requirement of standard (IEC, NEMA, ANSI/IEEE) specifications for continuous rms & peak over voltage capabilities and in-tank routine characteristics.

Typical MV rated Capacitors are indicated below. It is not practical to manufacture lower rated capacitors economically for this category of voltages.

System Voltage	3.3 or 6.6kV	11kV	22kV	33kV
Minimum rating of Capacitor Bank	75kVAr	200kVAr	400kVAr	600kVAr

LV capacitors are suitable for fluctuating loads, non linear upto 20%. When Capacitors are directly connected across motors ensure that rated current of capacitor bank is not > 90% of no-load current of motor to avoid self excitation and over compensation.

As a safety measure it has to be ensured that live parts of motors are handled a good 10 minutes (in case of HV equipment) after disconnection of supply.

Impact of non linear loads

% non linear loads	Type of Capacitor
≤ 15%	Standard
>15% to ≤ 20%	Heavy Duty
>20% to ≤ 25%	Super Heavy Duty
≥ 30%	Capacitor plus a Reactor is required

Configuration of Capacitors—Merits & Demerits

Cost is lower since neutral is not insulated	Common in industries	Used only at distribution voltages
Capacitor switch recovery voltages are low	Many parallel units to add up to total kVAr	Isolation of faulted unit does not cause over voltage in the other L-L connected loads
High in rush current may occur in station grounds	Usually use minimum 4, so that removal of one does not cause over voltage in the other three	
Used for smaller installations		
Grounded capacitor should not be used in un grounded or resistance grounded system to avoid zero sequence current that can mal operate E/F relays.		

As a general safety against over voltages it is necessary to have trained O&M personnel on system behavior for switching ON the capacitor banks.

Foot Note:

I didn't have opportunities to delve into this subject so long as I was doing power station jobs, but as soon as I was required to work for a fertilizer plant off sites, some 12 years later, I realized how important this was. The surprise was the size of the reactors and the need to find an acceptable location for all of them with so much oil within them.

In another plant operating engineers faced a problem of 'hunting' of capacitor banks causing switchgear wear. Selection of the right bank sizes and the PF relays that control their switching becomes very important.

24

Solar Power Systems

While a lot of emphasis is seen these days on large scale use of Solar Power to compliment utility generated power, our present discussions shall limit applications of Solar Power Systems for cases—such as a remote oil field or an off-shore platform. The reason is in such cases only a small amount of reliable power is needed for the control & instrumentation power needs and running power cables or locating in plant 'conventional' Diesel Generation systems are not feasible or are not economically worthwhile.

Our size of Solar Power Systems would comprise of

1) Solar array
2) Fully rated charge controllers/Regulators
3) Sealed Ni-Cd valve regulated batteries sized adequately for the no. of days without effective sunlight.
4) Other auxiliaries like solar array junction box, solar panel circuit breaker.
5) Associated housing for the batteries & components
6) Associated structures for the solar arrays
7) Associated lightning protection system

We are not discussing solar systems that need to parallel operate with grid, net metering etc.

System SLD

The schematic SLD below is self explanatory.

Under normal "sunny" conditions the solar array will feed the loads through the Charger Controller & inverter. When there is no sun, the batteries support the load. Need to add here that during sunny days the batteries get charged from the solar array.

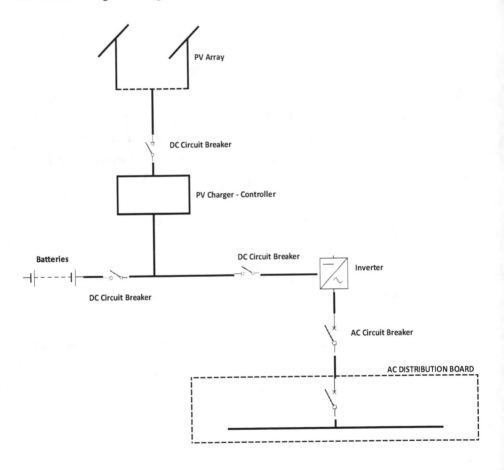

Solar Arrays

Solar Arrays constitute the 'heart' of the system.

Photo Voltaic Cells (PV Cells) constitute the basic building block of the system. PV Cells are essentially two layers of semi conductor materials composed of silicon crystals. Though on its own Si crystals are poor conductors of electricity, the 'doping' process of adding impurities in a controlled manner brings out unique properties. The top layer is doped with phosphorous to form the 'N' layer and the bottom layer is doped with Boron to form the 'P' layer. The resultant P-N junction produces the electric field. On entering of sun light, the photon energy there is converted into electron energy in the P-N junction that causes flow of electrons and thus a current source is created in the P-N junction.

Individual cells (about 4" square) generate very little power (<2 watts); so they are grouped together as 'modules'. Modules are then grouped into large panels encased in Glass or Plastic (for weather protection) Resulting in '**Arrays**'.

Three basic types of solar arrays are:

1) Single Crystal cells

   These are manufactured as long cylinders and sliced into hexagonal wafers. Such cells are very efficient—as high as 25%—but are very expensive.

   Roughly 30% of the global market is for such cells.

2) Poly crystalline cells

   Here molten silicon is cast into ingots and sliced as squares. While the process is cheaper the efficiency of such cells are lower—circa 15%. The square cells lend themselves for a closer assembly.

   Roughly 62% of the global market is for such cells.

3) Amorphous Silicon (a-Si) cells

These are somewhat different from the above. Here silicon is sprayed onto a glass or metal surface to form very thin films creating the whole module in one step. The manufacturing cost is very low here but the efficiency of such cells are also low—only about 5%.

Other equivalent improvements are under development like Galium-Arsenide (Ga-Ar), Copper-Indium-diselenide ($CuInSe_2$) and Cadmium-Telluride (CdTe) and these offer increased efficiencies and additionally can capture photons outside the visible light spectrum. However these are at present rather 'futuristic'.

The a-Si cells account for only 5% of the global market.

As we had seen the trade-off in all the three technologies above is Efficiency vs Cost.

The historic trend has been as follows:

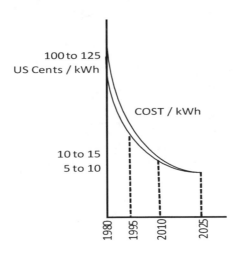

So essentially our industrial PV cell will be of either Type (1) or (2) above with a PV cell encapsulated—typically—between a toughened anti glare glass sheet on the 'sun' side and an Ethylene Vinyl Acetate sheet at the bottom covered by a Poly Vinyl Fluoride film.

These modules are rated by vendors as 'Peak Power' (W_p) under standard test conditions i.e., at 1000 W/m² of peak sun light at 25⁰C and air mass of 1.5. In reality the modules always produce lesser power than above since it depends upon the following:

➢ The amount of solar radiation
➢ The temperature of the module output decreases as the temperature rises
➢ The voltage at which the load and/or batteries are drawing the power

Panel Generation Factor

"Panel Generation Factor" is a term coined of late by a few. This is nothing but a slew of correction factors applied on the data provided by a vendor (typically) to arrive at a conservative design.

W_p of a PV panel is the rating using 1000 W/m² under "perfect" conditions.

The Application Engineer will do well to apply some correction factors to use the vendor data "with a pinch of salt".

15%	:	Losses for temperatures above 25⁰C.
5%	:	Losses due to sun light not striking the panel straight on caused by glass having increasing reflectance at lower angles of incidence
10%	:	Losses due to not receiving energy at the maximum power point. If we use a MPPT controller, this factor can be ignored
5%	:	Allowance for dirt
10%	:	Allowance for aging

Hence Total Power = $(1 - 0.15) * (1 - 0.05) * (1 - 0.10) * (1 - 0.05) * (1 - 0.10) = 0.62$ of the vendor provided W_p rating.

Batteries

The batteries commonly used are "Deep Cycle" VRLA batteries or sealed Ni-Cd batteries with nominal system volts of 16V.

Solar Charge Controller

Solar Charge Controllers regulate the voltage & current coming from the PV panels going to the batteries and prevents the batteries from overcharging under excessive sunlight, thus prolonging battery life.

Typically a charge controller has a 3-stage charge cycle as described below:

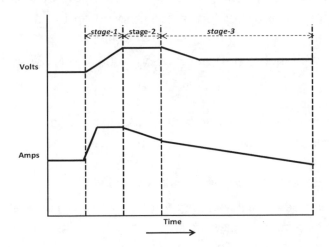

Stage-1 : During the 'bulk stage' of the charge cycle the voltage gradually rises to the bulk level (usually 14.4 to 14.6 V) and the batteries draw maximum current.

Stage-2 : The 'absorption stage' now begins. Here the voltage is maintained at voltage levels in (1) for a specified time (usually 1 hr) while the current tapers off as the batteries get charged.

Stage-3 : The 'float stage' begins when the voltage level goes down to float level (usually 13.4 to 13.7 V) and the batteries draw a small maintenance current until the next cycle

Presently available multi stage charge controllers are Pulse Width Modulation (PWM) types.

Newer versions are Maximum Power Point Tracking (MPPT) Controllers that match the battery voltage to the output of the solar panels to ensure maximum charging amps.

Typically a comparison is provided below:

	Normal	*MPPT*
Solar Panel Rating (say)	100W	100W
Current rating (say)	6A at 16.5V (6 x 16.5 = 100W)	6A at 16.5V
If battery is at	12.4V	12.4V
Current delivered	This will still be 6A	This will be (100/12.4) = 8A
Power Output	6 x 12.4 = 75W	100W

Sunlight (meteorological) Data at site

The sunlight data at site will be normally available in terms of "mean daily peak sun hours" at that location. The daily solar radiation is averaged out to give equivalent number of 'peak sun' or kWh/m^2.

Solar maps by public agencies provide monthly average daily solar resource information on grid cells.

"Solar irradiance" is a measure of how much solar power you are getting at your location. This irradiance varies throughout the year depending on the season. It also varies throughout the day depending on the position of the sun in the sky and lastly is dependant on the weather.

Satellite data are as yet superior to on-ground measurements that will just record the 'sun shine hours'. It will be a good engineering practice to use the kWh/m²/day data provide by satellites and use that as the 'average value' for the lowest month as the design basis. A 15% margin is taken over that to be on the conservative side.

In India our Ministry of New and Renewable Energy has a Solar Energy Centre who has brought out detailed SOLAR RESOURCE MAPs for the whole of our country after a detailed satellite based survey with US collaboration. The information is available in their web site.

Solar Insolation

Insolation is an acronym for Incident Solar Radiation—is a measure of the actual amount of sunlight or solar energy that strikes the surface of the earth (or the solar panel). The figures vary from country to country.

The insolation values represent the resource available to a flat plate collector, such as a PV panel, oriented due South (Northern Hemisphere)/North (Southern Hemisphere) at an angle from the horizontal equal to the latitude of the collector location.

Unit is kWh/m²/day.

Solar Insolation is a measure of solar irradiance over a period of time—typically over a period of a single day. We can also get these month wise and as Annual average solar resource data.

For a conservative design the Application Engineer should choose the coldest month.

Insolation is used by Solar panel vendors to calculate the optimum panel angles to capture sunlight, position of the panels and sizing of system. Usually vendors use their proprietary software to arrive at good results.

Equipment sizng

The Application Engineer needs to get familiar with the sizing of each & every equipment of the solar power system summarized as follows:

➢ Assessment of load, including a 30% margin to account for the losses in the system and considering thrice the value for those loads that are rotating in nature.

➢ Sizing of the PV array taking into account Insolation data of site, the number of days of autonomy required, the peak power data of the solar vendor and allowing for panel generation factor

➢ Sizing of Inverter—with 30% margin & matching voltage with that of the batteries.

➢ Sizing the batteries—taking into account battery losses, depth of discharge and no. of days of autonomy.

➢ Sizing the solar charger controller considering short circuit rating of the PV arrays and a 30% margin

---

Foot Note:

Use of these was observed in the later stage of my career in the oil & gas sector. Remote facilities, 'not electrified', needed the essential power from solar system and that provided the opportunity to learn. Believe me, in this field anyone would still be learning!

25

Motors

Motors account for about 65% of the energy consumed in a typically large industrial plant. Commonly used motors are of the AC squirrel cage induction type. Slip ring motors are also used in specific applications.

Motor is a very extensive topic that needs a basic understanding of how it works, types etc. Since you are going to be an Application Engineer, for this discussion we will straight away jump to buying motors and for that what you need to start off specifying—some essentials as listed below:

A) Rating

1) Rated frequency & variation limits—usually $\pm$ 5%
2) Rated voltage & variation limits—usually $\pm$ 10%
3) Combined maximum limits of voltage & frequency variation—usually $\pm$ 10%
4) No. of phases
5) Rated speed in rpm (n) (no. of poles would depend on this)
6) RATED OUTPUT in kW (P)
7) Rated torque in Nm = P*9550/n
8) Starting load inertia
9) Service Factor
10) Duty Cycle

B) <u>Environmental related needs for the motor</u>

1) Ambient temperature—if > 40°C
2) Site altitude—if > 1000m, some derating is needed
3) Cooling method
4) Degree of Protection needed—IP 55
5) Paint finish needed
6) Frame—Al or Cast Iron
7) Material of name plate
8) Material of screws

C) <u>Special needs</u>

1) Thermistors needed—3PTC
2) Separately mounted driven fan
3) Shaft height
4) Direction of rotation
5) Mounting arrangement

D) <u>For hazardous areas</u>

1) Zone—1—Ex e or Ex d?
2) Zone—2—Ex n

E) <u>Terminal Box</u>
1) Location
2) Type

F) <u>Anti condensation heater needs</u>

G) <u>Electrical parameters</u>

1) Rated voltage
2) Tolerance on rated voltage allowed
3) Insulation Class
4) Temperature rise allowed for the insulation

5) Full Load Current
6) Starting current

H) Testing Needs

1) Type tests
2) Acceptance tests
3) Routine tests
I) Noise limitations

J) Vendor would indicate some significant data in his offer that needs a good understanding:

A discussion on the importance of a few parameters will make you aware of why you need to specify those.

Insulation

Motors are usually available with insulation classes B (130°C), F (155°C) & H (180°C). The figures in the paranthesis indicate the temperature limits. Thus above an ambient temperature of 40°C the insulation permits temperature rises of 90, 115 and 140° rise. However in practice it is common to specify insulation of class F with temperature rise limited to that tolerated by Class B.

Effect of Voltage variations on performance

The effect of voltage excursions—with respect to the name plate voltage rating—are explained by the simple diagram below where the X & Y axis are in % values with respect to name plate values:

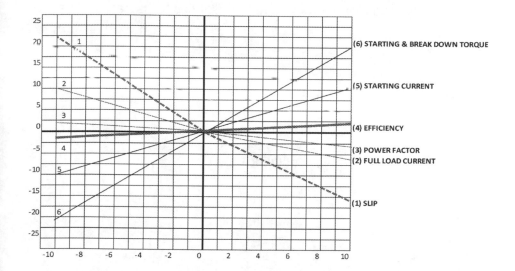

Note that voltage variations on either side will cause motor to operate hotter and hence prolonged operation under those conditions will result in insulation deterioration and reduced life.

The starting as well as break down torque varies as the square of the voltage and so is the slip (almost).
Increase in voltage results in reduced PF and vice versa.

Voltage unbalance

Even if it is small it can cause a large % imbalance in the impedance and so the current can be as high as 6 to 10 times the FLC flowing in the windings causing a huge amount of heating. Typically a 3.5% imbalance in voltage can cause 25% increase in temperature.

Slip

$$\% \text{ slip} = \frac{Ns - N \, rated \, full \, load}{Ns} \qquad N_s = 60f/p$$

Typically induction motors have a ≤ 5% slip. This can be even as high as 20% in case of applications requiring high starting torques such as conveyor drives

Torque, slip, current variations from start conditions

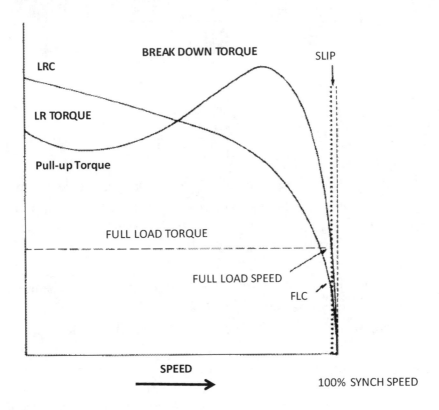

Coupling with the driven equipment

> Direct

Motors are normally connected directly with the driven equipment, but not always.

Direct connection is resorted to if the required load speed and the available motor speed match. Even then use of flexible coupling is common so as to avoid axial thrust of the load on to the motor bearing—usual in case of fans and pumps—and allow slight amount of mis alignment.

> Belt, Chain and gear drives

   Use of these will mean good application checks by the manufacturer for bearing loads and radial load capacities.

Efficiency (η)

Higher efficiency of motors will therefore make a significant impact on the energy consumed.

KYOTO protocol of 1997, 55 nations in the world agreed to implement energy saving measures. Between 2008-12 target was to reduce by 5% with 1990 as base.

By using high efficiency motors life cycle cost is saved.

If losses in the motor are low,
efficiency will be high since $\eta = \dfrac{Input\ power - Losses}{Input\ power}$

Losses in the motor

> No Load Losses

   o Friction & Windage losses
   o Stator Iron Losses
   o Stator I^2R Losses

> Load Losses

   o Stator I^2R Losses
   o Rotor I^2R Losses
   o Stray Load losses—these depend on the slot geometry, no. of slots, air gap length, rotor slot insulation, manufacturing process etc.

Duty Cycle of Motor

The duty cycle of a motor describes the load variations with respect to time—in cyclical terms, that result in variations in the current drawn by the motor.

> Continuous Duty—this demands constant load for an indefinitely long length of time. This is the most commonly occurring load. Here the motor hp is selected based on the continuous load.

> Intermittent Duty—here the motor operates intermittently thus—"load" and "rest", "load" & "no load" or "load", "no load" and "rest". The optimal rating of the selected motor can take the above into account and can be lower than the "load" rating thus allowing short time overloads. However if the operation is too frequent it can cause over heating. A good example can be a crane motor.

> Varying Duty—selection for such application is more involved. Here the load varies with discreet bits of time over a period and the cycle repeats all over again. Here the peak load is determined by computing the RMS loads over a time period and is computed (in simple terms) as follows:

RMS HP of load $= \sum HP_t^2 / \sum t$ where HP_t is the load for a time period t.

Good Engineering practice calls for a 10 to 15% margin to account for fluctuations.

Motor Service Factor (MSF)

MSF is the permissible amount of overload that the motor can handle for short durations, under rated voltage conditions without resulting in motor overheating beyond permissible temperature limits.

Obviously MSF is > 1 to handle occasional increase in loads.

MSF is a cover to operate motor

> ➢ To accommodate inaccuracy in correctly predicting intermittent loads
> ➢ To handle occasional overloads
> ➢ To allow operation for a short while above the rated ambient temperature
> ➢ To allow operation for a short while under voltage unbalance conditions

Frequent operation under such conditions may reduce motor speed, life and efficiency and the motor should not be expected to operate continuously with those factors applied.

Many manufacturers (and standards) allow an MSF of 1.15 for open type fan cooled cage motors implying that if the motor FL rating is say 20 HP, it can be loaded for short durations upto 23HP. This should however not influence selection for required starting & pull-out torques.

For fractional HP motors it is not unusual to come across MSF of 1.25 and even 1.5.

MSF is always 1 for motors operating in hazardous environment.

Starting Load inertia

The inertia of loads during start influences the starting torque needs affecting acceleration time and consequently has an effect on heating of the motor windings.

W_k^2 (referred to motor shaft) = $[\dfrac{rpm\ of\ driven\ equpment}{rpm\ of\ motor}]^2$ x W_k^2 (driven equipment)

The above formulae is useful particularly in case where motor is not directly coupled with the driven equipment.

Typically pumps are "low inertia" loads—that starts in < 1 sec

Reciprocating pumps are "high inertia" load—that takes a much longer time to start.

Bearing Systems

Anti friction deep grooved ball bearings are common.

Sleeve type bearings come with oil reservoir, ring oilers and drain points.

Lubrication of bearings is an important aspect of maintenance practices. The interval depends on the recommendation from the vendor typically as follows:

		Re lubricating interval
Easy type	Valves	1 to 10 years
Standard type	Pumps	6 months to 7 years
Severe type	Generally wherever vibration is there—usually where driven equipment is reciprocating	Varies from case-to-case
Very Severe type	Dusty areas Not high ambient areas	2 to 9 months

Accessories with Motor

- ➤ CTs
- ➤ Grounding provision
- ➤ Surge protection capacitors
- ➤ Thermal protection such as Thermostats, Thermistors and RTDs

Enclosure category

IPXX nomenclatures are normally used. What are those?

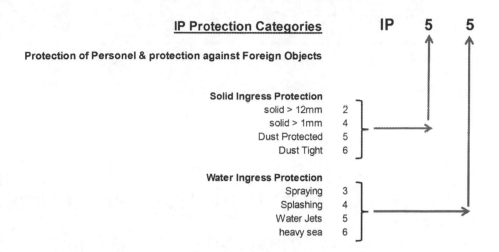

IP Protection Categories

For Indoor application an open type drip proof motor enclosures are good enough so long as the environment is free of dust and moisture.

Totally Enclosed Fan Cooled (TEFC) motors are very common for outdoor industrial applications where some amount of dust and moisture are expected. These are however not adequate for applications in area classified as hazardous. Such applications are discussed separately.

Motor Cooling

The cooling of motor is achieved by the surface of enclosure. It depends on

> ➢ The frame surface area
> ➢ The air flow over the motor
> ➢ The ambient air density

Ambient derating factors (typical)

Ambient temp (^{0}C)	30	40	45	50	55	60	70	80
% Rating	107	100	96.5	93	90	6.5	79	70

Altitude correction factors

Altitude above MSL (Ft)	1000	1500	2000	2500	3000	3500	4000
% Rating	100	6	92	8	84	80	76

Starting Time

Starting time of motor is a function of Load torque, inertia and motor torque

If starting time is high, motor can get hot.

Again frequent starting of motor means the motor is getting loaded with high currents too often and this can cause stress in the windings. Thus motors are required by manufacturers to have a certain no. of equally spread starts per hour—to allow the windings to cool off.

Special Design Features

Sometimes the Application needs would warrant additional design features such as

> ➤ Low starting current—instead of the "standard" value of 6 times FLC with a further 20% tolerance permitted; system requirements for voltage drop during starting might need starting current as low as just 3 times the FLC with no (+) ve tolerance. The extra cost involved might be worth it.
> ➤ Special temperature rise needs
> ➤ Special terminals to accommodate large cable sizes that are inevitable where long runs are involved that result in higher cable sizes to cap the voltage drop within permissible values.

Foot Note:

I was excited when I was required for the first time to witness Factory Acceptance Test of a motor for my project. The FAT witnessing gave me a 'feel'.

The ability to actually select the right motor size was not picked up so much in the initial stage of my career since it was mostly decided by the vendor and reviewed by the mechanical department. The quantum 'leap' in my understanding came when the clients in the paper industry would rather buy the motors separately to avail plant standardisation in the makes and also in the process hit a good bargain in discounts for bulk buying. Thus the client's compulsion became a good learning opportunity.

While most of the motors were of the cage type, purchasing EOT crane opened up opportunities to learn about slip ring motors.

Synchronous motors were rather elusive and could come across it in a big way in the late 90s in the course of compressor selection for a natural gas facility.

Reviewing the control schematics for a single phase motor driven valve for open-close duty was an opportunity to thoroughly go into the details of how actually a single phase motor works.

Who can ofcourse forget the lone dc motor that used to be there in every power station project for the emergency lube oil pump. Designing a starter for the DC motor was in itself a good learning too.

26

Variable Speed Drives

Why do we need variable speed drives?

Most of the Industrial processes involve some sort of speed control for the drive motors:

A few application examples are described below that are not exhaustive, but mentioned to provide an idea of the wide spectrum that such application covers:

> Mining sector:
> Conveyors, grinding mills, crushers, shovels, water pumps, ventilation fans, hoists etc.

> Oil & Gas and Petrochemicals sector:
> Oil pumps, Gas compressors, water injection pumps, cooling fans, cranes, hoists etc.

> Metallurgy sector:
> Rolling mill drives, cooling fans, pumps, extruders, coolers, furnace blowers etc.

> Off-shore and marine sector:
> Propulsion, thrusters, fuel transfer pumps, gas compressors

> Paper & pulp sector
> Grinders, winders, pumps, fans

> Cement sector
  Crushers, Fans, kiln drives, pumps

> Power sector
  Gas turbine starters, Boiler feed water pumps

Typically,

For a pump application—the motor selected is usually oversized thus requiring controlling the output by throttling the delivery valve, or providing a bypass valve controlled to achieve the desired output or even resorting to an on-off control.—all these, though simple in operation cause a huge amount of energy loss over the life of the plant

For maintaining hot air temperature in a cement plant kiln, the fan speed is controlled.

In an air conditioning plant (HVAC) the air flow requirement needs to vary depending on the room temperature and humidity. Hence the inlet & return air fans' speed are finely controlled.

As you all know the basic relationship for an a.c.motor is n = 120f/p and n is also a function of V/f where n is the speed in rpm, f is the system frequency of the supply to the motor, p is the no. of poles in the motor and V is the voltage supplied to the motor

Thus for achieving speed control n needs to be varied that can be achieved by varying V, f or p.

Varying p is practically difficult though two speed motors are in the market by switching on to two sets of windings.

We thus need to vary f, the frequency of voltage supplied to the motor or vary V, the a.c. voltage itself.

In general, a <u>VFD</u> in its most basic configuration controls the speed of a motor by adjusting the frequency of the power supplied to the motor.

Benefits of using VSDs

Energy Savings

The maximum benefits of VFDs occur with fans and pumps. The power that a pump or fan consumes is directly proportional to the cube of the velocity. This means if an operator can run a fan at 80% of full speed, it theoretically uses 51% of full load power.

Improved Process Control

By matching pump output flow or pressure directly to the process requirements, small variations can be corrected more rapidly by a VSD than by other control forms, which improves process performance. There is less likelihood of flow or pressure surges when the control device provides rates of change, which are virtually infinitely variable.

Reduction of maintenance

When using a VFD, we don't need to deal with the DC motor carbon brushes or mechanical speed-control gearboxes (transmissions).

Eliminates a number of costly and energy inefficient ancillaries,

such as throttle valves or bypass systems since the electronic control can match the motor speed to the load requirement.

Optimize motor starting characteristics.

VFDs bring motors up to full speed quickly and by drawing only 100% to 150% of full load current (FLCs). This ability to start at normal FLC is very important if the power supply cannot withstand the normally six times FLC across-the-line starting draw, or even the 350% FLC soft-start device current. VFDs achieve this by managing the magnetic flux of an induction motor. Magnetic flux is directly proportional to the voltage and inversely proportional to the frequency. By keeping the flux constant, the inrush current does not exceed the FLC rating of the motor, and full torque is maintained. This is a significant improvement on a soft-start, which has significant voltage drop problems and cannot start under full load.

Improved System Reliability

Any reduction in speed achieved by using a VSD has major benefits in reducing pump wear, particularly in bearings and seals.

Typically the system would be configured something like what is shown below:

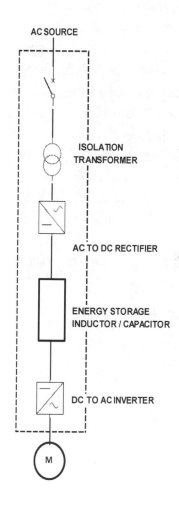

Thus the VSD is not a single piece of equipment, but that which is multi disciplinary in nature involving power electronics, electro mechanical systems, control systems, digital signal processing, FE analysis, thermodynamic and above all economics. However the technology has evolved over the past 50 years and even now different applications have different optimal offers from various manufacturers

Basically we have the following:

> Grid connected transformer(s).
> Rectifier or power converter
> DC link storage stage of the power converter—ether an inductor for voltage source converters—VSCs) or capacitor (for current source converters—CSCs). Successive switching over time of the CSCs/VSCs is what is called modulation
> Inverter—that provides the variable frequency, voltage, amplitude and adjustable phase angle for controlling the torque, flux and speed of the driven motor
> Control systems to achieve the desired feed back from the load and convert them into action by the VSD
> Load filters
> Connecting power cables to the motor

Technologies commonly available

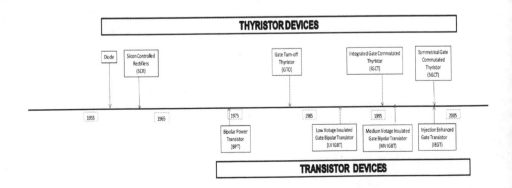

Insulated Gate Bi-polar Transistor (IGBT) is currently the dominating technology for low power and low voltage applications, essentially using two level VSCs.

Other than low powered ASDs, application of high power AFDs require attention to certain system design aspects to overcome a few challenges, some of which are listed below:

Heat dissipation

The frequency conversion process causes 2% to 3% loss as heat in the VFD that must be dissipated. The converter will have significant losses and therefore ventilation requirements for the electronics can be an important issue. The life expectancy of the converter is directly related to the temperature of the internal components, especially capacitors. The converter may require installation in a less onerous environment than the motor control gear it replaces. Electronics are less able to cope with corrosive and damp locations than conventional starters.

Operating a VFD in a potentially explosive atmosphere is not usually possible

Over voltage spikes

The high rate of switching in the PWM waveform often yields overvoltage spikes. Reinforced insulation "inverter duty" motors are often needed. Older motor insulation systems may deteriorate more rapidly due to the rapid rate of voltage change. Again, filters will eliminate this problem.

Problems with Long cable runs

The long length can cause "transmission line" effects, and cause raised voltages at the motor terminals. The carrier frequency pulsed output voltage of a PWM VFD causes rapid rise times in these pulses, the transmission line effects of which must be considered. Since the transmission-line impedances of the cable and motor are different, pulses tend to reflect back from the motor terminals into the cable. The resulting voltages can produce over voltages equal to twice the

DC bus voltage or up to 3.1 times the rated line voltage for long cable runs, putting high stress on the cable and motor windings and may cause eventual insulation failure. On LV systems and inverters with 0.1 microsecond rise time IGBTs, the maximum recommended cable distance between VFD and motor is about 50 m. Mitigation measures include minimizing cable distance, lowering carrier frequency, installing dV/dt filters, using inverter duty rated motors and installing LCR low-pass sine wave filters.

Harmonic current distortions.

The rate of the wave front rise can cause electromagnetic disturbances, requiring adequate electrical screening (screened output cables). Filters in the inverter output can eliminate this problem.

Motor Bearing currents

Voltages can be induced in the shafts of larger motors where the stray capacitance of the windings provides paths for high frequency currents that pass through the motor shaft end essentially leading to circulating currents, which can destroy bearings. Insulated non-drive-end bearings are commonly provided on all motors over 100 kilowatt (kW) output rating. Common mode filters may additionally be required for higher powers and voltages.

Prevention of high frequency bearing current damage uses three approaches: good cabling and grounding practices, interruption of bearing currents, and filtering or damping of common mode currents. Good cabling and grounding practices can include use of shielded, symmetrical-geometry power cable to supply the motor, installation of shaft grounding brushes, and conductive bearing grease. Bearing currents can be interrupted by installation of insulated bearings and specially designed electrostatic shielded induction motors. Filtering and damping high frequency bearing currents or, instead of using standard 2-level inverter drives, using either 3-level inverter drives or matrix converters could be a solution.

Since inverter-fed motor cables' high frequency current spikes can interfere with other cabling in facilities, such inverter-fed motor cables should not only be of shielded, symmetrical-geometry design but should also be routed at least 500mm away from signal cables.

Foot Note:

Use of VSDs were experienced by me, not so much in the course of engineering for power plants in the 70s but during the course of exposure to engineering for the paper & pulp industry in the 80s.

Interestingly the VSD used for the first time by me was in the early 70s for a Fast Breeder Test Reactor project where the liquid sodium used as a coolant/heat transporter was pumped with its speed controlled by a 'Ward-Leonard' set.

Later I had seen that use of VSDs were much more rampant in the processes involved in the oil & gas sector—from large compressor drives right down to small motors.

27

Safety Earthing

Need for Safety Earthing

Earthing of the body of any electrical equipment ensures that in the event of a SLG fault (due to insulation break down or mal operation) *and* in the event of accidental contact with the body of equipment by an operator, the fault current flows to ground through the earthing provided rather than through the person. The latter can turn out to be fatal even before an electrical isolation takes place at the source.

Considering the importance of this a *redundancy is always ensured*.

Objective of proper earthing system is therefore

> ➢ To reduce electrical shock hazard to persons
> ➢ To provide low impedance return path to ground fault current that will enable E/F relays to operate and trip the supply.
> ➢ To have proper ground fault current capability to also ensure there are no flash overs that could pose a fire hazard.

Codes & Standards

IEEE – 80 & 142
IS 3043
BS – 7430
IEC

Engineering Pratices commonly followed in Earthing

Various "good engineering practices" have evolved for different industries based on theoretical considerations, experience and practicability of construction.

Some of the typical arrangements are discussed below to convey some idea.

In Industrial Plants (Say, an Oil & Gas Plant)

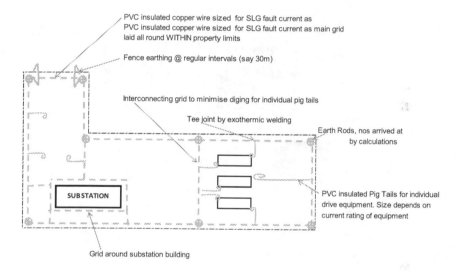

PVC insulated copper wire sized for SLG fault current as
PVC insulated copper wire sized for SLG fault current as main grid laid all round WITHIN property limits

Fence earthing @ regular intervals (say 30m)

Interconnecting grid to minimise diging for individual pig tails

Tee joint by exothermic welding

Earth Rods, nos arrived at by calculations

SUBSTATION

PVC insulated Pig Tails for individual drive equipment. Size depends on current rating of equipment

Grid around substation building

In Substation Buildings

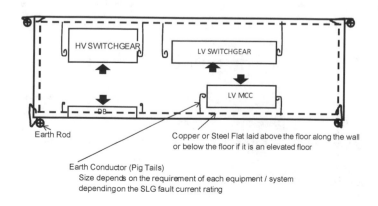

HV SWITCHGEAR

LV SWITCHGEAR

LV MCC

DB

Earth Rod

Copper or Steel Flat laid above the floor along the wall or below the floor if it is an elevated floor

Earth Conductor (Pig Tails)
Size depends on the requirement of each equipment / system dependingon the SLG fault current rating

285

The concept is to provide a dedicated, visible ground conductor all round the bulding and have all electrical equipment connected to it with adequate redundancy.

In EHV Switchyards, Power House Transformer Yards

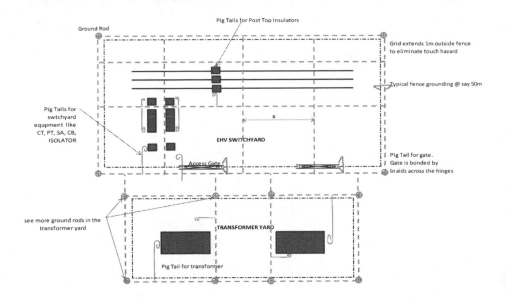

x depends on 'grid spacing' obtained by design (to IEEE 80) based on touch & step voltage considerations and allowed mesh potential.

No. of ground rods depend on total nos. arrived at as per design.

Pig tail sizing depends on the SLG fault level ratings of the equipment.

Choice of Earthing Conductor Materials (Copper or Steel?)

Mild steel offers a better choice as an earth conductor since it is cheaper when compared to copper. Normally MS rods for buried installation & GI flats for above ground installations are used.

a) Jointing & welding of conductors are easier in case of flats

b) Rod has better mechanical ruggedness and more suitable for bending at site.

Copper conductors/flats on the other hand are electrically superior. For underground connections at site exothermic CADWELD^R process is used where a mould with alloy on heating up will fuse weld the copper flats. Use of this technique is more popular in the Gulf and developed countries.

Corrosion Allowance for Buried Steel Installation

"Corrosion Allowance" is the allowance provided in over sizing of steel conductor. All other methods like cathodic protection, encapsulating in concrete or galvanizing are not economically suitable for very large installations.

Corrosion of earth conductor depends on the following properties of soil in which it is buried:

1) Acidity—rather empirical.
2) Electrical resistivity of soil—high resistance soils are usually non corrosive unless they are poorly aerated.
3) Salt content of soil—higher it is more the corrosion.
4) Moisture content—higher it is more the corrosion.
5) Aeration—poorer it is more the corrosion

Various empirical data are available for maximum corrosion (in mils) in 12 years for various soil conditions.

Typically one such study indicated 173 mils in 12 years in a particular environment. This was therefore factored as (173/12) mils/yr or 0.366mm/year in the grounding design.

Corrosion rate for steel is highest in the first 10 years and halves in the next 10 years and then it is negligible.

For a large project, like a coal fired thermal power station the average life span of the grounding grid is taken as 40 years including commissioning time and future expansion.

The total corrosion period for calculation purpose is taken as 10 + 10/2 + 20/4 (last value is taken to be on the conservative side, though it is zero) = 20 years.

Hence corrosion allowance for adding up to the diameter of calculated value is

2 x 0.366 x 20 = 14.64mm

So where a 26.7 mm dia rod was electrically adequate, as we had seen in the typical example, a 40mm dia rod is chosen on account of corrosion considerations.

Soil Resistivity Value (in Ohm m)

This is an important input for design of earthing system.

Practical measurements use the 4-pin Wenner method. Here 4 electrodes are planted on a straight line and a DC voltage injected in the two inner pins that leads to a current flow between the two outer pins. An Earth Megger directly computes the value of soil resistivity from the relationship

$V = 2\pi RS$ where

V = the injected voltage
R = so resistivity at depth S in ohm-m
S = spacing in m

Sizing of Earth Conductor

The famous ONDERDONK's equation (Ref IEEE-80) is a good empirical starting point.

$$A = I \sqrt{\frac{0.00104\,\alpha\,t\,\rho}{ds \log[(1 + \alpha tm)/(1 + \alpha t0)]}} \qquad \text{where}$$

A	=	Cross section of ground conductor in mm²
I	=	SLG fault current in Amps
A	=	Material temperature coefficient
T	=	Duration of fault current considered in seconds
P	=	Resistivity of earth conductor in micro-ohm-cm
D	=	Density of the material in gms/cc
S	=	Specific heat of material in Cal/gms/cc
t_m	=	Maximum allowable temperature in °C
t_a	=	Ambient temperature in °C

Typically we tabulate below the values for the two options we will usually have viz., steel & copper.

	Steel	Copper	Remarks
α at 20°C/°C	4.23 x 10⁻³	4.30 x 10⁻³	Ref. SIEMENS tables
ρ at 20°C micro ohm cm	15	1.72	- do -
d gms/cc	7.85	8.96	- do -
s cal/gm/°C	0.114	0.092	Ref. Electrical Engineer's Handbook by Fink & Beaty
t_m in °C	900/620	450	For welded/braced joints
	310		For bolted joints
t_a in °C	50	50	Typical condition in India

For a SLG fault current of 45kA, for 1 sec duration, the size of steel conductor works out to 560.25mm² or an equivalent dia of 26.7mm.

The values recommended in IS 3043 are somewhat lower since it apparently ignores the thermal expansion effect of the heat due to fault current that lowers the effective cross section.

Earth Pits

Vertically driven rods of copper/steel provide good earthing.

The resistance to earth (R) of a driven electrode improves as the length of the rod increases as per R = $\dfrac{\rho}{2\pi L}$ [ln{8L/D} – 1] where

ρ is the soil resistivity in Ohm-m

L is the length of the buried portion of electrode in m

D is the OD of the rod in m

Since it is the OD that is of consequence, the rod can be a GI pipe with similar OD for yielding almost similar values.

These rods are usually housed in concrete pits (bottom open) to facilitate connection to ground conductor, testing and watering and hence these are known as "Earth Pits".

There are however some do's & don'ts in locating the Earth Pits.

Prefer all corners of an installation since the voltage in the corner of an UG earthing system are experienced to be high.

Two adjacent pits must be at minimum twice the depth of the pit to be effective. If R is the resistance to earth of one pit, for two pits it will be R/2 provided they are L away, where L is the length of the rod buried vertically.

In general terms R_N = R.F/N where R_N is the effective resistance, R is the resistance of a single rod and N is a factor that approaches unity for spacing ≥ the buried length.

Earth pits need watering to maintain moisture to give low resistance values

The soil in the immediate vicinity of the electrode, if improved by adding bentonite or charcoal will dramatically reduce the resistance values.

Earth Mats (as per IEEE 80 Standards)

Unlike other standards, IEEE 80 recommends design of a mat (woven from a grid conductor) as the ideal choice to provide an equipotential surface that also keeps the 'step' & 'touch' potential hazards under control.

The conductor spacing limits in the mat (in both directions) are worked out by rigorous methods prescribed in the standard.

The practice is widely used in the power industry and in EHV switchyards.

Recommended Earth Resistance Values

Electrical Equipment earthing	:	$1\,\Omega$
Steel structures/non electrical equipment	:	$10\,\Omega$
Earthing for static discharge	:	$10\,\Omega$
Earthing for Lightning Protecton	:	$10\,\Omega$
Intrinsically safe Inst Earthing	:	$1\,\Omega$
Non intrinsically safe Inst Earthing	:	$5\,\Omega$
Telecom system Earthing	:	$5\,\Omega$

Voltage rise per m run of Earthing Conductor

Assuming resistive drop only, voltage rise in a ground conductor is given by

$\Delta V = I_k\,(\rho L/A)*10^3$ Volts where
    I_k = SLG Fault Current in kA
    ρ = Resistivity of Earth Conductor in Ω-mm
        Typically 15 micro Ω – cm at 20^0C for steel conductor

L = Length of conductor in mm

A = Cross sectional area in mm².

Thus ΔV works out to $150 * I_k / A$ Volts/m

For a 45kA Fault current $\Delta V = 6750 / A$ Volts/m

Below table will give you an idea of the high values likely to be encountered in the event of a SLG fault current of that magnitude flowing

Conductor size mm x mm	50 x 8	50 x 6	35 x 6	25 x 6	25 x 3	10 SWG or 3.251 mm dia or 8.3 mm²
Voltage rise/m	16.875	22.5	32.14	45	90	813.1

A "feel" of above will help you appreciate the measure we recommend for a safe installation.

Concept of Bonding/Tie-Ups/Transfer Potential

Transfer potential hazards exist between the "local earth" and a "Remote Earth" because of a pipeline/Cable connection that originates from another plant some distance away.

To avoid this

At entries of Pipelines, bond all Pipelines together and connect them to local earth. However special features are required in case of cathodically protected pipelines.

Within plant at every 100m ensure pipeline is bonded to adjacent pipes and grounded.

All pipe rack bottoms are grounded.

The transfer potential in the event of SLG faults can be calculated and the values can be quite high since the fault current values are high. The problem will be dormant during normal times but will manifest as flash over under fault condition. **A HAZARD!!**

Earthing Schematic/SLD

Conceptualise by an SLD how you are going to carry out Earthing for the whole plant by a simple sketch. This will help in identifying and accounting for each and every part of the installation to ensure full compliance.

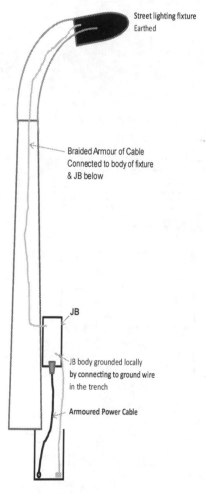

Street lighting fixture
Earthed

Braided Armour of Cable
Connected to body of fixture
& JB below

JB

JB body grounded locally
by connecting to ground wire
in the trench

Armoured Power Cable

Street Lighting Pole Earthing scheme

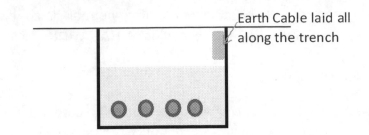

Earth Cable laid all along the trench

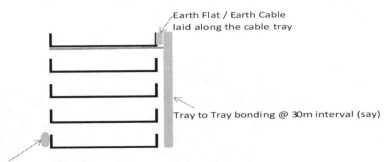

Earth Flat / Earth Cable laid along the cable tray

Tray to Tray bonding @ 30m interval (say)

Braided connection between two tray sections

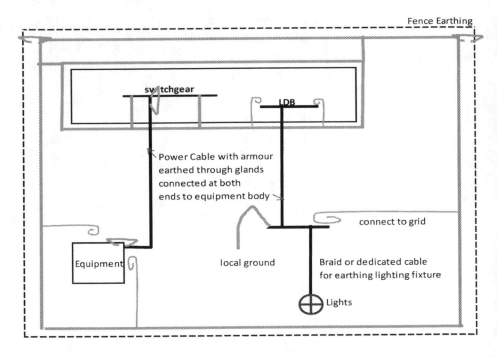

Fence Earthing

switchgear

LDB

Power Cable with armour earthed through glands connected at both ends to equipment body

connect to grid

Equipment

local ground

Braid or dedicated cable for earthing lighting fixture

Lights

Common Installation Practices

Equipment Earthing

Concept of redundancy is to be always followed. Always imagine that one of the connections would snap and remain undetected for some time. "Is the resultant earthing arrangement safe?" should be the question.

Connection should be flash proof. Ensure tight & proper connection for preventing arcing/flash over in the event of SLG fault current that can be at times hazardous.

Generator

Ensure earthing at two places for the generator body, cable boxes, Auxiliary terminal boxes etc. The neutral earthing needs have nothing to do with this and are dictated by SYSTEM EARTHING NEEDS.

Switchgear Assemblies

Usually FBAs have a dedicated earth bus run on the inside through & through. These are brought out at both ends for external earthing. Sometimes they are internally connected to the body of the switchgear, which in turn have externally provided bushes for further earthing.

It is mandatory to have the two earthing connections from the switchgear to be VISIBLE.

Motors

Body of motor is usually earthed from two bushings placed diagonally on opposite ends of the base frame. It shall be ensured that further connections for the local earthing system have redundancy.

Apart from the above, for HV motors, the terminal boxes & auxiliary terminal boxes are also earthed separately at two places.

Local Earth Bus

It is customary to have two local earth buses installed at the bottom for a group of equipment such as valves, fans etc. mounted atop a structure, to minimise cable clutter. We should not lose sight of redundancy in any case.

Transformers

Two dedicated ground connection to locally provided earth pits in the transformer yard is recommended. Additionally two separate earth connections for the HV & LV cable boxes and Marshaling boxes are also recommended to be interconnected to the body earthing system.

Flanges to radiators, tank tops etc are provided with jumper connections to ensure earth continuity.

Radiator cooling fans too have dedicated earthing.

The above has nothing to do with NEUTRAL EARTHING NEEDS that are as per the system earthing needs.

Lighting Fixtures

Lighting Poles/Towers

The pole/tower bottom has to be provided with a dedicated earth connection. Redundancy is usually ensured by the presence of earth continuity via the armour of the connecting cables.

Street/Flood lighting fixtures

Each fixture is ensured a dedicated earth connection that is brought down to the bottom Junction Box via the braided armour of the cable. Redundancy is provided by the armour itself via cable glands used for the fixtures.

General Fixtures

A dedicated earthing bush on the fixture is connected to a bare copper wire that is pulled through the conduit system that ultimately gets connected at the source ground bus.

Redundancy is ensured by the threaded conduit connection itself.

Industrial Power Sockets

The earth pin is usually connected to the earth of the source. The "body" is connected to the earthing conductor nearby. Two nos. are the recommended practice for redundancy.

Cable Termination/Joints

Cable glands generally get connected to the body of the equipment via the gland plate and the star washer used for tightening provides adequate electrical contact with the equipment. However for HV equipment as a matter of abundant caution, dedicated braided conductors are connected to local earthing conductor. To this braid, the insulation screen is also connected as per the needs of the terminating kits.

Straight through joints for long run of cables are also earthed at the point where the armours get connected up. This ensures that the armour at this point does not have dangerous voltages (as per V/m rise we saw earlier) in the event of SLG faults.

For 1c cables the need to do this has to be assessed in line with whether the armour is going to be earthed at both ends or at one end only for the current rating considered.

Cable Trays

Cable trays pre fabricated out of galvanized sheet steel are used widely. They come in standard lengths of 2.5m to 3.0m length— basically because of the "bath tank" size restrictions imposed in the manufacturing process and also due to transport restrictions.

It therefore becomes necessary to use 'fish plates" to connect up by bolting two adjacent sections for structural integrity. There is however no guarantee that such connections ensure electrical continuity.

The GI tray *per se* however will usually have adequate 'electrical cross section" to carry the SLG fault current of the cables that are laid on them.

It is therefore necessary to connect a bridging flexible (made of copper braid) across the trays. For 'redundancy' it is appropriate to provide on both sides of the tray.

There is also a practice of laying a 50 x 6mm flat right along the exterior of the tray to visually ensure that there is indeed an earth connection. However this is restricted to one for a bank of trays, with interconnected flats at "regular" intervals for the balance trays in the bank, with this tray. At what interval is dictated by what we had seen in the V/m rise in the event of a SLG fault. At every 50m is practical in reality.

Foot Note:

I had the opportunity early in my career to detail hands-on, way back in 1972—an earthing grid design for a nuclear facility where the IEEE—80 (then AIEE) method of designing a grid system was rigorously applied—what made it special was the use of Copper conductors, that was otherwise banned in the power industry then due to the fact that the metal was scarce & imported.

Later the same principle was extensively used in coal fired thermal power stations & EHV switchyards, but with bare round steel conductors. Comparing short time ratings of copper & steel conductors was a good learning.

While usage of bare steel was the order of the day in the power projects in the 80s, a great deal of refinement was experienced in the 90s in the oil & gas sector that had the practice of extensively using PVC insulated copper conductors for buried grids. The amount of detailing that goes into the safety earthing design in the oil & gas sector is phenomenal.

28

Lightning Protection System

Practical installation in Industry may require protection against lightning and to do so a good understanding of the phenomenon of lightning would help.

<u>Phenomenon of Lightning</u>

"Lightning" is formed as a result of natural build-up of charges in storm clouds.

Typically warm air rises from earth and that is replaced by cool air that drifts down. This sets in motion a convection process that causes cooing of the rising air to form clouds—as low as 7.5kms and sometimes well over 18kms above the earth.

By a hitherto unexplained phenomenon, the cloud separates the charge within it such that the top part carries (+)ve charges while the bottom part carries (−)ve charges.

The (−)ve charges in the cloud induces (+)ve charges on the top of structures (usually at protruding sharp points) and the stage is set for a "Lightning strike"—caused by movement towards the ground of the stepped downward leader in approximately 50 steps. This is not visible to the naked eye as yet.

When the stepped leader is close to the ground its relatively large (−)ve charge induces great (+)ve charges on the projecting objects on earth.

Unlike charges attract.

So the (+)ve charges move upwards (upward streamer) and when the two meet, the air in between ionizes and a complete conducting path is created carrying a massive current that attempts to equalize the potential between the cloud and the object on the earth. This is the "flash" of lightning we see—and called "Return stroke".

Lightning Stroke

Thus what strikes after a lightning is a huge current in several kA magnitude at its peak. It is capable of dissipating its energy in the form of heat with temperatures going upto 20,000°C for a few micro seconds apart from a part of the energy dissipating as sound and electro magnetic waves in the light & radio spectra. Each current wave is a 'strike" and looks somewhat like what is shown below:

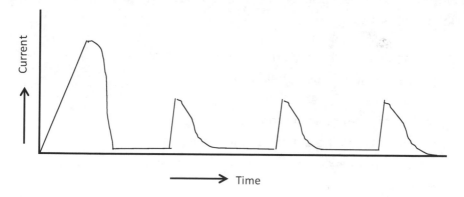

1st wave has a low $\dfrac{di}{dt}$ but high in peak value.

Next waves have high $\dfrac{di}{dt}$ but lower peaks. Typically we can have upto three of those.

Such huge current "strokes" need to be grounded by the shortest path/lowest impedance.

If the impedance is high the product IZ will cause a very high voltage that can flash over to neighbouring objects causing damage.

That is the reason why we need PROTECTION AGAINST LIGHTNING.

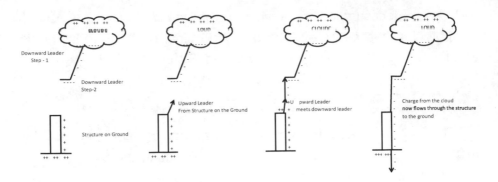

Decision on Lightning Protection

"To Protect" or "not to protect" is a techno-economic decision governed by codes that provide guidelines on assessing the risk involved considering

- The likelihood of the structure being struck
- The consequences of such a strike
- The 'use' of the structure
- The nature of its construction
- The value of the structure & its contents
- The prevalence of thunderstorms in the area (iso ceraunic data)
- The presence of additional structure nearby that may provide adequate protection

Irrespective of the risk assessment a few structures are always protected against lightning

- If they are or near where large number of persons congregate
- If they have essential public services
- If the area is known to have frequent lightning
- If t is a very tall or isolated structure
- If it is a structure of historic/cultural importance

Standard provides a spread sheet where the above risks are factored-in to ultimately calculate and indicate whether a separate Lightning Protection is required or not.

<u>How is protection against lightning provided?</u>

In simple terms, by providing a conductor at the top of the structure and effectively grounding it by the shortest path we can take care of protection.

- What type of conductor?
- Where to place them?
- How many?
- How to assess adequacy?
- How to ground them?

Above are some of the issues that should be of interest to the Application Engineer.

BS 6651 is a good reference.

<u>Roof Conductor or Air Termination Networks (ATN)</u>

Usually horizontal conductors (copper flats) laid on the roof, clamped rigidly to the roof structure/parapet wall/roof, interconnected between themselves and also interconnected with a few tall spikes placed in the roof corners as a minimum.

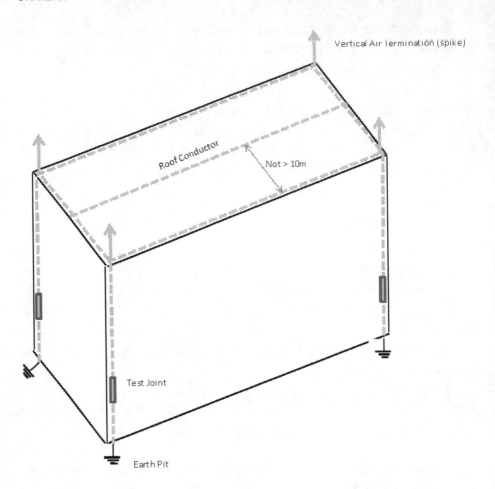

The general guideline is "no part of the roof shall be more than 5m away" from a horizontal conductor. Thus we need a 10m spaced mesh in one direction as a minimum on top.

The vertical spikes are usually solid copper rods of about 1m high rigidly supported at its base and have provision for good connection with flat conductors.

Down Conductors

Down conductors are copper strips run from the ATNs on the exterior of the structure to its own dedicated earth pit.

Provision shall exist for disconnecting and testing the resistance to earth of the earth pit and such disconnections are placed at accessible locations—circa 2m above the ground close to earth pit.

No. of down conductors depend on the area of the building & perimeter of the building whichever is more—1 per 100 sqm or 1 every 20m.

Checking of adequacy

Quick check is by considering the protection cone (45^0 on the outside and 30^0 within two structures). However a more accurate empirical method is by the ***Rolling Sphere Method.***

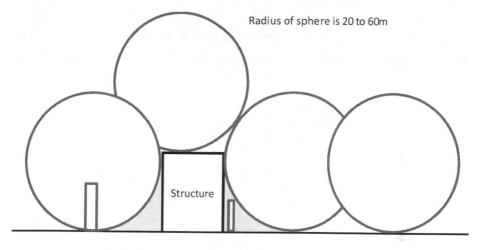

Radius of sphere is 20 to 60m

Structure

Shaded areas are protected since the sphere can't touch them

The top of the tallest lightning mast nearby provides a hemispherical surface of radius (say R_M) to receive the stroke.

R_M depends on many factors that can be calculated in a rigorous exercise and varies between 20m to 60m depending on the protection level needed.

We can thus imagine a sphere of radius R_M rolled on around a group of protected structures. Wherever the locus of the sphere touches the structure, additional protection is needed and portion included within the loci stands protected.

Protection Level	I	II	II	IV
Radius of sphere (m)	20	30	45	60

The 'rolling sphere' concept can be graphically applied and seen in 3D, whether an integrated protection against lightning has been accorded or not.

It can be seen that this concept also ensures that the tall vertical sides are also protected.

However theoretically no structure is 100% protected since all these are empirical.

Earthing of down conductor

Dedicated Earth Pits along the periphery of the structure—one per down conductor—are the usual practice. The Earth pit design has been discussed under earthing.

Modern Improvements

Recent improvements make use of an "Early Streamer Roof Top" installation that are however yet to find universal acceptability.

Foot Note:

Lightning Protection was treated with great seriousness right in the first project in 1972 where I was involved in the detail engineering for a fast breeder test reactor (FBTR) for Reactor Research Centre (RRC) then (now known as Indira Gandhi Centre for Atomic Research—IGCAR) at Kalpakkam in India and it was a thrilling experience to be responsible for the design of lightning protection system of the Reactor Building that had a flat dome top that added to the challenge. Even today when I have opportunity to pass through the place I wistfully look at the seven rods that are located on top of the dome doing its job of protecting the dome like silent sentinels.

Since then I had opportunities to assimilate different types of lightning protection applied with varied principles in the contemporary nuclear, thermal, coal & gas based power plants, switchyards and oil & gas facilities.

29

Cathodic Protection System

Corrosion

The phenomenon of corrosion is well known to all engineers. Corrosion can be categorized into two viz.,

1) Uniform Corrosion—those that can be evaluated & controlled by

   - Increasing material thickness
   - Coating
   - Adding corrosion inhibitors
   - **Providing CATHODIC PROTECTION** that supplements all the above

2) Non Uniform Corrosion—those that are highly localized (need specialized solutions) such as pitting, crevice corrosion,

   - Galvanic corrosion,
   - Intergranular corrosion,
   - Dezincification
   - Graphatisation
   - Filiform corrosion
   - Stress corrosion
   - Hydrogen blistering
   - Hydrogen embrittlement
   - Fretting corrosion
   - Cavitation, Erosion & Impingement

Basic Principle of Cathodic Protection (CP)

We will generally discuss in the context of steel.

Cathodic Protection is applicable only when there is an electrolyte i.e., "a corrosion medium" and cannot obviously be applied when the environment is just air or gas.

CP is defined as the establishment of a state of immunity or a perfect passivation (by PURBAIX 1966)

CP basically involves

> ➤ A CATHODE that is the object to be protected—say a buried pipe line, a metal tank or a steel structure
> ➤ An ANODE—which we shall call the "protector"
> ➤ An ELECTROLYTE—which is the one causing the corrosion in the form surrounding soil or liquid.

The basic principle is to make the potential of the whole surface of the steel structure sufficiently negative with respect to the surrounding medium in order to ensure that no current flows from the metal into the medium. Corrosion of steel in normally aerated soils is entirely prevented if the steel is maintained at a potential of not more positive than (–) 850mV with respect to a Copper—Copper Sulphate half cell or (–)800mV with respect to a Silver—Silver Chloride half cell.

We need to understand what these "potentials" and 'half cells' are all about, how the "protection potentials" are achieved etc in the course of our discussions on CP.

Types of CP

Two types of CP are employed:
> ➤ Sacrificial Anode (SA) System
> ➤ Impressed Current (IC) System

Sacrificial Anode System

A conceptual arrangement is shown below

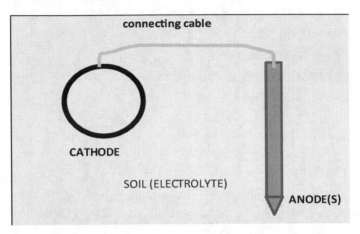

Here use is made of the galvanic action to provide the CP current. The surface of the structure to be protected is made "Cathodic" by connecting it electrically to a mass of less noble material as both are kept buried in an electrolyte (i.e., the soil or water). The anodes are referred to as "sacrificial anodes" because with the passage of time the anode is consumed in providing the protection and has to be replenished again. The number of nodes, type etc are chosen by the Application Engineer depending on the cost, soil involved and the object that is protected.

Impressed Current System

A conceptual arrangement is shown below

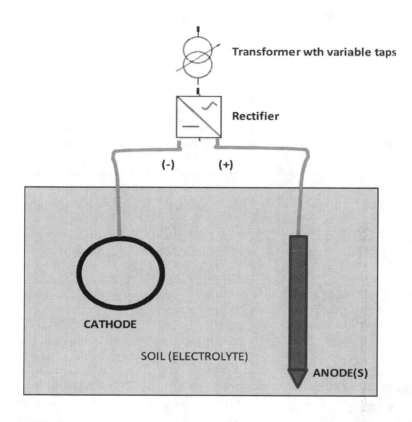

Here an external DC voltage is applied between the underground directly buried object to be protected and the anodes buried adjacent to the above at a few pre determined locations. The applied voltage is closely monitored and finely controlled such that the required protection potential is always maintained. Here the anode materials stay for a long time and need no replenishment. They are of graphite, high silicon iron rods, cast iron scraps, etc buried in good ground beds. Platinised Titanium anodes are used for marine applications apart from above to ensure long life.

Comparison of SA & IC systems

SA system	IC system
Simple system. Needs no external power	Complicated system, needs external power supply. Complication is more if auto control is provided.
Usually applied where protection current needs are small	System can be designed for any current requirement
Interference due to neighbouring structures are minimal	Interferences may arise from neighbouring structures
Over protection does not cause any problem	Over protection can be catastrophic since it may cause hydrogen embrittlement
Easy to install	Installation is somewhat complicated
Needs no maintenance	Needs regular maintenance
Protection is not precise	Protection is very precise since the protection potential can be precisely set.
System may not be cost effective in many cases	Very cost effective where long lengths of pipe lines, large tanks etc are involved
System is effective only where the soil resistivity is low	System is effective under all situations

Galvanic Chart

An understanding of the galvanic chart will be useful.

In a corrosion situation where there are two dissimilar metals and an electrolyte, you need to know which of the two metals would corrode and with what intensity. This is best read from a galvanic chart which is shown below in a simplistic form covering only those metals that are of interest to our Application Engineer.

Note that at one end of the chart is Magnesium, the "least" noble and at the other end is Gold, the "most noble".

1	Mg	Al	Mn	Zn	Cr	Fe	Ni	Sn	Pb	H₂	Cu	Hg	Ag	Pb	Au
2	(−)	(−)	(−)	(−)	(−)	(−)	(−)	(−)	(−)	0	(+)	(+)	(+)	(+)	(+)
	2.37	1.66	1.19	0.763	0.74	0.440	0.230	0.136	0.126		0.34	0.796	0.7966	1.2	1.42

Row (1) indicates the metal
Row (2) indicates the electric potential with respect to Standard Hydrogen Electrode (SHE) at 25⁰C in 1 bar Ag solution.

In any corrosion environment where there are two dissimilar metals, the one that is more electro negative would corrode. More the separation in the above galvanic table, more intense will be the corrosion.

Reference Electrodes

CP installations involve ascertaining the potentials of the object that is protected. In measuring the potential difference between the metal surfaces and the contacting electrolyte i.e, soil or water—the principle used is to form an electro chemical half cell, the second half being a "standard reference electrode" usually of $Cu/CuSO_4$ or $Ag/AgCl_2$.

The reference electrode mentioned above comprises of half cells i.e., a standard electrode immersed in an electrolyte of known concentration which therefore exhibit certain potentials vis-à-vis an arbitrarily fixed "zero" potential by Standard Hydrogen Electrode (SHE) that is not practical to use. Some of the commonly available Reference electrodes are:

Reference Electrode	Potential to SHE at 250C̊	Applications
Ag—AgCl$_2$ Noble metal with silver coating in HCl solution	(+) 198mV	For laboratory applications
Cu—CuSO$_4$	(+) 298mV	Rugged. Used for buried installations
Pure Zn	(+) 700mV	For marine applications
Saturated Calomel Electrode (Pt wire in mercurous chloride)	(+) 240mV	For laboratory applications

Protection Potential

Pourbaix diagram is a plot of the pH vs Electrode potential that can be used

- To predict spontaneous extent of reaction
- To estimate the composition of any corrosion product that can be found at particular combination of pH & potential
- To predict environmental changes 9solution composition, potential or pH that will accelerate or reduce corrosion.

The regions of "immunity", "corrosion" and 'passivation" are identified from the Atlas of Pourbaix for *any* metal.

Metal by nature tends to get oxidized and 'return' to its ore stage. If you recall, "Metallurgy" involves "reducing" the ore to metal while "corrosion" involves "oxidising" the metal back to ore form. Hence corrosion protection system should ensure that conditions are always there to facilitate a 'reduction' process only—meaning we need to ensure "addition" of electrons. By maintanng the corroding object at a more (–)ve potential "reduction" process can be ensured and corrosion retarded. But how much exactly?

Basic chemistry starting from ionic product of water and Nernst equation has established that a potential of (–)850 mV vs $Cu/CuSO_4$ electrode is a practically achievable value that can stop corrosion and thus provide effective Cathodic Protection.

Ready to use Protection Potential charts are in use, typically shown below:

Job	Empirical Protection Potential	
Steel in soil	(–) 850mV	Vs $Cu/CuSO_4$
Steel in sea water	(–) 800mV	Vs $Ag/AgCl_2$
Steel in anaerobic bacterial soil	(–) 950mV	Vs $Cu/CuSO_4$
Stainless steel in sea water	(–) 800 to 900mV	Vs $Hg/HgCl$
Lead in soil	(–) 550mV	Vs $Cu/CuSO_4$
Copper in sea water	(–) 100 to (–) 250mV	Vs $Cu/CuSO_4$
Galvanised steel in sea water	(–) 850 to (–) 900mV	Vs $Ag/AgCl_2$
Al in soil	(–) 800 to (–) 850mV	Vs $Cu/CuSO_4$
Al in sea water	(–) 850mV	Vs $Cu/CuSO_4$

Anode Selection

One of the critical elements of a good CP design is for the Application Engineer to decide on the type of protection (SA or IA) and select the right type of anodes before getting into quantification of those.

Sacrificial Anodes

Sacrificial Anodes should have the following characteristics:

- Should have a high driving voltage i.e., a high electrode negative potential
- Should not passivate due to anodic corrosion products
- Should give a high A-Hr/Kg to be economical
- 'castability' and 'fabricability' should be high
- Should be cheap & readily available
- Should corrode easily & uniformly

Use of Magnesium or Aluminium or Zinc or Manganese alloys are widely prevalent.

Some of the key characteristics of such typical anode materials are tabulated below. Actual values are to be obtained from vendors.

	Mg	Al	Zn
Theoretical A-Hr/kg capacity	2200	3000	800
Galvanic Efficiency	Max 60%	NA	High (90%)
Driving Voltage (vs $Cu/CuSO_4$)	850 mV	450mV	200 – 250mV

Pure Mg, is highly prone to "self corrosion" or "chunk effect". What is commercially available has Al & Zn added to it causing grain refinement. Mg has some Fe impurities that cause local cell formation. This is neutralised by adding Mn that has better affinity with Fe, so they are entrapped and leeched out. Mg alloy anodes are widely used for direct burial.

Al anodes are more active than Fe and are apparently ideal for CP. But after sometime Al passivates the surface and a passivated surface is more noble than Fe. Result is the object to be protected starts protecting the anode. Hence alloy of Al with Hg, indium or Gallium is used. Sometimes with Zn to achieve better mechanical properties.

The alloying easily form 'spots' on the anode, rendering them easily penetrable. Al anodes are widely used in marine environment.

Al-Zn-In alloys are widely used in marine environments to avoid Hg related environmental issues.

Mn anodes are commercially not so popular due to high cost and problems associated with its casting.

Impressed Current Anodes

Impressed current anodes should have the following characteristics:

- Should have a low rate of consumption for reasons of economy
- Should have a low anode polarization from point of view of driving voltage requirement
- Should have good electrical conductivity
- Should be highly reliable
- Should have sufficient mechanical strength particularly in case of deep buried anodes
- Should have good resistance to abrasion & erosion
- Should have low cost compared to the overall cost
- Should be available for easy fabrication to any shape

Some of the key characteristics of such typical IC anode materials are tabulated below. Actual values are to be obtained from vendors.

Anode	Consumption (kg/A-Yr)	Utilisation	Optimum Current Density
Platinum	5.9×10^{-6}	Not Available	Not Available
High Si Iron	0.25	50%	Not Available
Graphite	0.1 to 1.0	66%	11.3
Magnetite	0.005 to 0.08	Not Available	Not Available
Steel	6.8 to 9.1	Not Available	Not Available

IC Anodes are grouped under four categories:

1) Fully consumable anodes—these comprises of mainly active metals like Fe, Cast Iron, Al & Zn. Where ferrous anodes are required old engine blocks, scraps etc are welded together for several lengths and surrounded by a back fill of coke to avoid rapid anode dissolution. Where non ferrous anodes are required Al is used. It is non toxic and particularly effective where low conductivity of environment is there say a lot of fresh water. In such environments Al anode would not passivate.

2) Bulk non metallic conductor—these are Magnetite anodes or Carbon based graphite anodes, suitable for sea water environment since they are inert in a chloride environment. These are suitable for low current densities but are brittle and prone to frequent "anode failures".

3) Partially passive metals & alloys—these are High Silicon Iron (14 to 18%) and are very popular. The hydrated SiO_2 form a protective layer on the anode. However are susceptible to pitting in saline water and in such cases High Silicon Chromium Anodes are used.

   Pb/PbO_2 Anodes are used mainly in sea water applications. The anode here is an alloy of Lead & Silver or Antimony or Inert Platinum. The last two metals ensure formation of PbO_2 that adheres well and is a good conducting film. Even if the film is damaged it easily regenerates.

4) Fully Passive Anodes—these are essentially small anodes operating at high currents. Typically bulk Platinum anodes or Platinum plated over Nb, Cr or Ti subtrates are used. For a Low operating voltage of < 12V $Pt-TiO_2$ is suitable. If the same is >12V upto 40V the TiO_2 breaks down and hence use of Platinised Niobium or Tantalum is resorted to. These are widely used in marine environments such as Jetties, Oil platforms etc.

Practical Design

The actual design of CP systems need a lot of specialized training and experience and is not dealt with for the present discussions other than a brief summary below.

For CP system design we need to collect a lot of field data, coating resistance data, coating efficiency data etc to begin with. Current density values are assessed by experience from where the current requirements are worked out. Anode resistance is computed from where the number of anodes is arrived at after checking for their Life expectancy in case of SA system. Then a layout is worked out with anodes located below ground in such a way that they can 'see' the object buried under through the soil.

IC system of CP is automatically controlled by sensing the actual potential of the object and comparing it with a preset protection potential, amplifying the difference and use it to vary the voltage of the transformer that powers the rectifier. Over protection cut offs are employed to ensure there are no dangers due to over protection.

Foot Note:

I had a welcome opportunity to attend a week long training on CP system principles at the Central Electro-Chemical Research Institute (CECRI) at Karaikudi in Tamil Nadu, India in 1988. Subsequently the same was used for protecting the raw water line run from Pechiparai in adjacent state of Kerala for the infrastructure needs of the now famous Kudankulam nuclear power project. Much later the principles learnt were delightfully handy while delving into the engineering of CP systems that were applied in the oil & gas sector during my stint in the gulf where the CP system of protection are extensively used for protecting oil & gas pipe lines, bottom of crude tanks etc.

30

Interface with other Disciplines

Engineering for a large project is a multi discipline group activity and it is no intention to try and list them out here. Electrical engineering involves interfacing with practically all other disciplines in the course of the project work

- ➢ To provide inputs for their further engineering
- ➢ To obtain inputs for Electrical engineering
- ➢ To ensure the engineering is well coordinated

Interfacing with Process Engineering Group

The interfacing with this discipline is mainly for activities on

- ➢ Load List
- ➢ Continuous, Intermittent & Standby loads
- ➢ Identification of lines & equipment and stipulating the temperature needs for Electrical trace heating

Interfacing with Safety Engineering Group

The interfacing with this discipline is mainly for activities on

- ➢ Hazardous Area Classification Layouts
- ➢ Fire Detection, Alarm & Protection needs

Interfacing with Mechanical Engineering Group

The interfacing with this important discipline is mainly for activities on

- ➤ Rotating Equipment—need for proper selection of motors, power supply & cabling
- ➤ Package Equipment—need for proper selection of motors, power supply & cabling.
- ➤ Static Equipment—need for CP for tanks

Interfacing with HVAC Engineering Group

Almost all indoor located electrical equipment needs climate controlled environment—by a proper heating, ventilation or cooling—to ensure that the temperatures needed for proper operation and performance of the equipment are adhered to.

The interfacing with this important discipline is iterative because the source of the heat is the electrical equipment itself and the climate control needs will mean addition of more equipment that in turn might spew out more heat and so on.

The interfacing activities will be on

- ➤ Heating Loads
- ➤ Ventilation Loads
- ➤ Air Conditioning Loads
- ➤ HVAC Layouts
- ➤ HVAC Equipment vendor drgs

Interfacing with Civil & Structural Engineering Group

The interfacing with this important discipline is mainly for activities on

- ➤ Plant Layout showing drains, trenches etc
- ➤ Pipe Rack/support layout

- Building Layout & Details
- Electrical Equipment Foundation Layout & Details
- Sunshade location & details
- Floor cut out location & Details for all Electrical Equipment
- Platforms, Hand Rails—Location, Elevation and Details
- Stairs—layout & Details for ALL areas
- Column & Beam Schedule and Layouts for ALL buildings
- All in plant trenches, culvert location & details
- Oil soak pits
- Transformer foundation details
- Fire walls around transformers

Interfacing with Piping Engineering Group

The interfacing with this important discipline is mainly for activities on

- Piping Layout
- Pipeline Layout
- Pipe Supports & Structures
- Understanding insulation provided on lines & equipment that needs Electrical trace heating

Interfacing with Architectural Group

The interfacing with this discipline is mainly for activities on

- Plant Layout
- Fencing layout with access locations
- In plant road layout
- Security Fencing Layout & Details
- Gate House Layout
- Fire Station layout
- Control Room Layout
- Equipment Room Layout

- Administration Building Layout
- Canteen Layout
- Stores Layout
- Workshops Layout
- Clinic Layout
- Door details for ALL above buildings, since the equipment will need to be taken in!!

Interfacing with Instrumentation & Control Group

In many organisations the Electrical and the Inst & Control group function as one monolyth group.

The interfacing with this discipline is mainly for activities on

- AC UPS Power needs
- DC UPS Power needs
- Instrument Room Layouts
- Special Cabling needs for Motors—RTDs, BTDs etc.
- Interface needs with Power Modules
- Vendor Drgs confirming above needs

Interfacing with Telecommunications Group

The interfacing with this discipline is mainly for activities on

- Main Exchange building Layout
- Telecom Room Layout in various Locations
- DC UPS Power needs
- AC UPS Power Needs
- Vendor drgs confirming above needs

Self learning exercise

In order to ensure that the Application Engineers grasp the importance of the interaction needs with various other disciplines, the reader is encouraged to think through all by himself the interface needs using the templates provided below.

I would however prefer to conduct this as part of my training session in the form of a mini workshop.

Note that the Application Engineering aspects of the Equipment/ System listed in the LHS column have all been covered in the previous chapters.

	Equipment / System	Process	Safety	Rot Eqpt	Pkg Eqpt	Static Eqpt	HVAC	Piping	Civ & Str	Control & Inst	Telecom	Architectural
1	Load List	x										
3	Transformers - Dry Type											
3	Transformers- Distribution - upto 5 MVA								xx			
3	Transformers - Distribution > 5 MVA		xx						x			
3	Transformers - EHV - Upto 160 MVA		xx									
4	Generators - LARGE		xx		xx	xx		xx		x		
4	Generators - SMALL		xx		xx		xx		xx			x
6	System Grounding									x		
7	Switchgears											
7	Switchgears - HV GIS								xx			
7	Switchgears - HV & MV (WITH SF₆)								xx			
7	Switchgears - HV & MV (WITH VCB) 33,22,11,6.6kV								xx			
7	Switchgears - LV DRAW OUT MCC / PCC / PMCC								x			
7	Switchgears - LV FIXED TYPE MCC / PCC / PMCC								x			
7	Switchgears - FIXED - For Package Equpment				xx				x			

Equipment / System

		Process	Safety	Rot Eqpt	Pkg Eqpt	Static Eqpt	HVAC	Piping	Civ & Str	Control & Inst	Telecom	Architectural
8	EHV Switchyard - as EPC		XX						XX			x
8	EHV Switchyard - Lightning Arrestors								x			
8	EHV Switchyard - SF$_6$ Circuit Breakers								x			
8	EHV Switchyard - CTs & VTs								x			
8	EHV Switchyard - CCVTs								x			
8	EHV Switchyard - Isolators								x			
8	EHV Switchyard - Connecting Hardware								x			
9	Overhead Lines		XX									
10	Cables - HVXLPE								x			
10	Cables - LVPVC								x			
10	Cables - CONTROL CABLES								XX			
10	Cables - COMMUNICATION CABLES JELLY FILLED								XX			
10	Cables - FIRE ALARM CABLES		XX									
11	Bus Ducts - MV								XX			
11	Bus Ducts - LV								XX			

	Equipment / System	Process	Safety	Rot Eqpt	Pkg Eqpt	Static Eqpt	HVAC	Piping	Civ & Str	Control & Inst	Telecom	Architectural
12	Lighting Fixtures & Accessories (certified for hazardous)		x						x	x		
12	Lighting - Plugs & Hand Lamps (Flame Proof)		x						x	x		
12	Lighting - Control Panels (Flame Proof)		x						x	x		
12	Lighting Fixtures - for non hazardous areas						x		x	x	x	
12	Lighting - High Mast											x
12	Lighting - Transformers								x			
12	Lighting & Small Power Panel								x	x		
12	Lighting - ELCBs											
13	Batteries Flooded LA		x						x	x	x	x
13	Batteries VRLA		x						x	x	x	
13	Batteries - NICAD		x						x	x	x	x
14	DC UPS		x	x	x				x	x	x	x
15	AC UPS		x						x	x	x	x
16	Electrical Protections										x	
17	Control of Power Distribution - Control Station - Weather Proof		x	x	x				x			
17	Control of Power Distribution - Control Station - Flame Proof		x	x	x				x			
17	Control of Power Distribution - PB & Indicating Lamps											
17	Control of Power Distribution - TIMERS											
21	Equipment for Haz areas - JUNCTION BOX FLAME PROOF		x									
21	Equipment for Haz areas - LIGHTING DB - FLAME PROOF		x						x			
21	Equipment for Haz areas - CABLE GLANDS											
21	Equipment for Haz areas - CABLE TERMINATION & JOINTNG KITS											

Equipment / System

	Equipment / System	Process	Safety	Rot Eqpt	Pkg Eqpt	Static Eqpt	HVAC	Piping	Civ & Str	Control & Inst	Telecom	Architectural
22	Electrical Trace Heating	xx			xx	x						
23	Power Factor improvement								xx			
24	Solar Power systems								xx			x
25	Motors - MV - Industrial Safe Area		xx		xx				x			
25	Motors - LV - Industrial Safe Area		xx		xx							
25	Motors increased safety for Zone 2		xx		xx							
25	Motors -LV-Type e & n - zone 2		xx		xx							
25	Motors - Synchronous		xx						xx			
26	Variable Speed Drives	xx					xx			x		
27	Safety Earthing		xx			xx			xx			
28	Lightning Protection Systems		xx									x
29	Cathodic Protection Systems							x				

31

Project Implementation

What is a Project?

A project in a general sense is a temporary endeavor undertaken to create a unique product or service. For purposes of this discussion we may narrow it down to an effort involving thousands of person hours spread over a good length of time—in months or even years—to construct an Industrial facility. The facility could be a thermal power station, an oil & gas plant, a refinery, a process plant or just an EHV substation.

Team involved

Typically as soon as the project work is awarded to an organization, a "Project Manager" (PM) takes charge of all the activities of the organization for execution of the Project. The PM has an Engineering Team headed by a "Project Engineering Manager" (PEM) reporting to him to carry out ALL the engineering activities for the project and as Application Engineers you should be primarily interested in that.

The PM also has a Project Procurement Team headed by a Project Procurement Manager (PPM) reporting to him.

A Project Construction Team headed by a "Project Construction Manager (PCM)" also reports to the PM.

Later on a Project Commissioning Team and a Project Operations & Maintenance Team are constituted to take over site activities as the construction work nears completion.

While we had stated that Application Engineers should primarily focus on Engineering aspects, this is not to suggest that they have no role in Procurement, Construction, Commissioning or O&M activities. All these activities are challenging and exciting and need significant skills for sure.

The Project Engineering Team

The Engineering Team is usually constituted specifically for the Project—either whole time dedicated to only the particular project or at times for a few projects executed simultaneously in various stages of execution depending on the complexities involved, availability of engineering resources etc.

The team comprises of various disciplines of Engineering viz., Process, Mechanical, Piping, Architectural. Civil & Structural, Electrical, Control & Automation, Telecommunication etc. Each discipline is lead by an experienced "LEAD ENGINEER" to whom a team of specialized/experienced and at times lesser experienced engineers are assigned to assist him to execute the project on behalf of his discipline. As an Application Engineer you can expect to be beginning your career in an engineering organization as part of such a team.

The entire project team has to work as a closely knit unit to achieve the project execution goals to Budget, to Quality and to Schedule. Your Lead Engineer is there to push you to achieve the above three objectives.

Typical ACTIVITIES of the Application Engineers

> ➤ Be clear about the objectives of the Project—viz., what it is all about. What goes in as inputs, what is processed and what comes out as output.
> ➤ Have clarity on the environment data viz.,
>   o Ambient temperatures—minimum & maximum

o   Altitude above mean sea level (MSL)
o   Wind speed—every day and maximum
o   Soil Resistivity

Your Engineering activities hinges on the above.

➢   Obtain/Compile a LOAD LIST including HVAC and Lighting & Small Power Loads.
➢   Compute maximum Power Demand.
➢   Decide on in-house power generation needs—normal as well as under outage of normal power (called "Emergency" generation)
➢   Know where, at what voltage and how the incoming power from elsewhere is received.
➢   Obtain a PLOT PAN and try to identify the above details in the same to begin with.
➢   Assess the LOAD CENTRES where it makes sense to probably locate the substations.
➢   Develop an SLD.
➢   Assess system Fault Levels at various voltages.
➢   Develop a Front End Engineering Design (FEED) narrative.
➢   "Specify" major Electrical Equipment such as Generators, Transformers, HV/MV/LV switchgears and MCCs, Cables etc. based on available data.
➢   Work out equipment sizes to have first pass on the inputs for room sizing to enable other disciplines such as Architectural & Civil engineering disciplines to move further in firming up their requirements.
➢   Revise all layouts.
➢   If load list is reasonably certain, fine tune the equipment specifications and obtain vendor quotes. You will always be in a HURRY to meet tight schedules because if you delay ordering the whole project will be delayed.

> It is a good engineering practice to develop a preliminary estimation of the quantities of Power, Control & Instrumentation cables at this stage

> Evaluate the bids received and as you do that use the data received to revise the layouts—you still have opportunity to correct what you did earlier.

> Order major long lead equipment including spares needed while commissioning.

> Review vendor drawings. Chase & get them in time. Some of the critical drawings might need your specific approval before the manufacturing starts.

> Witness the Factory Acceptance Tests (FAT) as required depending on the criticality of the item. Normally standard off the shelf products do not need witnessing of FAT but tailor made items such as Switchgears/MCCs need FAT witnessing to spot anomalies and rectify them in the shop floor before the equipment are shipped to site. It is also a good practice to witness FAT for critical items even if they are manufacturer's standard products to ensure you get the right equipment that meets the criteria specified.

> Review ALL Test Reports even if FAT witnessing has not taken place. This will help weed out non conforming products from reaching site.

> Update earlier drawings (SLD, Layouts, Room sizes) and develop Detailed Design Drawings.

> Estimate Lighting and Small Power needs and develop detail engineering drawings including layouts. Developing Power distribution drawings for the above will help arrive at accurate Cable MTOs.

> Update your estimated quantities of Cables for Power, Control, Instrumentation etc. Do not forget to include requirements for Cathodic Protection and Electrical Trace Heating.

> Order CABLES.

➤ Estimate Earthing & Lightning Protection needs and develop detail engineering drawings including layouts.

➤ Order BULKS. This includes all the hardware items needed for installation such as Cable Trays & Fittings, Termination & Jointing kits, Cable Glands, Cable tiles, covers, etc. Significant time goes in working out these quantities and as a young engineer you can be normally expected to assist in the task.

➤ Prepare CABLE SCHEDULE.

➤ Release all drawings to site FOR CONSTRUCTION.

➤ Prepare Interconnection Chart/Schedule/diagrams.

➤ Work out Relay Coordination Diagrams and setting charts

➤ Write (based on vendor inputs) a PLANT PRE-COMMISSIONING MANUAL/CHECK LISTS.

➤ Develop Plant O&M manuals.

➤ Order O&M SPARES.

➤ Prepare Engineering CLOSE-OUT REPORT narrating the broad details, deviations if any from what was originally required, deviations if any from customer standards and the "lessons learnt" that will be invaluable for yourself and your organisation to pay attention to the next time around.

You are now ready to play a larger role in the next project and so on. You will keep learning as you move up the ladder as an EXPERIENCED APPLICATION ENGINEER.

32

Electrical Deliverables in a Project

Below is a generic listing of what is normally produced by the Electrical Department as an Engineering Deliverable for a typical Project. The numbers vary depending on the size of the project, its complexity and geographical spread. The list is indicative and by no means should be considered as exhaustive.

1) Key SLD
2) Detailed SLDs—EHV/HV/MV/LV and DC systems
3) Electrical Plot Plan
4) Load List
5) Engineering Calculations—for various systems
   - Electrical systems study—using computerized tools for Load Flow, Short Circuit and Motor starting studies apart from other studies as required such as transient stability studies, Harmonic studies etc.
   - Generator/Emergency Generator sizing
   - EHV outdoor switchyard design, if applicable
   - NER sizing
   - Cable sizing
   - Lighting
   - Earthing
   - Lightning Protection
   - Equipment sizing to decide on room sizes/yard sizes
   - Battery capacity sizing—for DC & AC UPS
   - DC & AC UPS sizing
   - PF improvement capacitor bank sizing

6) Electrical Equipment Layout—for indoor substations
7) Cable Trench & Tray Layout drawings
8) Lighting & Small power Layout drawings and Distribution SLDs
9) Earthing Layout drawings
10) Lightning Protection Layout drawings
11) Installations Details—Cable Trenches & Trays and Cabling
12) Installation Details—Lighting & Small Power
13) Installation Details—Earthing
14) Installation Details—Lightning Protection
15) Electrical Trace Heating Layout drawings & distribution SLDs
16) Installation Details—Electrical Trace Heating
17) Electrical Protection Coordination studies, curves and setting charts
18) Cable Schedule
19) Cabling block diagrams
20) Interconnection Charts/diagrams

33

Potential Recruiters

To assess the number of potential recruiters is a formidable task if you take into account the diverse nature of organisations where you can easily find an entry level slot if you fare well in the interview process.

Broadly we can summarise the organizations under the following heads:

1) **Owner organizations**

   These are companies owning and operating industrial facilities such as Power stations, Refineries, process plants etc. They can be in the

   - Public Sectors (PSUs).
   - Government bodies
   - Private Sectors

   Usually large PSUs/Governmentt bodies have a transparent selection process through press releases etc. Selection process is usually rigorous. We need not attempt to peg the numbers.

   Large Private sector Owner organizations should be seen in the following sectors

   - Power
   - Oil & Gas

- Refineries
- Paper
- Cement
- Iron & Steel
- Mining
- Fertiliser

2) Consultancy/Engineering Companies

These are in the following categories

- Public Sectors (PSUs)
- Private Sectors
- Engineering Back Offices of overseas Companies

Usually large PSU Consultancy companies have a transparent selection process through press releases etc. Selection process is usually rigorous. We need not attempt to peg the numbers.

Reputed consulting Engineering firms in the private sector are plenty and may run into well over even fifty.

Engineering back offices of large Engineering/Contracting Companies operating overseas have mushroomed in the last decade such as Foster Wheeler, Bechtel, Fluor, Technip, Saipem, Petrofac, McDermott, FL Smith etc.

3) Large Contracting Organisations

These are large companies who take up big projects/contracts on a turn key basis to Engineer, Procure and Construct (EPC route). They exist both in the Public as well as Private sectors.

- Public Sectors (PSUs)
- Private Sectors

The numbers should be seen in the following sectors

- ➢ Power Generation
- ➢ Power Transmission
- ➢ EHV switchyards
- ➢ Oil & Gas plants
- ➢ Pipelines
- ➢ Refineries
- ➢ Paper
- ➢ Cement
- ➢ Iron & Steel
- ➢ Mining
- ➢ Fertiliser

4) <u>Vendor Organisations</u>

These are the manufacturers who actually **make** the products/ equipment that the Application Engineer working in the organisations described earlier under (1), (2) & (3) seek to use in his/her projects. Typically in any well developed country in the manufacturing sector the number of equipment vendors are huge with manufacturing spread over the entire country. It will be very useful for the Application Engineer to stay abreast on who are all the vendors manufacturing a particular equipment/component. Towards this objective a list of vendors in alphabetical order can be attempted to be compiled in an EXCEL format showing details of the product(s) that each vendor manufactures. *The list, obviously can become obsolete by the day*. However it could be a good starting point for the young engineer to be aware and probably probe and ascertain his chances of walking into one of such organizations under a product vertical that effectively could total to well over 400.

The above segregation under (1) through (4) gives you an idea of what to look for in a structured way. *You are encouraged to scour the internet and research on the organisation you would like to approach for an opening.* Only very few out of the above would have visited your college for a campus recruitment. Bulk of the companies will usually have intake of electrical graduate engineers in very limited numbers and one of them could be **YOU.**